THE HUMAN RIGHTS WATCH GLOBAL REPORT ON PRISONS

THE HUMAN RIGHTS WATCH
GLOBAL REPORT ON PRISONS

Human Rights Watch
New York · Washington · Los Angeles · London

Library of Congress Catalog Card No.: 93 78608
ISBN 1-56432-101-0

Cover design by Robert Kimzey.

The Prison Project
The Prison Project, established in 1988, cuts across the five regional
divisions of Human Rights Watch to focus on a single issue: prison
conditions worldwide. The Prison Project has investigated conditions for
sentenced prisoners, pre-trial detainees and those held in police lockups.
It examines prison conditions for all prisoners, not just political prisoners.
The work of the Prison Project is guided by the Prison Advisory
Committee, whose chairman is Herman Schwartz. Other members are
Nan Aron, Vivian Berger, Haywood Burns, Alejandro Garro, William
Hellerstein, Edward Koren, Sheldon Krantz, Benjamin Malcolm, Diane
Orentlicher, Norman Rosenberg, David Rothman and Clarence Sundram.
The director of the Project is Joanna Weschler. Anthony Levintow is the
associate.

For a catalog of publications, please call (212) 986-1980.

HUMAN RIGHTS WATCH

CONTENTS

Country Sections

Appendices

ACKNOWLEDGMENTS

Joanna Weschler, the director of the Prison Project of Human Rights Watch is the principal author of this report, and Aryeh Neier, the former executive director of Human Rights Watch, its editor. The introduction and preface were written by Herman Schwartz, the chair of the Prison Project's Advisory Committee; sections were also contributed by David Rosenberg, a lawyer and consultant with Human Rights Watch.

The following staff members and consultants for Human Rights Watch wrote or researched the country chapters: Mary Jane Camejo, Holly Cartner, Allyson Collins, Erika Dailey, Rachel Denber, Timothy Gellat, Eric Goldstein, Patricia Gossman, Sidney Jones, Robin Kirk, Lydia Lobenthal, Ellen Lutz, Bronwen Manby, Anne Manuel, Juan Méndez, Aryeh Neier, Benjamin Penglase, Alexander Petrov, Luis Felipe Polo, David Rosenberg, Peter Rosenblum, Virginia Sherry, Mickey Spiegel, Joanna Weschler, and Lois Whitman.

The authors were assisted and guided in their work by a group of advisers comprising staff and board members of Human Rights Watch and prison specialists. They were: Alice Brown, Eric Goldstein, William Hellerstein, Gara La Marche, Judge Morris Lasker, Kenneth Roth, David Rothman, Kenneth Schoen, Herman Schwartz, Andrew Whitley and Lois Whitman.

Dr. Herbert F. Spirer and Dr. Marilyn Duecker of the American Statistical Association's Committee on Scientific Feedom and Human Rights helped with interpreting statistical data.

The report was copyedited and designed by Robert Kimzey. Anthony Levintow provided production assistance.

PREFACE

The Human Rights Watch Global Report on Prisons summarizes six years of work by the Prison Project and divisions of Human Rights Watch in investigating prison conditions in some twenty countries worldwide.

The project was established in 1987 to focus attention on the circumstances in which *all* prisoners—not only those accused of politically-motivated offenses—are incarcerated; and to put these problems on the world's human rights agenda. At the request of Human Rights Watch Executive Director Aryeh Neier, Professor Herman Schwartz of the American University in Washington, D.C., a pioneer in litigation securing rights for prisoners in the United States, undertook investigations of prison conditions in Poland and Czechoslovakia in 1987 and 1988 respectively. At the time, neither country permitted access to its prisons. Nevertheless, we were able to gather sufficient information to publish detailed, comprehensive and, we believe, reliable reports.

In an attempt to extend our efforts to other parts of the world, Human Rights Watch assembled an advisory committee of prison experts whose names appear in an appendix to this report. Working with the staff of the regional divisions of Human Rights Watch—Africa Watch, Americas Watch, Asia Watch, Helsinki Watch and Middle East Watch—the project launched investigations of prisons and jails in selected countries around the world. An indispensable three-year grant from the Edna McConnell Clark Foundation supported the work of the project. In 1990, Joanna Weschler of the staff of Human Rights Watch, succeeded Professor Schwartz as director of the Prison Project and Professor Schwartz became Chairman of the Advisory Committee. Ms. Weschler is the principal author of this report.

Our investigations covered North America, South America, Europe, Asia, and Africa and the six largest countries in the world, Brazil, China, India, Indonesia, Russia, and the United States. The other prison systems we investigated were those of Cuba, Czechoslovakia, Egypt, Israel and the occupied West Bank and Gaza Strip, Mexico, Jamaica, Mexico, Peru, Poland, Romania, South Africa, Spain, Turkey, the United Kingdom, and Zaire. We thus covered virtually every part of the world as well as countries with very diverse political, economic and demographic circumstances. In addition, we benefitted from information on prisons collected by Human Rights Watch during its many investigations of general human rights conditions around the world. (The work of the Human Rights Watch Prison Project did not include an examination of mental institutions, institutions for the criminally insane, institutions for juvenile offenders or clandestine prisons.) Because *The Human Rights Watch Global Report on Prisons* is based almost exclusively on reports previously published by Human Rights Watch, citations in the text were kept to a minimum. A comprehensive bibliography appears in the back of this report.

In every case, we sought access to prisons by contacting the appropriate authorities well in advance of our planned investigation. To avoid being shown "model" prisons, and to follow up on what preliminary inquiries showed to be troubled institutions, we specified the prisons we wanted to see. In many cases, permission was granted, though sometimes only after prolonged efforts; or, as in the case of Poland, after we first issued a report based on interviews with ex-prisoners and publicly available information. Permission was often denied in countries considered democracies: Turkey, Spain, Brazil (Rio de Janeiro), and India. In Spain and Rio de Janeiro, we nevertheless gained access to some prisons. By contrast, even under the Communist regime, the Soviet Union and Poland allowed free and uninhibited entry.

Where permission was denied, we worked with local human rights groups in arranging for our representatives to interview men and women who had recently emerged from penal institutions. With the help of a lengthy checklist that the project developed over the course of our investigations, we conducted in-depth interviews both on-site and with ex-prisoners. In our conversations with inmates, we insisted that prison staff should not be present, and were usually successful. In many cases, stories were cross-checked by asking different prisoners interviewed separately detailed questions about the same incident, and by examining documentary sources. In some countries, such as Czechoslovakia and Turkey, domestic human rights groups had previously issued reports based on their own investigations, and we were able to build on these. We are gratified that in no case has any government been able to refute our findings by identifying substantial errors. A copy of the most recent version of the checklist, which is being continually refined, appears in the appendix. We used the U.N. Standard Minimum Rules for the Treatment of Prisoners, which also appears in the appendix, as a standard against which to measure prison conditions around the world.

In these investigations, Human Rights Watch has not evaluated and chosen among penological theories or alternatives, nor do we call for the abolition of prisons. Similarly, we do not at this time propose revisions in penal or procedural codes, although it is likely that deficiencies in these contribute significantly to prevailing human rights abuses in prisons. Our focus, in this report, is solely on the human rights problems that are endemic in penal systems worldwide and it is our hope that the information we have assembled here will promote increased efforts by the international community generally, and the United Nations in particular, to secure compliance with the international standards for the treatment of prisoners.

INTRODUCTION

Jails and prisons do more than deprive their inmates of freedom. The great majority of the millions of persons who are imprisoned worldwide at any given moment, and of the tens of millions who spend at least part of the year behind bars, are confined in conditions of filth and corruption, without adequate food or medical care, with little or nothing to do, and in circumstances in which violence—from other inmates, their keepers or both—is a constant threat.

No one should be surprised by the routine cruelty of imprisonment. Despite international declarations, treaties and standards forbidding this, it is tolerated even in countries that are more or less respectful of human rights, because prisons, by their nature, are out of sight; and because prisoners, by definition are outcasts.

By and large, it is not possible for prisoners themselves to call attention to the abuses they suffer. Except for political prisoners, the great majority are not skilled in organizing or in communicating; while in prison, they are cut off from the rest of the world; and, once out of prison, they are eager to avoid continuing identification with prisons. Accordingly, it is up to others, acting out of a willingness to concern themselves with the suffering of their fellow human beings and out of a commitment to the rule of law, to concern themselves with prisons.

The institutional mechanisms that have been devised to deal with suffering and that promote adherence to the rule of law include nongovernmental human rights organizations and the human rights bodies of the United Nations. Unfortunately, these agencies have done little to challenge the routine cruelty of imprisonment.

Though prison conditions have long been a central concern for such bodies worldwide, the focus has been on the conditions under which those confined for politically-motivated offenses have been held. At the time Human Rights Watch launched its Prison Project six years ago, with some notable exceptions, groups defending human rights in their own countries had not extended this concern to suspects in common crime cases. This failure to pay attention to the treatment of the vast majority of those imprisoned worldwide was also generally true of those nongovernmental organizations established to protect human rights internationally and of the human rights bodies of the United Nations.

They too focused on prison conditions almost exclusively insofar as they affected political dissenters and others incarcerated in security-related cases.

This focus is, of course, to be expected. Worldwide, most human rights groups were founded during periods of political repression to defend the victims (although it is important to remember that a few countries, especially in Europe, have a rich tradition, dating back to the nineteenth century, in which specialized groups defend the general prison population against abuses). Even in the United States, where prison conditions have been an important issue to domestic human rights groups for the past quarter of a century, neglect of common prisoners by such groups had previously been the rule. The largest human rights group in the United States, the American Civil Liberties Union, was founded following World War I in response to the political persecution of those who had opposed the war and to defend political radicals victimized by one of the country's periodic "red scares" in the aftermath of the war. It was not until the late 1960s, nearly a half century after its establishment, that the American Civil Liberties Union began to concern itself systematically with the conditions under which common crime suspects are imprisoned.

In many countries, human rights groups remain small, beleaguered organizations that are hard pressed to try to defend political dissenters and lack the capacity to go further to try to deal with such questions as prison conditions as they affect the general prison population. Moreover, in some other countries—for example, China, Syria, or Malawi—the general climate of repression is so severe that it has not yet been possible to establish human rights groups that operate openly. But in a few countries, established human rights groups have begun to turn their attention to prison conditions as they affect the great majority of prisoners.

Human Rights Watch welcomes this development. The prohibitions in international human rights agreements of such practices as "torture or cruel, inhuman or degrading treatment or punishment" (International Covenant on Civil and Political Rights, Article 7) and guarantees that "All persons deprived of their liberty shall be treated with humanity and with respect for the inherent dignity of the human person" (International Covenant on Civil and Political Rights, Article 10) apply to all those incarcerated and not only those whose offenses were political. We believe it is essential for the international human rights movement generally, and for the United Nations bodies charged with seeking compliance with international agreements on human rights, to adopt this view not only in principle but also in practice.

Human Rights Watch is, of course, also concerned about the treatment of those confined for political or security offenses. Their cases figured prominently in our investigations. We take it as a given that the international human rights community will do its utmost to protect them. In publishing this report, we call on the international human rights movement also to concern itself with all the others also victimized by the denials of human rights that we have recorded in this volume. We also call on the United Nations to launch a campaign to secure compliance with the provisions of the Universal Declaration of Human Rights, the International Covenant on Civil and Political Rights that concern prisons, and the United Nations Standard Minimum Rules for the Treatment of Prisoners (see the chapter titled "The Role of the United Nations in Monitoring Prisons" for our specific recommendations with respect to such a campaign).

A likely response to many of our recommendations will probably be that the proposed improvements are costly and few countries in the world have resources to meet the needs of the majority of their citizens who have not assaulted, stolen or committed other crimes. If food and medical care are inadequate in prison, they are often also inadequate outside.

This concern is obviously justified, and yet it is not a complete answer. When the state deprives someone of liberty, it has an obligation not to punish the person beyond the penalty prescribed by law and the country's poverty cannot be an excuse. It must ensure that the conditions of confinement do not cause excessive suffering.

Equally important, many reforms require only will, not money, as reform-minded prison directors in Poland and the former Czechoslovakia have demonstrated. A change in attitude, policy and practice at the top, and a willingness to insist that prison staff adhere to those changes, were all that were necessary to virtually end physical and verbal abuse in Poland and the former Czechoslovakia, in both of which beatings, insults, curses and the like had been pervasive. Also, if a country cannot afford to deal with overcrowding by constructing adequate facilities, it can consider other means, including a change in sentencing policy, modification of its pre-trial detention policy, and different ways of dealing with minor offenders.

Changes with respect to such matters as staff behavior, mail and visiting practices, discipline and practices that foster the subjugation of some inmates to other prisoners—few of which involve significant costs—are at the heart of our recommendations. Among the most important of our recommendations is a general call to open the prisons to the public in every way possible, to make them visible. Citizens in a democracy have a right to know what goes on in public institutions, the operation of which affects them so deeply. Openness is the best preventive of abuses.

Much can therefore be done that involves little or no cost. This is not to say that true prison reform costs nothing. Ancient buildings must be replaced, facilities must be upgraded, and staff salaries must attract competent people for a difficult job. All this does indeed cost money. But if a society deprives its transgressors of liberty as a penalty, it does so to uphold the inviolability of human dignity and to make clear its insistence on upholding its laws. By treating criminals and those accused of crime in an inhuman and degrading manner, and by imposing penalties on them not authorized by law, a society betrays the very principles that its criminal laws purport to uphold.

The world community must begin to take seriously its responsibilities toward people in prison. Domestic politics and indifference, reinforced by financial stringency, often block any attempt to improve prison conditions, and outside pressure is necessary to produce change. The United Nations should be deeply involved, especially at this time when it is becoming a leading moral authority in the world. Also, though U.N. standards have been much criticized for vagueness and imprecision, they are widely known and are accepted in principle. Yet many of these standards are clearly violated routinely and systematically throughout the world. For example, Rules 9-14 on decent accommodations; Rules 27-32 on discipline and the ban on corporal punishment; and Rules 35-36 on the availability of rules and fair disciplinary procedures.

The U.N. Criminal Justice Branch of the Center for Social Development and Humanitarian Affairs must be strengthened. It requires more staff and resources. Additionally, there must be a serious effort to monitor and enforce compliance with U.N. standards, preferably by a special body of the world organization charged solely with that responsibility.

Treatment of the ordinary prisoner is a crucial test of a society. Condemned for often serious offenses, without powerful supporters, often poor and inarticulate, disproportionately comprising members of minorities suffering from discrimination—for example, blacks in the United States, Gypsies in Romania, lower caste Indians—and removed from public view, prisoners are highly vulnerable to our worst impulses. They are fellow human beings and are entitled to be treated as such. Unhappily, that is frequently the exception and not the rule. It is time for the international community to stop averting its eyes and to insist that its lofty pronouncements should be respected.

SUMMARY OF FINDINGS AND RECOMMENDATIONS

By any accepted standards, whether the often vague United Nations Standard Minimum Rules for the Treatment of Prisoners or any other criteria, prison conditions, policies and practices usually fall below the level of decency. From torture in a police lockup to degrading conditions and abuse by guards or other inmates in a long-term prison, prisoners all over the world are abused in gross violation of their rights under international and domestic law, almost invariably without recourse or remedy.

What follows is a summary of the topical sections of this report. The subject headings deal with issues of vital importance to anyone concerned with abuses of human rights in prisons.

PRE-TRIAL DETENTION

The conditions of pre-trial detention are generally much worse than those of long-term incarceration. Pre-trial detainees are often held in police stations and other facilities that are poorly equipped, overcrowded and dirty. In many places, pre-trial detention is ruled by the interests of the investigation and inmates are isolated and subject to harsh interrogation and physical abuse. The length of pre-trial detention—which should be brief—often reaches several months and sometimes years in Turkey, Spain, Poland, Peru, Zaire and elsewhere. Detainees are thus held for long periods in facilities equipped for only short-term stays.

PHYSICAL CIRCUMSTANCE

Overcrowding and inadequate physical circumstances cause a great deal of suffering among the world's prison population. Many prisoners not only are packed together with many other prisoners without adequate clothing, cell furnishings, plumbing, light, and in extremes of heat and cold.

Overcrowding, especially in pre-trial facilities, is so severe that, in many countries, inmates have almost no place to sit or even move. In some prisons, even turning over while asleep or stretching is impossible. Overcrowding was taken to an extreme in a Jamaican prison when nineteen men were confined in an eight-by-seven foot room causing three of them to die of asphyxiation. Prisoners in Russia, the United States, Egypt, Kenya, Brazil, Peru and Poland also suffer because of severe overcrowding.

In many prisons, the cells are barely furnished. Not all prisons have beds, and those that do often arrange them so close to each other that there is no room even to sit and tie one's shoes. When tables and chairs are provided, there is not always room for them to be used comfortably.

Plumbing, an essential ingredient in a humanely-run prison, is often faulty or, even in relatively prosperous countries entirely absent. In 1991, nearly 40 percent of British cells had no plumbing (though the situation is now being corrected) forcing the prisoners to use plastic buckets which they were allowed to empty periodically. In Jamaica and Egypt, buckets are the main toilet facilities available.

Many prison systems force inmates to live with too little—and, in a few places, too much—light. In cells without natural light, authorities often provide insufficient artificial lighting. When adequate electric light is provided it is often out of the inmates' control and thus a source of discomfort and frustration.

Inmates the world over complain of insufficient supplies of clothing and toiletry. These inadequacies can have a terrible impact on prisoners' morale. In Britain, Cuba and the United States, Human Rights Watch encountered prisoners who complained of policies that left them in dirty or otherwise inadequate clothing.

FOOD

Complaints about food are among the most frequently voiced during interviews with prisoners all over the world. In some cases, they concern the quality and taste of the food, but in many, the complaints focus on insufficient amount. In countries such as Egypt, Indonesia,

Brazil or Mexico, inmates get along by supplementing their prison diet with food brought in by relatives. Deaths from starvation and diseases brought about by severe malnutrition have been reported in Zaire and Peru.

A NOTE ON MEDICAL CARE

Inadequate medical care, like inadequate food, is one of the most common complaints we heard when visiting prisons throughout the world. Prisoners in almost all prison systems complain of indifference, neglect and an attitude of suspicion on the part of medical workers. Worse, in some countries denial of proper medical care is used as a form of punishment.

The proportion of HIV positive prisoners is usually significantly higher than among the general population of any given country and there is great suffering from AIDS in the world's prisons. In addition to the pain and misery of the disease itself, many prisoners with AIDS suffer discrimination by the authorities and do not receive adequate medical care.

CLASSIFICATION

Classification systems are often primitive or nonexistent and expose vulnerable or weak prisoners to violent offenders. In many countries, violent criminals are held together in large groups, often mixed with those convicted of lesser, nonviolent offenses. Predictably, this victimizes the nonviolent offenders who lack the ability and the disposition to protect themselves. Similarly, when juveniles are housed with adults, severe exploitation and abuse are likely to result. Human Rights Watch encountered cases of juveniles housed with adults in South Africa, Brazil, Indonesia, Romania, Peru and the United States. With few exceptions, the prison systems we visited segregate prisoners by gender.

Some prison systems separate prisoners using criteria that are patently unfair. In India, for example, prisoners are officially classified according to their social and economic status. Those classified as belonging to the richer classes receive far better treatment than poorer inmates. A similar, though unofficial, practice exists in Brazil, Mexico and Zaire.

WOMEN

Because women constitute fewer than 7 percent of the world's prisoners, their needs—particularly regarding menstruation, pregnancy and motherhood—are often ignored by prison administrators. Although the level of violence among inmates is much lower in women's prisons, the inmates are more vulnerable to abuse by prison staff.

In a number of prison systems, including Romania and Kenya, female inmates are denied access to sufficient supplies of tampons and sanitary napkins. Worse yet is the abuse and inadequate care many women suffer during pregnancy in prison. Although some countries provide decent care and conditions for pregnant women, many pay little regard to medical needs and others inflict deliberate cruelty upon pregnant women.

For women with infants, the conditions in prison vary widely. In most countries, authorities allow new mothers to keep their babies with them in prison. The United States is a conspicuous exception. Most U.S. prison systems, including the Federal system, do not allow newborn children to stay with their mothers. Some prison systems impede contacts between mothers and their non-infant children, banning them completely or allowing visits to take place only through a glass partition.

Women in prison often suffer from inferior opportunities for work, education and recreation. In many countries, they are assigned lower-paying and more menial jobs and often have extremely limited options for education by comparison to the offerings for men.

Since women tend to be poorer than men, they often have fewer possessions while incarcerated. In many countries, prison authorities do not take into account that the families of women may not have the means or the desire to assist them with food and clothing and other needs.

As there are comparatively few women in prison, many countries have only a handful of institutions that house women prisoners. In large countries such as Egypt or the United States, this makes visiting difficult for the families of women from distant regions.

MASTER/SERVANT RELATIONSHIPS

Many prison authorities ignore, and sometimes encourage, exploitation by strong inmates of the weak. This is often the case in prison systems in which the authorities do not provide adequately for all the prisoners' basic needs. In these situations, some prisoners are forced to rely on other prisoners to meet their daily needs for food and clothing. The result is that the poorer prisoners become enslaved to the more well-to-do, performing everyday chores as well as sexual favors, in return for basic goods.

Another kind of relationship of domination between prisoners arises when authorities sanction so called "convict officers." In a number of countries, officials designate certain prisoners to positions of authority to perform duties customarily assigned to prison staff. These prisoners thus exercise a great deal of power over other inmates. This results in a startling amount of abuse and subjugation of certain prisoners.

DEATH ROW

Human Rights Watch opposes the death penalty under all circumstances primarily because of its inherent cruelty. This inherent cruelty is made worse by the fact that prisoners on death row are often made to suffer pains and penalties beyond those of other prisoners. These can endure many years and may include strict isolation and denial of any activity; the use of leg-irons and other restraints; confinement to dark and silent cells or cells lit twenty-four hours a day; and subjection to verbal taunts by prison personnel. Such conditions pervade death row in many of the countries we investigated, including China, Jamaica, Russia, Indonesia, South Africa and the United States.

ACTIVITIES

Though boredom is endemic in all prisons, prison authorities generally provide few opportunities for diversion and productive activity. In many countries, prisoners languish in their cells nearly all day with only a scattered few minutes of diversion. Such idleness is particularly difficult in overcrowded conditions and can lead to hostility among inmates and ultimately to violence. In contrast, in other countries, the authorities go to great lengths to provide recreation, work and extensive education opportunities for the inmates.

WORK

Prison labor has many benefits for the prisoner and society: it makes time pass quickly; it teaches good habits and skills; it provides income for the inmate and his or her family; and it can provide a way to earn an early release. But prison labor can also be a means of exploitation and punishment of the prisoner, virtually enslaving him to the state.

Some prison systems attempt to earn profits or at least achieve self-sufficiency through the labor of prisoners. This tends to promote abuse of prisoners in the authorities' quest to be more efficient and productive. The abuse can take many forms. In China, prisoners are sometimes held beyond the length of their sentences and forced to remain at their prison jobs, often for the rest of their lives. Chinese prisoners are also often punished for refusing to work or for failing to meet quotas. In many countries, prisoners perform unsafe and highly unpleasant work, evidently because it would be too expensive to pay a free citizen to carry out the task. The compensation for this or any other work in prison is almost always very low.

AVAILABILITY OF PRISON RULES

An absolute necessity for the observance of human rights in prison systems is the existence of rules that set forth prisoners' rights and obligations and that provide mechanisms for oversight of prison conditions. To be effective, rules must meet three criteria: they must conform to international standards; they must be made readily available to all prisoners, staff and outsiders; and they must be followed consistently.

The rules of almost all countries conform to international standards. But this is all too often merely lip service; they exist to allow governments to cite them in response to complaints rather than to take action against the violation. Equally troublesome is the fact that, while the rules exist, many inmates and staff are completely unaware of them. Rules and procedures that are unknown to prisoners are useless. The promulgation and availability of rules that are taken seriously are essential to the maintenance of adequate prison conditions.

DISCIPLINE

Many of the most appalling human rights abuses that take place in the world's prisons are perpetrated in the name of maintaining discipline. While discipline is an absolute necessity in prisons, prison authorities the world over attempt to achieve that goal by inflicting punishments that are cruel, humiliating, arbitrary and lacking in due process. Furthermore, a great many of these punishments are unauthorized, violating not only international standards but also the standards established by the prison system itself.

It is generally accepted that penalties should be imposed on prisoners who destroy property, commit violent acts, or seriously disrupt order. However, many prison authorities impose harsh penalties for much less serious offenses such as disobeying restrictions on reading, speaking too loudly, failing to keep a tidy cell or failing to report infractions by others.

Only two countries (Egypt and South Africa) whose prisons were visited by Human Rights Watch authorize corporal punishment. Nevertheless, in varying degree, physical violence is used in virtually all the prison systems we investigated. Moreover, the violence in Egypt and South Africa exceeds what the laws in those countries envision. We are aware of prisoners in Egypt who were beaten to death for minor infractions or for simply speaking their minds. A common tactic is for several guards to participate in a ruthless beating that focuses on the most sensitive parts of the prisoner's body.

Many countries, China in particular, use isolation as a form of punishment. While Chinese law forbids solitary confinement for more than fifteen days, some prisoners there have been isolated for several years. Similar outrages take place in Cuba, South Africa and the United States. Some inmates in isolation have to endure additional punishments such as limited diets and prolonged standing. Isolation cells are often designed to inflict punishment on their occupants; many are tiny, dark, crowded, without ventilation and infested with insects or deliberately unsanitary.

Physical restraints are a universal and necessary tool in law enforcement and incarceration, but their use in many countries is excessive and cruel. In a number of countries, devices such as chains, leg irons, fetters and shackles are used to punish inmates for alleged infractions and not only to restrain a prisoner who poses a security risk.

Other excessive and unfair forms of punishment include curtailing family visits, transferring the prisoner to another facility remote from family and certain bizarre practices such as forced prolonged standing and denial of clothing and other so-called privileges.

Due process is frequently denied the prisoner when disciplinary action is taken. In most countries we visited, the authorities regularly fail to allow prisoners an opportunity to defend themselves and to appeal a decision even when such procedures are required by law. This results in arbitrary and disproportionate punishment for many prisoners. Frequently, collective punishments are imposed on large groups of prisoners.

Some prison systems, such as those in the United States and Israel and the Occupied Territories impose punishments without declaring them as such. Authorities isolate prisoners in the name of security when the real reason is punitive retaliation for an alleged infraction.

BEATINGS AND RESTRAINTS

Many prisoners are forced to endure beatings and other abuses that serve purposes aside from punishment. Though the most frequent perpetrators of these abuses are police, prison officials also inflict unwarranted beatings that are a regular part of prison life. These beatings may be used to extort bribes, to intimidate prisoners or as part of cell searches. At other times, however, they are seemingly random sadistic outbursts by prison officials.

In many countries prisoners are routinely beaten on arrival in an attempt by officials to make clear who is in control. Frequently, during a cell search, guards not only destroy all the possessions of the prisoner, but they beat and humiliate him as well. This takes place in a wide spectrum of countries, including China, Turkey, Jamaica and Egypt.

Women are particularly vulnerable to abuse in prison. Rape is often used as a means of intimidation. As it does in the outside world, it is also employed as an act of violent domination.

AFTER A RIOT

A great many appalling human rights abuses occur in the wake of prison riots. While force is sometimes legitimately used to suppress riots, the purpose is often to exact revenge on the rioters. Extrajudicial executions and summary beatings of prisoners are frequent in the aftermath of prison riots.

Following several riots in 1986 in Peruvian prisons, no fewer than ninety inmates were killed by authorities after the rebellion was clearly over. Similarly, scores of inmates were killed by Brazilian prison authorities after violence had subsided in a number of riot incidents since 1989. Human Rights Watch has also documented extra-judicial killings in the aftermath of protests in Venezuelan and South African prisons. We also have documented brutal beatings of prisoners in apparent revenge after riots in Spanish, Polish and American prisons.

CONTACTS WITH OUTSIDERS

Contacts with the outside world—visits, mail, access to media, packages, phone calls—are all vital to a prisoner's well being and eventual reintegration into society. Furthermore, the flow of communication between prisoners and the outside is crucial in exposing and preventing human rights abuses.

In many prison systems a number of policies are prevalent that severely inhibit contacts. Among these are the use of incommunicado detention and the failure of authorities to notify relatives about an arrest. These policies leave prisoners cut off from the outside world for extended periods. Prison authorities also frequently put limits on prisoners' correspondence, visits (from relatives, friends and lawyers) and access to information sources such as newspapers and television.

NONGOVERNMENTAL MONITORS

Much abuse of human rights in prisons occurs when governments prevent outside groups from investigating conditions. Abuses are much less likely to occur if prison authorities know that outsiders will inspect and that abuses will be publicized and denounced.

A number of different types of organizations play important roles in monitoring prisons. Though local human rights groups are often in the best position to monitor, they are not always allowed access to prisons and prisoners. International human rights organizations such as Human Rights Watch may be permitted to visit prisons from which local groups have been excluded. In addition, the distinctive role of the International Committee of the Red Cross and its standing under international law provide it with special access to perform humanitarian services.

Publicizing the findings of prison visits is a key element in the effective monitoring of prison conditions. Dissemination of the findings through the press and through other sources can generate serious discussion of the reported abuses. An exception to this rule is the ICRC. Though its findings are confidential, it is frequently effective against torture and other abuses, because of the frequency of its visits and the material help it can offer to inmates.

THE UNITED NATIONS

The United Nations had addressed prison conditions in a number of human rights agreements including the Universal Declaration of Human Rights and the International Covenant on Civil and Political Rights. It has also adopted the Standard Minimum Rules for the Treatment of Prisoners as well as mechanisms for the implementation of those rules. The U.N. conducts periodic surveys on the implementation of the rules and on demographic trends in the world's prisons. While these agreements and efforts by the U.N. are important signs of concern for those incarcerated, they have been largely unsuccessful in improving the conditions under which prisoners live.

THE NUMBERS

Though the public perception is that imprisonment affects only a marginal number of people, the statistics tell a different story. In the United States, there are 455 prisoners per 100,000 people at any given time. While this is the highest reported rate in any sizeable country in the world, there are several countries whose rates approach that of the United States. The global data are woefully incomplete, however, as such countries as China and India have not given full accounts of their prison populations. Estimates suggest that the world rate is approximately 106 prisoners per 100,000 population, or about 5,300,000 people in prison at any given time. These numbers do not adequately reflect the much larger number who are detained or held in jail and police lockups for short periods. In the United States, a total of 3,483 per 100,000 people find themselves behind bars for some period of time during each year.

Worldwide, the total number confined at some point during any given year is in the tens of millions and much higher yet over the course of a lifetime. The scope of these numbers suggests that imprisonment is by no means a marginal issue.

RECOMMENDATIONS

At the end of each of the topical chapters that follow, Human Rights Watch provides a series of detailed recommendations aimed at minimizing abuses and at improving conditions. We stress in particular the improvements that can be achieved through policy and attitude changes alone, and to a lesser extent, with substantial investments. We also draw a line below which no government may go in its treatment of prisoners; poverty is no excuse for deficiencies that cause excessive suffering. In summary, Human Rights Watch recommends:

- pre-trial detention should be avoided whenever possible and should be replaced by a bail system; it should always count as time served and never exceed the maximum sentence for the offense a detainee is charged with; and its duration should be limited by law;
- investigating authorities should never be given jurisdiction over the conditions of detention under which suspects are held;

- regardless of how severe the economic conditions in any given country, the government must provide certain physical amenities for those it decides to incarcerate; in particular physical conditions must not be harmful to an inmate's health. Sufficient lighting, bedding, and clothing must be provided, so as not to cause hardship or such diseases as skin ailments;
- deliberate infliction of harsh physical conditions should cease;
- regardless of how poor a country is, it must provide adequate food to its prisoners: unspoiled, sufficient in caloric intake, and balanced so as to afford needed vitamins and other essentials. Prison management must also provide drinkable water in amounts sufficient for the climate and the time of year. There is no justification for going below this minimum;
- medical care is an aspect of prison conditions where improvements often require financial expenditures. Recognizing this, Human Rights Watch believes that there are certain minimum standards that must be met by every country. As a minimum we recommend that every prison should have a primary health care professional and a primary health care center equipped to provide vaccinations, first aid and basic medications for common illnesses. Patients in need of more sophisticated care should be referred to a primary care doctor, a specialist or to a hospital;
- a problem related to medical care that is pervasive in prison systems worldwide and that *can* be remedied without increased expenditures is the frequent attitude among prison officials that any medical complaint by a prisoner is evidence of malingering. Prison administrators should ensure that officials deal with medical complaints by inmates with appropriate seriousness and concern;
- every prison system has an obligation to consider the problem of AIDS and to devise a set of policies that would address such concerns as the need to provide proper medical care to those who require it; that would protect the privacy and other rights of those who are infected; and that would help to limit the spread of AIDS among prisoners;
- it is essential to separate the most dangerous inmates from the more vulnerable, and a classification system should be in place at *every* stage of incarceration, starting with police detention.

Furthermore, juveniles should never be housed in adult institutions, regardless of whether they sleep in separate cells or not; dormitory housing should be used as sparingly as possible; in particular, its use should be avoided in police lockups and jails, and they should never be used in maximum security institutions;

- efforts should be made to address specific problems of female prisoners, both physiological and social, as well as those due to women's low numbers in prisons and the resulting scarcity of female institutions;

- newborn babies should be allowed to stay with their mothers and prison authorities should provide adequate living conditions for the babies, including proper sanitary conditions, access to fresh air and medical care. The medical care should involve all the prophylactic procedures, such as shots, that should be administered in the given country to all babies. Efforts should also be made to facilitate mothers' contacts with their other children and their right to direct their upbringing;

- no inmate should ever be placed in a position to exercise significant authority over other prisoners. Though we advocate the employment of inmates in a variety of maintenance jobs in prisons, we are firmly opposed to assigning inmates positions of power over fellow prisoners. The institution of convict officers must be abolished;

- awaiting execution is, in and of itself, one of the greatest sufferings a human being can experience. Though we advocate abolishing the death penalty altogether, countries that retain it should undertake all efforts to avoid exacerbating the suffering;

- no inmate, regardless of the institution's circumstances, should be deprived of the right to daily time outdoors. In addition, there are many things prison administrators can do to alleviate boredom and reduce tensions with little money or through policy changes alone, including: inmates should never be banned from reading and should always have access to periodicals and broadcast media; there should be no limits on the number of letters received and mailed by prisoners; inmates should be allowed to have radios and TV sets in their cells;

- on the basis of our research in several countries, it appears that most human rights violations related to prison work occur when prisons are assigned to fulfill income-generating goals. When it imprisons its citizens, a government assumes a variety of responsibilities for them, including an economic responsibility. Provisions must be made in the national budget for the cost of the prison system. Prisons should not be required to generate income for the national economy;

- prisoners should not be required to work more than the standard weekly number of work hours in the country; if overtime is needed (during harvest time, for example), it should be voluntary and with compensation, such as extra pay, vacation from work at a later time, or eventual reduction of the sentence;
- prison labor should take place under safety conditions that are not inferior to those in the country as a whole;
- demeaning or excessively arduous labor and increased production quotas should never be used as punishment;
- prisoners should be paid for their work;
- the availability of the rules, and access to legal documents by all prisoners, are crucial in safeguarding human rights in prisons. Every prisoner should be issued a copy of the rules upon his or her arrival in the prison; if for technical reasons it is impossible to provide each prisoner with a personal copy, regulations should be posted in a place accessible at all times by all prisoners. A system should be established for illiterate prisoners to be thoroughly informed about the regulations;
- prison libraries accessible to all prisoners should have copies of the country's prison-related laws and of the U.N. Standard Minimum Rules for the Treatment of Prisoners;
- sanctions for violating the rules are necessary in prisons, as they are in any society or community if it is to function properly. But, as our research demonstrates, a fundamental right—freedom from cruel and unusual punishment—is often ignored when it comes to punishing prisoners. To eradicate cruelty inflicted on prisoners by prison staff is not a matter of huge investments. What is needed most of all is a policy decision at the central level of the country's prison administration and the will to enforce this policy. We believe that disciplinary measures, whether authorized or not, should be closely scrutinized by all those monitoring prison conditions: official prison inspectors, judges, nongovernmental organizations, and international bodies;

- violence by those charged with law enforcement—that is police and prison staff—is a serious and troubling phenomenon and reflects a low regard for the rule of law. But in contrast to some other aspects of prison conditions, violence and cruelty on the side of the prison staff can be decreased by changes in policy and attitude, and do not require large investments. Governments must make it a priority to eradicate violence from their places of confinement.

- so as to allow identification of assailants and thus decrease the possibility of assault, prison staff should always wear identification badges. The failure to wear such a badge should be considered a disciplinary infraction;

- in countries where practices of physical abuse are reported by the press or by domestic or international human rights monitors, independent investigative commissions should be established to examine these accusations, identify those responsible for such abuses and to take the disciplinary measures required to eliminate such behavior and provide the information to law enforcement agencies required to initiate prosecutions;

- the period right after a prison disturbance has been quelled is often the moment when the most extreme human rights violations are likely to occur. The level of tension is usually extremely high; events tend to occur very fast; and those who normally run the prison are not necessarily in full control, especially after emergency forces have been deployed. When there are casualties on the side of the government, troops often seek revenge. Riot gear frequently makes future identification impossible and, thereby, increases the likelihood of abuse. To minimize violence and other forms of summary punishment, we recommend that members of forces that may be deployed in subduing prison uprisings be given thorough training as to when and what type of force may be used; use of violence against individuals who have surrendered must be banned; and any prison disturbance that results in serious injury or death, or in which a shot is fired, should be the subject of an independent inquiry, and the findings should be disclosed publicly;

- Human Rights Watch believes that contacts with the outside world are among the most important aspects of prison conditions, both as a means of preventing abuses and as a way to help an inmate stay out of prison after he or she is released. This is also one of the aspects of prison conditions where a lot can be achieved through policy changes and without great financial cost. Consequently, we call on prison administrations to undertake all efforts to facilitate contacts by prisoners with the outside;

- particularly because of the history of abuse, incommunicado detention should be prohibited;
- the next of kin must be notified of an arrest within twenty-four hours; prison administrations must also notify prisoners' next of kin about a transfer, serious illness or death of a prisoner within twenty-four hours. The same should apply to notification of a prisoner about a close relative's death or serious illness;
- prisoners in pre-trial detention should have contact privileges (visits, mail, access to newspapers and broadcasts) that are at least as broad as those for sentenced prisoners;
- Human Rights Watch believes that for a prison system to function properly and to minimize abuses, a system for access by independent human rights organizations as well as by the media must be established. Exclusion of such visits usually means but one thing: the government has something to hide;
- a system for ongoing access to prisons by local human rights organizations and for access by international groups that demonstrate an ongoing concern with prison conditions should be established;
- a policy for providing access to prisons by members of all media (including broadcast), and for confidential interviews with all prisoners should be implemented;
- the results of prison inspections should be made a matter of public record except to the degree that the confidences of inmates may be violated or in the special circumstances of investigations by the International Committee of the Red Cross;
- with respect to the United Nations, we believe that creating a U.N. body with a mandate for inspecting prisons is the key to more effective implementation of the Standard Minimum Rules. We also believe that a permanent Working Group on prison conditions, along the lines of the Working Group on Disappearances, would play an important part in the improvement of human rights conditions in prisons worldwide. Such a Working Group should undertake prison inspections, hold

hearings and publish its findings in reports for general distribution. Using information reported by the Working Group as well as other U.N. agencies, the secretary general should publish an annual report on prison conditions. In addition, we call on the secretary general to undertake annual demographic surveys of prisons worldwide, in place of the current quinquennial surveys, and to publish the findings within the year following the year to which the surveys refer. We also call on the U.N. to sponsor periodic international conferences on prison conditions. These conferences would be effective in stigmatizing the world's worst violators before the eyes of the international community;

• finally, since the conditions, trends and methods of incarceration undergo constant change, the U.N. should undertake periodic examinations of the rules for the purpose of revising them to keep pace with these changes.

CONDITIONS

1
PRE-TRIAL DETENTION

Throughout the world, Human Rights Watch found that pre-trial inmates are generally confined in far worse conditions than those endured by prisoners convicted of the most heinous crimes. This was also true in those countries with legal systems that presume innocence before guilt.

One reason is that pre-trial detainees are usually held in facilities meant for short-term stays, such as police stations or jails that lack facilities such as recreation areas, dining halls or work places. Police stations, the first stop for many inmates, are usually the worst; not only are the conditions bad, but also they are usually where most physical abuses occur. (See chapter on "Beatings and Restraints.") They are filthy, often stuffy and dim, and seldom offer opportunities for exercise or recreation. Cells are often far more cramped and overcrowded than within the country's prison system. The same is often true for pre-trial facilities in countries where unconvicted prisoners are held in separate institutions. In Russia, whose prison system as a whole is used under its stated capacity, pre-trial facilities in large cities such as Moscow hold twice as many inmates as they have beds, and prisoners often have to sleep in shifts.

POLICE LOCKUPS

Recently apprehended prisoners are usually confined together, regardless of the charges against them: those suspected of minor offenses, such as driving while intoxicated or shoplifting, may find themselves sharing a cell with those suspected of violent crimes.

Many countries have legal limits on the length of time a person may spend in a police station, but in practice these are often extended.

In South Africa inmates are supposed to be transferred to a prison within forty-eight hours of the arrest, but a judge may significantly extend that period. In one police station in a black township near Pretoria, we encountered several juvenile prisoners whose stay in that police station that day was being extended for another three weeks. They

3

were living in a dark, crowded cell, with absolutely nothing to do, with no exercise facilities other than a small patio adjacent to the cell, and with no facilities or established system for family visits.

In Romania prisoners under investigation are held in police lockups and are only sent to prison to await trial after the investigative procedure has been completed. Human Rights Watch found that some detainees are held in lockups for two or three months, and occasionally for as long as twenty months. Cells in police lockups are extremely overcrowded and stuffy. They usually lack toilets or sinks, and inmates are let out of their cells just three times a day to use the bathroom. Otherwise, except for interrogation sessions, many inmates are continuously confined in their cells. Though some facilities have small outdoor exercise areas, many make no provision whatsoever for exercise.

ISOLATION

In some countries pre-trial detention is ruled by the interests of the investigation. Inmates are under the jurisdiction of the prosecuting authorities and they, and not the prison administration, make all vital decisions regarding conditions of incarceration. They routinely prevent detainees from communicating with the outside world or inmates other than their cellmates, to make it impossible for them to influence the testimony or conduct of other involved parties, whether suspects or witnesses.

In Russia pre-trial detainees often see no one but their cellmates or guards. They may not receive visitors or send letters unless the investigator in charge authorizes it.

Similarly, in Poland, the prosecutor oversees a pre-trial detainee's contacts with the outside world. Visits must be authorized and correspondence is censored by the prosecutor, with mail sometimes withheld for weeks at a time.

In Romania inmates under investigation are not allowed to send or receive any correspondence, and, though in theory they are entitled to two visits per month with immediate family, they usually are not allowed to see any visitors until the completion of the investigation. In the lockups, inmates are not allowed to communicate with anybody other than their cellmates; and windows are kept shut, even in the summer, to prevent any possible contact with accomplices.

Under these conditions, a prosecutor is given enormous power over the detainee, who, by virtue of recent arrest, is at the most vulnerable stage of his or her incarceration.

The isolation of pre-trial detainees, on the pretense of preventing concealment or meddling with evidence, has the additional effect of putting pressure on the suspect. That pressure, sometimes indirect, is in other cases quite open. In Romania we documented instances of outright blackmail by the prosecution. One inmate reported that the investigator told him: "You are a rascal and so am I. If you confess to some of these charges, I'll let you see your girlfriend."[1] Another told us his visits and packages were halted because he refused to plead guilty. Other Romanian inmates also reported that their packages were stopped because they did not cooperate with the criminal prosecution.

DETENTION OF WITNESSES

The Prison Project of Human Rights Watch ordinarily focuses on conditions of confinement, not the reasons for imprisonment. In this instance, however, we depart briefly from this rule to highlight an appalling phenomenon we encountered in India: the detention of victims of rape to assure their appearance in court as witnesses. According to human rights lawyers and women's rights advocates we interviewed, the Indian authorities frequently detain female rape victims and place them in "protective custody." Ostensibly this is done because of the stigma an Indian woman suffers if she has been raped and the authorities fear that the victim will not appear in court to testify against her rapist, so she is incarcerated to make sure that she will testify. This is even done in cases when the rapist has not been apprehended. Astonishingly, such "protective custody" confinement has been known to last for as long as three or four years.

---

[1] See Helsinki Watch, "Lockups in Romania," *A Human Rights Watch Short Report*, vol. 5, no. 2 (January 1993).

THE DURATION OF PRE-TRIAL DETENTION

The length of pre-trial detention, which often reaches several months, and sometimes years, is another matter of serious concern.

In Turkey, Human Rights Watch documented a case of a young female university student who was held in prison for five years, until a judge decided when her case came to trial that there was no evidence against her—she was a victim of mistaken identity—and ordered her release. Also in Turkey, in some political trials involving multiple defendants, the pre-trial period has been known to extend as long as nine years (see chapter on Turkey).

Pre-trial detention of a few years is not uncommon in other countries as well. According to a Polish study, as of August 31, 1990, 249 people had been held in pre-trial detention for between one and two years, and forty-two others for more than two years. The situation has not changed dramatically since this study was published because the law has remained the same. It allows for indefinite imprisonment, as long as a court authorizes such a detention.

In Spain, the legal maximum for pre-trial detention is four years, and many individuals are held close to that time before they are brought to trial. The Ombudsman of the Spanish region of Catalonia told us that it is not infrequent for an individual to serve the entire sentence corresponding to his or her crime by the time a trial starts.

In Peru where the justice system has been backlogged for the past several years, many pre-trial prisoners have been detained longer than the maximum sentence for the crime of which they were accused. Pre-trial prisoners or those awaiting sentence account for 77 percent of that country's prison population.

In Zaire pre-trial detention may last for years and only 15 percent of the country's prison population has been convicted.

In Mexico and India more than half of all inmates are awaiting trial or sentence. Among the most disgraceful cases Human Rights Watch encountered was that of a man in Kenya who was found innocent in October 1990 after being held in remand for nine years on murder charges.

Apart from all other human rights concerns, holding unsentenced prisoners beyond their maximum potential sentence exacerbates overcrowding. Getting rid of that backlog would be an efficient way to deal with this problem that plagues many prison systems, including those of Spain and Peru.

In at least one country where we investigated prison conditions—South Africa, where prisons are severely overcrowded—pre-trial detention does not automatically count toward the sentence. A judge may, but is not required, to count time served before conviction. Pre-trial detainees account for about 25 percent of the prison population.[2] Automatically crediting the time spent in pre-trial detention toward any eventual sentence would obviously decrease overcrowding.

RECOMMENDATIONS

Our principal recommendation with respect to pre-trial detention is that it should be avoided whenever possible; that efforts should be undertaken to establish a bail system in countries where one does not yet exist; and, in those places where there is a bail system, its use should be the rule, not the exception.

To diminish the hardships and human rights violations related to pre-trial detention, Human Rights Watch recommends:

- implementation of careful classification from the moment of detention. Prisoners accused of violent crimes should never be held with those detained on suspicion of minor offenses;
- pre-trial detention should always count as time served and never exceed the maximum sentence for the offense a detainee is charged with;
- the duration of pre-trial detention should be limited by law and should not exceed three months in cases in which the maximum penalty is no more than a year in prison; six months where the maximum penalty is no more than five years; and a year in all other cases. The only exception should relate to delays caused by the accused or his or her counsel;
- investigating authorities should never be given jurisdiction over the conditions of detention under which suspects are held;

---

[2] *SA Barometer*, vol. 6, no. 19 (September 25, 1992).

- pre-trial detainees should be arraigned within twenty-four hours of arrest. If they are to be held while awaiting trial, it should be under the custody of an agency that does not have police duties;
- pre-trial detainees should have, at a minimum, the same rights regarding visits, correspondence, packages from home and recreation as those enjoyed by sentenced prisoners.

2
PHYSICAL CIRCUMSTANCES

Overcrowding is perhaps the most pervasive problem Human Rights Watch encounters in prisons worldwide. It is a principal factor adversely affecting physical conditions, for when too many people use any building, the living conditions deteriorate no matter how solid the original structure. In many countries where the infrastructure was poor to begin with, recent overcrowding has resulted in living conditions that can only be described as abysmal. Several countries still make use of old and dilapidated prisons, and some, like a fourteenth-century former convent in Poland, were never intended for use as prisons. Other facilities that were never meant to hold prisoners for long periods of time, such as jails in Brazil or pre-trial facilities in Moscow or St. Petersburg, in fact incarcerate people for years.

It is difficult, if not impossible, to achieve meaningful improvements in the physical conditions of incarceration without investing significant sums of money. But lack of funds is no excuse for any government—no matter how poor—to subject its citizens to subhuman conditions that not only violate human rights but minimal standards of decency as well. Even in this aspect of prison conditions, there are modifications that could be made through policy changes that do not require huge financial expenditures.

OVERCROWDING

In virtually every country where Human Rights Watch conducted prison investigations, overcrowding was either systemic or a problem in at least one type of facility. In Russia labor colonies or camps, where most prisoners serve sentences, are not overcrowded, but other types of institutions suffer from tremendous overpopulation. It is also worth pointing out that when an institution or system is said to be close to 100 percent capacity, it is actually overcrowded, since at any moment some cells are not used for housing due to repairs or for other reasons.

Among those prison systems in countries that provided us with statistics, Brazil's is the most severely overcrowded. As of late 1992, the country held about 124,000 prisoners in institutions designed for fewer than 52,000. Not all the prisons were overcrowded, which means that some prisons held significantly more than two and a half times as many inmates as their stated capacity would allow. Among the prisons we saw in Rio de Janeiro and São Paulo, cells were so packed that there was barely room to move. At the Agua Santa prison, most cells measures approximately 450 square feet and held between 25 and 35 prisoners. One 750-square-foot cell in that prison held 90 people, providing 8 1/3 square feet per prisoner. In Guarulhos, near São Paulo, an average of 20 prisoners were housed in 186-square-foot cells. In some institutions, we saw shoes stuck between the bars in the front of a cell. We were told that the cells were so crowded that prisoners took off their shoes inside to avoid hurting one another when they inevitably stepped on each other's toes while trying to move around.

In Russia's pre-trial facilities, especially those in large cities, the overcrowding is horrendous. In Moscow inmates sleep in three separate shifts; some suffer from swollen legs from standing for many hours a day because there is not enough room to sit.

In 1990 when a Human Rights Watch delegation was in Jamaica, we saw a 400-square-foot cell that held 50 inmates at the time of the visit, providing 8 square feet per prisoner. The superintendent of that prison volunteered the fact that this particular cell sometimes held up to 150 men. In October 1992, in a horrible example of overcrowding and police negligence, 19 men were confined in a 8-by-7-foot cell at the Constant Springs lockup in Jamaica. The only ventilation came from holes drilled into the solid door of the cell. The men were held in the cell for 40 hours while police ignored their cries for air. Three men died of asphyxiation.

In the United States in January 1992, the courts found that overcrowding was so severe that it violated the constitutional prohibition on cruel and unusual punishment in forty states, the District of Columbia, and more than 500 jail jurisdictions.

In Egypt, we visited a windowless cell that measured approximately 20 by 100 feet, holding 147 men.

In Kenya, an inmate in the Kamiti Maximum Security prison in Nairobi said that because of the overcrowding, "While sleeping at night, one could not turn unless the whole lot in the cell turned."[1]

---

[1] Africa Watch, *Kenya: Taking Liberties* (New York: Human Rights Watch, 1991), p. 159.

On several occasions, we observed that overcrowding was exacerbated by the uneven distribution of inmates within the existing facilities. During our 1989 visit to Poland, we saw some severely overcrowded police cells, while adjacent cells were empty. We encountered exactly the same pattern in Egypt in 1992. Similarly, in the Casa de Detenção prison in São Paulo we saw cells occupied by one or two prisoners, while most others of similar size held five or more.

It is also noteworthy that in most cases, prisoners held under these conditions spend nearly all of their time confined in these cells.

CELL FURNISHINGS

In some prisons we visited in the course of our research we found no furnishings whatsoever. In South Africa many prisons, especially those that had been designated originally as "black prisons" (see the South Africa chapter) do not have beds. In the Rio de Janeiro Agua Santa prison, inmates slept on thin foam rubber mattresses on bare cement. In Egypt, many inmates slept on sheets of cardboard, provided by relatives. In Indonesia, inmates are frequently forced to sleep on bare, damp cement and often suffer from painful joint diseases as a result.

In countries such as Spain, Russia and Romania, inmates ordinarily do get beds assigned to them, but because of overcrowding bunk beds are often stacked as high as four levels. The distances between levels may be two feet or less, creating an intolerable sense of stuffiness and overcrowding.

Prisoners usually accumulate some personal belongings in the course of their incarceration. Lack of personal space to store them was a frequent source of complaints. In Brazil, we observed clotheslines strung across many of the cells we visited on which personal belongings were hung in plastic bags. The same happens in the Russian Krasnopresnenskaia facility. The use of clotheslines increases the sense of crowdedness.

Some prison systems provide their inmates with tables and chairs, making it possible to write and study. But frequently, there are fewer chairs than inmates in the cell. In Poland, where we observed this shortage frequently, the situation was exacerbated by the fact that beds were almost always double bunks and the space between the two bunks was often too narrow to allow inmates to sit comfortably. Polish prisons usually lack dining halls; inmates took their meals in their cells, crouching on their bunks.

PLUMBING AND SANITARY CONDITIONS

Proper sanitary conditions are obviously among the key elements of humane and decent treatment. They have an impact on prisoners' health, morale and to a large extent determine the quality of life in prison. A basic question to ask when examining physical conditions in any prison is whether inmates have free access to toilets and water. While in most cases, among the countries we studied, the answer was "yes," this was not always the case. One of the most disturbing features of the British prison system at the time of our visits there in 1991 was that about 40 percent of all cells did not have plumbing. Inmates had to use plastic buckets as toilets, and were allowed to empty them a few times a day. They told us in interviews that they considered the necessity of living with the presence and smell of these buckets one of the most degrading features of prison life. Currently, a nationwide remodeling campaign is underway, and authorities hope to have plumbing installed in all cells by the end of 1994.

Virtually all the prisons we visited in Jamaica in 1990 lacked the basic necessities for personal hygiene. The cells in the two main prisons lack plumbing and inmates must use slop buckets. In the Kingston General Penitentiary, inmates were required to empty their buckets into non-functioning toilets: the floors of the toilet areas were wet and filthy and the stench was overwhelming. In one prison, we saw human excrement gathering on the grounds of the facility. In the Halfway-Tree lockup, in Kingston, toilets were not functioning at the time of our visit and the stench was oppressive. We were told that toilets were periodically scooped out and the excrement was dumped behind the building. In some cells, inmates urinated through the bars into gullies in front of the cell.

In Egypt, some cells we visited in 1992 had no toilets or running water and inmates there too had to resort to buckets. We also received reports of cells that lacked even such buckets. One prisoner described the conditions in the Cairo el-Makhoum prison in the following way: "During the period the door was locked [from 4 P.M. to 8 A.M.] we were forced to urinate and defecate in a raised area in the cell, in front of the door. This area was about 1 by 1.5 meters [3.2 by 4.9 feet]. There was no drain . . . everything collected in this area until the morning, when it was removed by a sentenced prisoner."[2] Another Egyptian prisoner wrote to Human Rights Watch describing the situation at the Tora Istikbal prison: "There was no provision for defecation and urination. The cell is closed by 3:30 P.M. and opened at 8:30 A.M. The following morning when [the cell is] opened one is obliged to pay [the] equivalent of twenty cents before one is allowed to defecate and shower in the unhealthy lavatory situated within the detention premises."[3]

Many of the prisons we visited throughout the world were dirty. Some were in serious need of painting and general renovation, but many were just filthy due to lack of cleaning—an astonishing fact, since all prisons have a readily available work force. In Puerto Rico, a court-appointed monitor observed trash piling up on the grounds of one of the facilities, and in Spain the cells we visited were generally clean and neat, but the patios and day rooms were full of trash.

LIGHTING

We received many complaints about lighting so inadequate as to make it impossible to read or write in the cell. At the Spanish Town lockup in Jamaica, where some inmates spent as long as five months, the cells were pitch-dark even during the day. In the main police lockup in Warsaw where some inmates formerly spent as long as six months (due to the new regulations, the maximum time of detention at police facilities is now 48 hours), cells were located in the basement and there was hardly any natural light. The electric light was so weak as to make it difficult to distinguish facial features. Punishment cells in Cuba, in which some prisoners have spent extended periods, are completely or almost completely dark.

---

[2] Middle East Watch, *Prison Conditions in Egypt*, (New York: Human Rights Watch, 1993), p. 51.

[3] Ibid., p. 50.

In Spain, in the brand-new police lockups in Madrid and Barcelona, characterized to us as "models," the cells had no windows, and the electric light was dim.

The presence or absence of a light switch inside the cells is another feature that is important to the quality of life in a prison. When light is switched on and off by the guards from outside the cell, it adds to the sense of total loss of control over one's existence, a feeling that is obviously strong to begin with in a prison context. In addition to complaints about the lights going off too early, we also encountered situations in which they were *never* turned off, making it difficult for some inmates to sleep. For example, we heard reports of lights left on continuously in some cells at the Westville prison in Indiana; in all of the Death Row cells at the Pretoria Maximum Security prison in South Africa; and for some political prisoners in China.

CELL TEMPERATURE AND VENTILATION

In overcrowded cells, ventilation is frequently one of the chief problems, exacerbated by the fact that in most prisons a significant proportion of inmates smoke.

When a Human Rights Watch delegation asked prisoners in Romania what was the worst thing about the police lockups there, the first thing most mentioned was the lack of fresh air. "Even ten minutes a day of fresh air would be a relief," they told us.[4] In Spain, we found the police lockups extremely stuffy even when cells were empty: they were located in the basement and had no windows. We found similar conditions even in the two newly-designed facilities, described to us as state of the art.

Extreme temperatures (too hot in the summer and very cold in the winter) were a further source of complaint virtually everywhere we visited, as in the case of Boniato prison in Cuba, where the small barred windows lack glass.

---

[4] Helsinki Watch, "Lockups in Romania," *A Human Rights Watch Short Report*, vol. 5, no. 2 (January 1993), p. 6.

INSECT AND RODENT INFESTATION

Unsanitary conditions often lead to rodent and insect infestations in prisons. In Brazil, we saw rats in at least one prison, and were told of their presence in several more. We also saw insects, including huge cockroaches. In addition, some inmates showed us signs of insect bites all over their bodies. The lack of glass in the windows in Boniato prison in Cuba makes mosquitoes a severe problem during certain seasons.

We heard reports of similar problems from former prisoners in Turkey. One former female prisoner told us of an incident in which some of her fellow inmates had to be hospitalized because their noses were bitten by rats.

INMATES' CLOTHING AND PHYSICAL APPEARANCE

Clothing, sheets and blankets are obviously basic necessities for sheer survival. Clothing and overall physical appearance, in addition, have an impact on a prisoner's morale. While in the majority of countries we visited clothing appeared adequate, at least from the climatic, if not aesthetic standpoint, we did hear some complaints. In England prisoners complained about not receiving changes of fresh underwear often enough. In Kenya, female security prisoners were forbidden to wear underwear, apparently as a means of humiliation. In Cuba, prisoners we saw in punishment cells were naked or near naked. In Florida, inmates told us of suffering from rashes because they had to put on their underwear when still damp after a wash.

We heard many complaints about insufficient or nonexistent personal hygiene supplies such as soap, toothpaste and toothbrushes. We were also told of a past practice in Poland where inmates had their heads shaved upon arrival in prison. This practice was discontinued when other important changes in prison regulations were also implemented but in Romania and China it is used as of this writing. In Poland, at the time of the other changes in prison regulations, women were also authorized to wear makeup, and many commented that this particular privilege was of great importance to their sense of self-esteem.

PUNITIVE USE OF PARTICULARLY HARSH
PHYSICAL CONDITIONS

In at least three countries, we observed how particularly harsh prison conditions were deliberately imposed on specific groups of inmates.

In the United States, prisoners held in super-maximum security institutions—either because of infractions they had committed in the past or because of their perceived dangerousness and speculation about acts they might commit in the future—are subjected to particularly harsh physical conditions. These inmates are usually housed in sparsely furnished individual cells. For example, in the Florida State Prison at Starke, at the time of our 1991 visit, cells for inmates under "close management" featured only a bed, a sink and a toilet. Some inmates in addition had a trunk for their personal belongings, but none had a table or a chair. Inmates sometimes spent a few years in these conditions, some of them leaving the cell for only a few minutes three times a week to shower, and never going outdoors. A small group of inmates in that prison confined in such conditions also lacked windows. Inmates complained to us of back pain from years of not being able to sit on a piece of furniture that would give them support. Similarly, most inmates at the federal prison at Marion live in single cells without chairs or tables. In the Maximum Control Complex at Westville, Indiana, inmates are housed in cells that have lights on twenty-four hours a day.

In Egypt, we observed that physical conditions under which security prisoners were housed were particularly harsh. For example, security prisoners at the Tora Istikbal prison are often held in small first-floor cells that are deprived of light or ventilation due to a cinderblock wall that runs parallel to the cells, creating a dark ten-foot wide hallway that blocks the entry of light and air from the building's atrium. Many security prisoners also reported they were denied the customary time out of cell afforded to other inmates, especially during the first month or so of their incarceration.

In Cuba, punishment wings in all the men's prisons we saw were dark and provided no more than a concrete bunk.

RECOMMENDATIONS

Regardless of how severe the economic conditions in any given country, the government must provide certain physical amenities for those it decides to incarcerate. In particular:

- physical conditions must not be harmful to an inmate's health. Sufficient lighting, bedding, and clothing must be provided, so as not to cause hardship or such diseases as skin ailments;
- all inmates should have access to toilets and running water at all times;
- light switches should be located inside the cells;
- every inmate should have a bed and a set of bedding adequate for the season of the year;
- every inmate should be provided with basic articles of personal hygiene;
- all inmates should be provided with a place to hold their personal belongings;
- deliberate infliction of harsh physical conditions should cease;
- prisons should be kept clean, including both cells and general areas;
- in prisons with overcrowding, efforts should be made to use the existing cell space evenly;
- when overcrowding is severe, efforts should be made to alleviate the hardships inmates are forced to endure by extending the length of time they spend out of the cells each day;
- the wearing of makeup by women and facial hair by men should be allowed, and heads should never be forcibly shaved.

3
FOOD

The one aspect of prison conditions that provoked the most frequent and bitter complaints in interviews with prisoners is food. Food-related problems included insufficient amounts, monotonous diet, the presence of spoiled foods in the diet, a lack of vital components, such as vitamins, and insufferable taste. Another frequent complaint was the lack of special diets, for health or religious reasons.

Though complaints about prison food were present virtually everywhere, the situation has been life-threatening and even fatal in Zaire, where cases of death from starvation have been reported in 1993.[1] Absence of medical care and severe malnutrition have been endemic in Zairian prisons for a few years now, contributing to an extremely high mortality. Similarly, cases of deaths from starvation have been reported in the Lurigancho prison in Lima, Peru.

In many prisons, there are no dining halls and prisoners take their meals in their cells. Since the cells usually contain a toilet, separated from the living area by a low partition under the best circumstances, and smack in the middle of the living space in most, inmates in many countries are forced to eat their meals in the midst of the unappetizing smell of their toilets. Another unpleasant and often humiliating aspect of prison life with regard to food is the lack of proper utensils. In Brazil, a Human Rights Watch delegation saw inmates using old margarine containers as bowls; in the course of our 1989 visit to Poland, we observed a woman eating her "special diet" meal from a piece of cardboard. Most Jamaican prisoners must make do by eating with their hands.

In addition to complaints about the terrible taste and insufficient quantities of the food served, prisoners frequently told us that there were too few meals, or mealtimes were spaced unevenly throughout the day so that prisoners were frequently hungry for many hours in the evening.

---

[1] Sam Kiley, "Inglorious death for soldiers in Zaire's civil war," *Times* (London), February 9, 1993.

In China, according to our interviews with former political prisoners, inmates receive only two meals at 10 A.M. and 4 P.M. In the United Kingdom, prisoners receive three meals but the last of the day is served between 3 and 4 P.M.; as a result inmates go without food until after 8 A.M. the next morning, when breakfast is served. Similar mealtimes are kept in Jamaica.

In many countries, relatives may bring in food during visits or send packages containing food. In Egypt and Mexico, Human Rights Watch delegations were repeatedly told that the food brought in by relatives is the key to survival because prison food is insufficient.

In the course of prison interviews, we frequently hear the charge that food is being siphoned off by the staff and that inmates with money can purchase it from the management. This seems to be especially true in poor countries and in those with food shortages.

The testimony Human Rights Watch took in Indonesia, from an inmate who served eleven years before release in 1989, is typical: "There was meat twice a week, but the pieces of meat were only the size of a single finger joint. Prison officials siphoned off the rest. Sometimes they took meat away before it even reached the kitchen, because there were hundreds of prison officials who had to be fed as well as the prisoners. Sometimes the head of the prison took the meat away. Sometimes the inmates who worked in the kitchen could see the meat being sold and rich convicts could afford to pay for extra portions."[2]

This former inmate had suggestions for how he thought corruption might be controlled. He told us: "Between 1978 and 1983 there was less corruption because the administrator of the prison was so strict and prisoners could complain directly to the officials. After he left, in 1983, things got worse."[3]

RECOMMENDATIONS

Though we support allowing family members to bring food to prison, the foods brought in from outside should be a supplement and

---

[2] Asia Watch, *Prison Conditions in Indonesia* (New York: Human Rights Watch, 1990), p. 19.

[3] Ibid.

relatives must never be forced to replace what should be provided by the prison. The same is true for purchases from the commissary. Inmates should be allowed to buy a variety of foods from a prison shop, but should never *have to* buy it in order to survive. Whenever food is supplied by sources other than the prison itself, prisoners without relatives or money become extremely vulnerable. This is the situation of foreign prisoners, particularly from other African countries, who are incarcerated in Egypt. They are forced into virtual enslavement to more well-to-do prisoners, performing chores and services for those prisoners to obtain necessary food in exchange.

Solving food problems, unlike some other aspects of prison conditions, in most cases requires money. As noted earlier, Human Rights Watch considers that when a government takes custody of an individual, it automatically assumes responsibility for meeting that person's basic needs and protecting that individual against harm. Consequently Human Rights Watch believes that an essential tenet of all penal systems should be: "You should not detain them if you cannot feed them." Regardless of how poor a country is, it must provide adequate food to its prisoners: unspoiled, sufficient in caloric intake, and balanced so as to afford needed vitamins and other essentials. Prison management must also provide drinkable water in amounts sufficient for the climate and the time of year. There is no justification for going below this minimum.

In addition, Human Rights Watch recommends:

- mealtimes should be spaced so that prisoners do not go hungry for long periods;
- proper utensils should be provided;
- dining halls should be provided wherever possible;
- closer managerial oversight is needed in prisons where food is likely to be pilfered by the staff;
- special diets due to medical requirements or religious beliefs should be accommodated;
- to encourage efforts to maintain the quality and taste of prison food, prisons where prison staff receive their food on the premises should require they receive the same food as the inmates. (This rule is applied in U.S. federal prisons. Not surprisingly, among the prison systems we visited, it was the one where prisoners had the fewest complaints about the food.)

4
A NOTE ON MEDICAL CARE

There were no doctors among the members of the Human Rights Watch delegations that visited prisons, and because of our lack of medical expertise, we have not focused on the quality of health care in prisons. Complaints about the medical care, or lack thereof were, however, among the most frequent we heard in prisons throughout the world. We see an urgent need for specialized investigations by medical professionals that focus particularly on the medical aspect of imprisonment. For now, we offer only a few general comments.

A complaint we heard almost everywhere was that prisoners were denied medical care because of indifference, neglect, and an attitude that could be summed up by the words of a Polish prisoner who said during our 1989 visit: "the medical examination is only verbal. Everybody here is considered a cheater . . . [According to the doctor] nobody is ever seriously sick."[1]

In some countries, denial of medical attention or delay in providing it is used as punishment or a way of putting additional pressure on a prisoner. Particularly gruesome reports about denial of medical attention come from Cuba. In February 1992 Francisco Díaz Mesa, a twenty-four-year-old prisoner in Alambradas de Mancas prison, died after a beating he received in retaliation for banging on the bars of his cell to demand medical attention. Two prisoners in Santa Clara, both reportedly suffering from tuberculosis, were beaten in March 1992 for complaining about the lack of medical attention.

A Chinese political prisoner, Xu Wenli, who developed a lump on the side of his neck in 1983, has been denied medical treatment, even though a top-flight medical unit, the Binhe Hospital, is situated within the Beijing No. 1 prison where he is held.

In the U.S. two federal inmates convicted of politically motivated offenses experienced delay in receiving medical treatment for potentially life-threatening diseases. Silvia Baraldini, who is serving a long-term sentence, endured a six-month delay before surgery was performed on a

---

[1] Helsinki Watch, *Prison Conditions in Poland: An Update* (New York: Human Rights Watch, 1991), p. 23.

lump she discovered that was eventually diagnosed as cancer. According to her testimony, she was initially accused of making up an illness. Dr. Alan Berkman, a physician who suffered from lymphatic cancer while serving a ten-year sentence, experienced repeated delays in obtaining proper treatment. At one point, it took a court order for the Federal Bureau of Prisons to send him to a qualified cancer center.

In Spain a diabetic prisoner in Barcelona who needs insulin shots before all his meals told us that he often received them too late for the shots to take effect by the time he eats. On the day he complained about this to a judge, he did not receive a shot until 11:15 P.M., which he interpreted as a reprisal for making the complaint.

Health care for most of the world's poor is inadequate; for prisoners, often the poorest of the poor, it is usually miserable. Inadequate diet and unhygienic living conditions—frequent problems in prisons—contribute to an extremely high rate of disease and death. According to official statistics, eight percent of the Zairian prison population died in 1991 (in contrast, one quarter of 1 percent of prisoners died in the United States in 1989, the last year for which such data is available); and in March 1993, the director of the Lubumbashi prison in Zaire told us that 173 out of 350 prisoners in his institution were sick. Health care is virtually nonexistent in Zairian prisons and most prisoners suffer from severe malnutrition.

AIDS

An important aspect of the medical situation in prisons is HIV and AIDS. Virtually all prison systems have inmates who are seropositive and in many prisons there are inmates suffering from AIDS. The institutions that we investigated vary greatly in their response, ignoring the problem entirely in some cases while other prisons require that all their inmates should be tested and segregate those who are seropositive.

Though the extent of HIV incidence in prisons reflects the rate of infection in the society at large, the percentage of HIV positive prisoners is usually significantly higher than among the population at large in the same community. Also, as with other afflictions, the suffering that is caused by AIDS is often intensified in prisons. Prisoners with AIDS tend to die sooner than their counterparts outside due to lack of appropriate care.[2] They are also targets of overt or hidden discrimination and, in some cases, victims of serious human rights abuses such as virtual solitary confinement for months or years on end.

Though Human Rights Watch has not undertaken the research that would allow us to propose a specific set of measures to deal with the problem of AIDS in prisons, we believe that every prison system has an obligation to consider the issue and to devise a set of policies that would balance such concerns as the need to provide proper medical care to those who require it; to protect the privacy and other rights of those who are infected; and that would help to stop the spread of AIDS among prisoners.

RECOMMENDATIONS

Medical care is an aspect of prison conditions in which improvements often require financial expenditures. Recognizing this, as in the case of food and physical conditions generally, Human Rights Watch believes that there are certain minimum standards that must be met by every country:

• as a minimum we recommend that every prison should have a primary health care professional and a primary health care center equipped to provide vaccinations, first aid and basic medications for common ailments. Patients in need of more sophisticated care should be referred to a primary care doctor (either within the prison system or in the community). That doctor, in turn, should send a patient to a specialist or to a hospital as required. In countries where prison services do not have hospitals, the country's system of medical services, from primary health care workers all the way to acute care hospitals, must cover prisoners too;

• a problem that is pervasive in prison systems worldwide and that *can* be remedied without increased expenditures is the frequent attitude among prison officials that any medical complaint by a

---

[2] See Catherine M. Bergman, Nancy Neveloff Dubler and Hon. Marvin E. Frankel, "Management of HIV Infection in New York State Prisons," *Columbia Human Rights Law Review* (Spring 1990), p. 363.

prisoner is evidence of malingering.   Prison administrators
should ensure that officials deal with medical complaints by
inmates with appropriate seriousness and concern.   Prison
officials responsible for neglecting medical problems should be
disciplined appropriately.

INMATES

5
CLASSIFICATION

Virtually all prison and detention systems must cope with violence by inmates against their fellow prisoners. One crucial means of controlling and preventing such violence is proper classification of inmates to avoid housing potentially dangerous and predatory prisoners with the vulnerable.

CLASSIFICATION IN JAILS

Proper classification is a particularly important and challenging task at the earliest stages of imprisonment, when inmates are new and many of them completely unknown to their jailers. Unless there are single cells for each inmate, or a system allowing the separation of individuals likely to be dangerous or violent from those detained for minor offenses, someone arrested for a traffic violation may be confined in the same cell with a dangerous criminal. The consequences, as illustrated by the following example (drawn from a U.S. court's records), can be tragic.

Timothy Ryan was arrested and charged with a minor motor vehicle violation. Because he could not post bail, Ryan was sent to jail, where he was placed in a cell with nine other inmates. One of them was Maurice Scott who had already been involved in several violent attacks during the two months of his incarceration. Jail documents showed that Scott had been convicted of a violent crime resulting in the injury of another person. Five days after Ryan's arrest, Scott attacked Ryan in a dispute over some food, breaking his neck and rendering him a quadriplegic for life.[1]

The type of housing and the physical layout of a jail also significantly affect safety because they determine the guards' ability to monitor the situation inside the cells.

---

[1] Ryan v. Burlington County, N.J., 889 F.2d. 1286 (3d Cir. 1989), cited in Human Rights Watch *Prison Conditions in the United States* (New York: Human Rights Watch, 1991), p. 21.

On Rikers Island, a giant, 20,000-inmate jail complex in New York City, where assaults among inmates are frequent, classification is often deficient or nonexistent. The institution's computers do not keep records of recidivists' past behavior in jail, and those with histories of violence toward other inmates may be housed in open dormitories.

In the police lockup in downtown Cape Town, South Africa, the male part of the lockup consists of 14 cells with a capacity of up to five detainees each, and one large cell with a capacity of 15 inmates. That larger cell is the furthest from the guard's station (about 80 feet) and is separated from the guards by a two-inch-thick steel door and a bend in the hallway. There is no buzzer in the cell to summon help. Not surprisingly, violence is a particular problem in the Cape Town lockup.

CLASSIFICATION AND MIXING OF SENTENCED PRISONERS

Most countries have some system of classification for sentenced prisoners, usually according to the type of offense for which they have been convicted, resulting in confinement in prisons with different security levels. Safety problems obviously arise most often in maximum security institutions where all inmates have been convicted of serious offenses and most are deemed dangerous and violent. One important safety measure in such institutions is to avoid housing large groups of inmates together. We at Human Rights Watch were particularly distressed when we found dormitory-style housing in such institutions, as in the U.S. and South Africa where large numbers of extremely dangerous individuals were often left unsupervised for the night and thus free to inflict considerable violence on one another.

In Russia, the current classification system places offenders convicted of the most serious and violent crimes in the highest security category alongside repeat offenders, regardless of the type of crime. As a result, recidivists who have never committed a violent crime—such as compulsive shoplifters—are housed together with the most dangerous prisoners in the system.

PROTECTIVE CUSTODY

Some inmates may be particularly vulnerable and likely to be abused by other prisoners. For example certain offenses, such as child abuse or killing a member of the clergy, make an inmate likely to be assassinated by other inmates in some prison systems. Sex offenders or homosexuals are also likely to suffer harassment or abuse in prisons in some countries.

Prison administrations have used protective custody, that is segregation from the general population, to prevent such violence. But protective custody may mean significantly inferior living conditions when compared with life in the general prison population, because such inmates may be housed in virtual isolation and have no access to activities afforded to other inmates. This is apparently often the case in Britain, where we received many complaints to this effect. In one Cuban prison, we encountered a prisoner who had been held for years in the punishment block of Kilo 7 prison in Camagüey and, though his cell had more amenities than the others in that block, he had no access to the work, education or recreation available to the general prison population.

SEPARATION OF JUVENILES FROM ADULTS

The Human Rights Watch Prison Project has not investigated conditions in juvenile detention facilities. Yet during the several years of our prison investigations, on numerous occasions Human Rights Watch encountered juvenile offenders held in adult institutions.

The maximum security Pollsmoor prison in South Africa holds, in addition to more than 2,500 adult offenders, several hundred juveniles. The two groups are housed separately, but the juveniles have some contact with the adults as they are transported to court together. We came upon children as young as ten in that prison. In some Indian prisons, juveniles as young as twelve are confined in adult prisons and mingle with the general prison population in the daytime but sleep in separate quarters.

In Brazil, we encountered four juvenile offenders in an adult prison at Taubate. One sixteen-year-old told us he had tried to commit suicide. We were later told that when he was only fifteen, he had been sexually assaulted in a jail prior to his transfer to prison.

In Indonesia, our delegation observed boys as young as twelve detained in adult prisons. A twelve-year-old boy in Malang prison was in a cell with many adult men.

In the U.S., we documented the case of Jason Iaquinta, who had turned eighteen two weeks before being incarcerated in a jail cell with several older inmates where he was raped and otherwise harassed. The guards finally separated him from the other inmates, placed him in a single cell but failed to supervise him. He committed suicide.

In Romania, juveniles are often housed in adult institutions. Even though they sleep in separate cells, the "cell boss" (see the "Master/Servant Relationship" chapter) is always an adult.

CLASSIFICATION BASED ON ECONOMIC AND SOCIAL STATUS

In the prison system in India, inmates' classification is based on their economic status, and reportedly, a similar system remains in effect in other former British colonies in South Asia. Prisoners are classified "A", "B" or "C", but not on the basis of their crimes; rather, the higher classifications are reserved for those who, according to one of the Jail Manuals, "by social status, education and habit of life have been accustomed to a superior mode of living." In general, those classified "A" or "B" are provided with decent conditions in prison, while "C" prisoners live in more overcrowded cells, get less and poorer-quality food, may correspond less frequently, are not entitled to receive as many publications, must perform menial tasks and are subject to the fetters and handcuffs that are not used on the higher class of prisoners.

In several countries, including Brazil, Mexico and Zaire, though there was no official regulation providing certain inmates with more amenities in prison, some inmates lived under dramatically better conditions than the rest of the prison population. That was generally true for more well-to-do inmates, as well as for prominent drug dealers and convicted policemen and other former officials.

CLASSIFICATION BASED ON RACE

Until late 1988, South African prisons were segregated by race and prisoners of different races were supposed to be held in separate institutions. In addition, non-white guards were never employed in all-white prisons. That situation, legally at least, has been changing over the last few years. During our 1992 and 1993 visits, we saw both former "white" and "non-white" prisons. The majority of inmates in each category of prisons were still black in former black prisons and white in former white prisons. The formerly white prisons had dramatically better conditions that those previously used to house only non-whites.

GENDER SEPARATION

In almost all the prisons we have visited over the years, inmates were separated by gender. But on at least three occasions we encountered situations in which men were housed together with women.

The Mexican Human Rights Commission, a governmental body that conducted visits to many prisons in that country in 1991 and 1992, identified three prisons where male and female inmates were intermingled. In 1990, Human Rights Watch saw one such prison.

In Turkey, we interviewed a sixty-five-year-old Kurdish woman who had been detained after going to the Parliament to protest prison conditions in Diyarbakir, in eastern Turkey, where her son was held. She spent ten days in a large cell in an Ankara police station, along with some twenty other detainees, men as well as women.

In Peru our representatives documented cases in Castro Castro prison and CRAS-Ayacucho where men and women mix with relative frequency.

A related though separate problem is the use of guards of the opposite sex. Some prison systems make an effort to use guards of both sexes on the grounds that contact with the opposite sex makes conditions inside prisons similar to those outside.

In many prisons in the U.S., we saw guards of both sexes in male and female institutions. In Puerto Rico as well, male guards are employed in female institutions.

Human Rights Watch received reports of sexual assaults against female prisoners by male prison staff or police guards in the U.S. and Puerto Rico, India, Kenya, and Jamaica. We discuss these in the chapter dealing with physical abuses.

In some facilities we also received complaints that the guards violate inmates' privacy by entering cells unannounced. In one jail on

Rikers Island, for security reasons, toilets were not shielded by any partition. The toilets were located directly in front of a guard's station, separated by a glass wall. The guard was female, the inmates male. We received many complaints that inmates felt humiliated having to use the toilets in full view of a woman.

RECOMMENDATIONS

Human Rights Watch is not opposed in principle to the use of guards of both sexes in prisons and jails. Indeed, the presence of females in what would otherwise be all-male institutions can have a significant effect in mitigating violence. We believe, however, that guards of the opposite sex must observe a strict rule of announcing themselves when entering cells or other areas where undressed inmates may be present. In places where for security reasons no privacy can be assured, only guards of the same gender should be employed.

As for the necessary separation of the most dangerous inmates from the more vulnerable, we stress the importance of a classification system at *every* stage of incarceration, starting with police detention. In addition:

- juveniles should never be housed in adult institutions, regardless of whether they sleep in separate cells or not;
- men and women should always have separate sleeping areas;
- dormitory housing should be used as sparingly as possible; in particular, its use should be avoided in police lockups and jails, and it should never be used in maximum security institutions;
- in post-sentencing classification, dangerousness alone and not such additional factors as recidivism should determine the type of institution an inmate is assigned to;
- inmates should never be classified according to their economic or social status or race;
- protective custody should be used with an inmate's consent; when an inmate requests to be returned to the general population, his or her wish should be granted;
- prison administrators should compensate with additional amenities, whenever possible, the loneliness and virtual solitary

confinement that is often a result of the need for protective custody.

6
WOMEN

In most countries, women constitute between 3 and 7 percent of the total prison population. For that reason, most prison systems are designed and managed primarily with male inmates in mind. As a result, women are frequently at a clear disadvantage compared with male inmates. In addition, in some countries prison administrators fail to address women's vital needs related to menstruation, pregnancy and motherhood.

The level of violence in women's prisons is significantly lower than in male institutions and usually there is less overcrowding. Women are, however, more vulnerable to abuse, including rape, by the prison staff and police. Human Rights Watch discusses these matters in the chapter on "Beatings and Other Forms of Physical Abuse."

HYGIENE

The availability of sanitary napkins or alternative materials, a strictly female necessity, is a simple but important measure of the administration's attention to women's basic needs. The lack of napkins is especially burdensome and humiliating during imprisonment, especially where sanitary conditions are poor and there is limited access to substitutes, such as rags.

In Romanian lockups women are rarely supplied with sanitary napkins and most are obliged to tear up their clothing for use during their menstrual periods. Kenya provides an even more extreme example for some female prisoners are not allowed to wear underwear, nor permitted to use any sanitary protection during menstruation.

PREGNANCY

Women who are pregnant at the time of their incarceration pose a separate set of health concerns. They require regular checkups, an adequate diet and, in cases where a high risk pregnancy has been

34

determined, careful medical supervision and often treatment throughout their pregnancies. Though we observed efforts to provide proper medical care and living conditions to pregnant women in a number of countries, in some places conditions were far from adequate, and we found a few instances of deliberate cruelty to pregnant women.

In its report on India, Human Rights Watch cites a document by a group of Bombay lawyers that describes a case of a pregnant woman taken from jail into police custody for investigation in a new case. The next day she was produced before a magistrate and was found to have been whipped; she had huge black bruises on her hands and legs.

In Turkey a twenty-three-year-old woman who was two months pregnant at the time of her arrest told us of being tortured by police in Istanbul. She said she was blindfolded and stripped, then given electric shock while suspended by her wrists, beaten and raped with a truncheon. She was released from custody after ten days; fortunately, she did not lose her baby.

During a visit to the California Institution for Women, we encountered a sizeable group of pregnant women. They complained about excessive heat in their cells (our visit took place in May) and lack of access to a doctor, especially late in the pregnancy.

CHILDREN

Authorities in most countries where we studied prison conditions allow new mothers to keep their infants with them in prison. The period varies, but it is usually at least a year, allowing mothers to nurse their newborns. In some places, children of up to a few years of age may live in the prison if the mother desires. Some prison systems allow small children, regardless of whether they were born in the prison or not, to live with their mothers.

A notable exception is the United States. Most U.S. prison systems, including the federal system, do not allow newborns to stay with their mothers for any length of time.[1] After a prisoner gives birth,

---

[1] On the other hand, some prisons in the United States make significant efforts to maintain ties between imprisoned mothers and their children. The law of New York State provides that mothers should be allowed to keep their infants until the baby is one year old. In the maximum security prison at Bedford Hills,

usually in a local community hospital, the baby is taken from the mother, to be placed either with relatives or in a foster home, while the mother is returned to prison.

A tearful young mother we interviewed in the minimum security federal prison camp at Danbury, Connecticut, told us that she had delivered a baby a few weeks prior to our interview, spent a few days with him in the hospital, but had not seen him since because her relatives were unable to travel and bring him for a visit.

Many female prisoners leave their children behind when they are incarcerated. It is a truism to say that contacts between mothers and children are vital to both sides (they are equally vital between children and fathers; it is worth noting, however, that many women, especially among those in prison, are single mothers and that their children in practice have no fathers). Yet in some prison systems the regulations make these contacts extremely difficult and often unpleasant; and some countries, such as Jamaica, ban them outright.

In South Africa, due to a "privilege system" under which only inmates of the highest privilege group are allowed contact visits, most women inmates have to see their children through a glass partition and have no physical contact whatsoever with them. It takes at least a year, and in practice frequently more, to advance from the entry level privilege group to the highest, and to be able even to touch one's child. Women tend to have shorter sentences and, as a result, ironically, it is usually only those who commit more serious crimes and consequently have longer sentences, who eventually achieve contact visits.

In Spain where most routine visits do not permit contact (although there is a system of contact and conjugal visits for certain categories of prisoners and a generous system of furloughs for certain groups), children are only allowed to talk to their parent through a glass partition, in visiting areas that are dirty and depressing.

New York, we observed not only an exceptional nursery but also became aware of a system making it possible for older children to maintain regular contact with their mothers. The prison provides buses from the two major cities the majority of inmates come from, making it possible for the children to visit without the necessity of being escorted by another relative. In addition, in the summer, the prison runs week-long programs for inmates' children who are housed with local families and spend the days with their mothers on prison premises.

WORK, EDUCATION, AND RECREATION

In the countries where prisons afford meaningful education, work, or recreation, women usually have fewer opportunities than their male counterparts.

In the U.S. federal camp in Danbury, which is adjacent to a larger male prison, women get the lower-paying, less-skilled jobs. In a plant making equipment for the Department of Defense, men perform a variety of electronic jobs, while women do the packing. Similarly, in a visit to a prison in Shanghai, China in 1988, we saw the men employed in electronics while the women worked in needle trades.

In the U.S. federal institution in Marianna, Florida, female inmates in a prison that held eighty-four prisoners at the time of our visit, complained that they had fewer educational opportunities than the men, held in a larger institution next door. They also had significantly fewer recreational facilities than the men.

AMENITIES

Female prisoners tend to be poorer than male. That was especially visible during our prison inspections in countries where prisoners are allowed such private possessions as radios or TV sets in their cells. One explanation may be that families are willing to make a larger sacrifice for a male member of the household than a female. In our Mexico report, we observed: "In contrast to male prisoners, many of whose wives and families visit regularly and bring them food, blankets, clothing and other necessities, incarcerated women get much less of that type of support."[2] There is also a particular stigma attached to female imprisonment in some countries (as opposed to the way the male is regarded in the same culture), and a female prisoner becomes an outcast in her own family.

---

[2] Americas Watch, *Prison Conditions in Mexico* (New York: Human Rights Watch, 1991), p. 23.

VISITS

Because of the low numbers of female prisoners, in some countries there are few female institutions. In nations with large territories, this makes visiting very difficult.

Poland, a country with relatively poor train and bus networks, currently has four female institutions nationwide. Inmates complained to us that many seldom or never received visits because it was burdensome and costly for their relatives to travel. They pointed out that the male inmates housed in the same complex were all from the local area and could take full advantage of the visiting policy.

In all of Romania there is only one female prison.

In Egypt few people, especially in rural areas, own cars, and travel is generally difficult. Yet more than 75 percent of all female inmates are incarcerated in the country's main institution for women in the Cairo area, despite the fact that slightly less than half the country's population is urban.

The institution in Marianna, Florida is the only federal women's prison in the United States that, in addition to other security levels, also houses maximum security inmates. As a result, most prisoners there find themselves hundreds and often thousand of miles away from their relatives. One woman we interviewed there commented that there had not been a single visitor in the prison on the previous Mothers' Day.

The small number of female inmates, either in particular categories, or in general, sometimes leads to total isolation. During our February 1993 visit to Brixton prison in London, a male institution, Human Rights Watch was told that for several months the prison had housed one female inmate as well. She was a defendant in a highly-publicized security-related trial underway in London. According to prison officials, because of the nature of her alleged crime, she had to be held in a maximum security institution; she could not be held in the other such institution in London because of concerns for her safety. Brixton officials expressed concern about that inmate's well-being in an interview with Human Rights Watch. We were unable to interview her (she was in court at the time of our visit), but we did see the area in which she was held. It was separate and significantly different from the other cells we inspected in that prison, consisting of a room with good natural lighting and an adjacent area containing an exercise bike, a TV set and a fish tank. It was obvious that prison officials made efforts to compensate with better living conditions for the isolation that the woman was forced to endure.

The situation described above resulted from a combination of unusual circumstances. Yet in some countries, the number of female inmates is generally low, and women are often regularly confined in conditions of semi-isolation. In Spain, where female institutions are often annexes to male prisons, some hold as few as two inmates. Prison management should be sensitive to these problems and make all possible efforts to alleviate isolation.

RECOMMENDATIONS

Among issues related to the imprisonment of women, perhaps the most controversial is the presence of babies and children in the prisons. Opponents argue that the prison environment is detrimental to babies and that no child should be raised in a prison. Some countries have a policy of allowing a new mother to postpone serving her sentence until her baby is at least a few months old. In the absence of such a policy, however, which is the case in most countries, the advantages of allowing the mother to nurse the baby and to care for the child in the early stage of the infant's life outweigh any disadvantages. Human Rights Watch believes that newborn babies should be allowed to stay with their mothers and that prison authorities should provide adequate living conditions for the babies, including proper sanitary conditions, access to fresh air and medical care. The medical care should involve all the prophylactic procedures, such as shots, that should be administered in the given country to all babies.

In women's institutions, prison administrators do not need to invest as much effort, resources and energy in preventing violence as in men's prisons. Since the prevention of violence is frequently the chief preoccupation of prison management (and properly so), there may develop a perception that female prisons are less of a problem and hence do not require the same degree of attention as the male institutions. But, as shown above, there are several areas in which women are affected in a more severe way by prison life, and the same attention that is paid to the male population needs to be devoted to female inmates, only with a different focus. Efforts should be made to address specific female problems, both physiological and social, as well as those due to women's low numbers and the resulting scarcity of female institutions.

In addition, Human Rights Watch makes the following recommendations with respect to female prisoners:

• female inmates should be given sanitary napkins or substitutes and have daily access to showers or their equivalent during menstruation;

• work and educational opportunities should be available on an equal basis to both men and women;

• where visits to female inmates are severely limited because of the long distances relatives must travel, the authorities must make efforts to compensate (by subsidizing relatives' travel or through some other system);

• pregnant prisoners should be given regular pre-natal checkups and an adequate diet;

• nursing mothers should get an adequate diet;

• efforts should be made to facilitate mothers' contacts with their children and their right to direct their upbringing.

7
MASTER/SERVANT RELATIONS

Prisons often spawn complex power structures among their inmates. Such power structures naturally emerge in many types of groups or societies, but in groups whose members are criminals and where coercion is often the way of life, they can become particularly dangerous and abusive. In addition to gang-related power structures—a subject Human Rights Watch does not attempt to examine in depth in this report—we observed at least two types of power-based relationships among inmates. The first arose directly from abysmal prison conditions and was, in a sense, forced upon certain inmates by the authorities' failure to take care of even their most basic necessities. The other sort was more deliberately promoted and designed by prison administrators who singled out trusted prisoners and assigned them positions of authority over other inmates.

DEPENDENCE CAUSED BY NECESSITY

In several countries, we observed the virtual enslavement of poor inmates to their fellow prisoners with greater resources. This occurs most often in those prison systems that fail to provide the most basic necessities: when not enough food is provided to survive and inmates have to rely on relatives; when no bedding is provided and all bedding articles are brought from the outside; and when there is not enough clothing and everything has to be obtained from outside of the prison. In these cases inmates without relatives or those whose family members are too poor to help are forced into dependence on other prisoners and must perform a wide variety of services for them in order to obtain articles they need to subsist.

In Egypt we encountered a number of foreign prisoners, most of them from other African countries, whose situation was precarious because they lacked the crucial support from an network on the outside. One such prisoner wrote to Human Rights Watch in October, 1992: "Most of the foreigners from Third World countries do not receive money from their parents and have to clean the rooms, toilets, clothes and

41

sleeping places of the affluent inmates, who reward them by providing them with food, clothing (prison uniforms), plates, stoves and pots, etc."[1]

In Mexico where inmates rely to a high degree on food brought in by relatives, those without family visits have to rely on handouts or enter into arrangements in which they receive food in exchange for favors or work.

As described in the chapter on classification, Indian prisoners are classified by prison rules according to their social and economic background, dividing them into Class A, B, or C. Diet and prison amenities are allotted depending on this classification. Class C prisoners, the most numerous and the poorest, receive a diet that is generally insufficient for survival. To get food supplements, for example, or blankets in the winter, Class C prisoners must fan the long-term prisoners who are designated as "convict officers," or massage their legs, or even perform sexual services for them.

DEPENDENCE PROMOTED BY THE AUTHORITIES

The Use of "Convict Officers"

In several countries, we encountered situations in which prisoners were used to perform duties customarily assigned to prison staff.

In India this category of inmates actually has a name and is recognized under the law. The Punjab Jail Manual establishes three grades of convict officers: watchmen, overseers, and warders.[2] Appointments to these posts are made by a prison director, who chooses from among the long-term prisoners, most of whom are those convicted of the most serious crimes. These long-term convicts have served varying portions of their sentences and have gained positions of authority depending on the class within the prison structure to which they are appointed. As a result, convict officers effectively run the prison through the practical enslavement of the rest of the prison population. The consequences are particularly severe for newcomers: they are teased,

---

[1] Middle East Watch, *Prison Conditions in Egypt* (New York: Human Rights Watch, 1993), pp. 41-42.

[2] Similar manuals, which spell out prison rules in great detail, are used in other Indian states.

harassed, abused, even tortured, as part of the process of breaking them in. In some prisons, convict officers have the authority to determine to which ward a newcomer will be assigned, using their authority to transfer them to a somewhat better location as a way of exercising power.

A similar situation has prevailed in Puerto Rico's State Penitentiary, where the Court Monitor has noted the presence of inmates performing duties normally assigned to staff, such as handling communications between staff and the prison population, keeping records and maintaining order in parts of the institution never visited by guards. As the monitor noted: "It is evident that staff do not go into these areas for security inspections, and from all indications, the different floors are in fact managed by inmate building tenders."[3] In the same report, the monitor remarked about another institution, Bayamón 292, where inmates were also assigned to a variety of jobs involving authority over other prisoners: "In the Consultant's view, the only reason the inmates have not gained control of this institution is that they evidently do not want to."[4]

In Zaire one of the more striking aspects of prison life is the power exercised by some prisoners. Inside the prison, authorities are rarely visible. Every prison has a "chief of staff"; beneath him are regional "governors," "pavilion leaders," and "guards," all of them prisoners.

In Brazil some prisons have relatively few staff members to manage the prisoners. In the country's largest prison, the 7,000-inmate Casa de Detenção in São Paulo, prisoners largely run many aspects of prison life. On the day of the infamous 1992 massacre in Pavilion 9 of that prison, there were fifteen guards in the building holding more than 2,000 prisoners. Cells are opened at 7 A.M. and locked at 5:30 P.M. and inmates are free to move throughout the five floors and the patio of the pavilion all day. On the day of our visit, just a few days after the massacre, only eleven guards were on duty in this building.

In Kenya long-term prisoners are often promoted to the status of prison guards as a reward for cooperative behavior. According to

---

[3] Report 113 of the Court Monitor; cited in Americas Watch, "Prison Conditions in Puerto Rico," *A Human Rights Watch Short Report*, vol. 3, no. 6 (May 6, 1991).

[4] Ibid.

testimony gathered by Human Rights Watch: "Those older prisoners have a lot of power; they are given power by the prison authorities and then try to prove they are more strict than the authorities themselves. . . . The authorities encourage all forms of intimidation by the senior prisoners."[5]

A particular cause for concern when considering this phenomenon is that the inmates given these positions of authority tend to be those serving the longest sentences. Guards know them best and trust them. Accordingly, as the longest sentences generally are imposed on those convicted of the most serious crimes, those exercising the most power over their fellow inmates are often the most violent criminals.

The "Cell Bosses"

Some prison systems use inmates not only to serve as the keepers of their fellow prisoners but also to report back to the authorities. In Romania in an obvious legacy of the Ceausescu era, each cell has a boss designated by the prison administration. The boss is responsible for organizing activities for the cell and maintaining its cleanliness. The boss is also responsible for reporting to prison officials about the activities of the cell. In theory, the cell boss is selected because he or she has more education, was convicted of a lesser crime, and behaves well. Inmates in several prisons reported, however, that the cell boss was abusive and frequently had a longer prison sentence. One inmate told us that his cell boss "was convicted of murder ... even so, he seems to get special benefits, such as furloughs."[6]

The cell boss system is also used in Romania's juvenile institutions, and there too those appointed to this duty tend to be those with the most violent history. In a prison hospital, our delegation interviewed a youngster recovering from a beating he suffered in a reeducation school. He told us: "I was arrested for stealing and sent to the reeducation school until my trial. I was put in the room with other boys who had already been convicted. The boss of the room had been convicted of murder and was in for five years. The first night, he and four others tried to force me to have sex with them. They beat me up.

---

[5] Africa Watch, *Kenya: Taking Liberties* (New York: Human Rights Watch, 1991), pp. 164-65.

[6] Helsinki Watch, *Prison Conditions in Romania* (New York: Human Rights Watch, 1992), p. 30.

I reported this to the guard. When the guard talked to the others and found out that the boss was involved, he said I was lying and punched me in the stomach and hit me with a hammer. I am afraid to go back there with what is going on. I am afraid to go to sleep. The guards know about the problem and pick the toughest one to be boss."[7]

Prisons and labor camps in China operate a complex system of internal terror and control, which is also known as the cell boss system:

> This system is the scourge of prisoners' daily life, for it undermines all guarantees for even their most basic physical safety and security. Although strictly banned by the government, the cell boss system flourishes throughout the Hunan prison system. Moreover, the prisoner-thugs who act as cell bosses are specifically appointed to play that role by prison officials themselves. The prisoners act as the latter's direct agents within the cells, and as a reward for this service they receive specially favorable treatment and conditions. Prisoners are usually even more afraid of these cell bosses—the system's unofficial hit men—than they are of the actual prison staff. Cell bosses have numerous specific ways and means of tormenting other prisoners and making their lives intolerable.[8]

The same report describes in detail twenty main varieties of such unofficial persecution and torture.

China also uses a system of work unit bosses, or "recorders," who report their fellow prisoners' work-related activities: infractions of the rules as well as "achievements" (officially recorded achievements are needed for release).

According to recent testimony collected by Human Rights Watch, a system similar to the structure of prisoner-bosses is also used in Vietnam. In labor camps, where most inmates serve their sentences, prisoners are divided into labor groups and each group has a leader

---

[7] Ibid., p. 31.

[8] Asia Watch, *Anthems of Defeat: Crackdown in Hunan Province 1989-1992* (New York: Human Rights Watch, 1992), p. 83.

designated by the camp's management. It is never a security prisoner, but usually a hardened criminal. These leaders engage in daily abuse of their fellow prisoners, according to the testimony.[9]

A related problem, though one that we have not investigated in depth and only flag here, is the situation that develops when large groups of security prisoners are given substantial autonomy within the prison. This was formerly the case in Spain, continues to be so Palestinian detainees in the Israeli occupied territories, and is still the case in Peru. Though Human Rights Watch does not object in principle to granting a certain degree of autonomy to security prisoners, we are concerned about abuse of authority and pressures within any group confined in a prison, including security prisoners.   Almost inevitably, political hardliners among the prisoners gain the upper hand and those who do not share their political views may suffer. Prison authorities have a duty to prevent situations in which some inmates are persecuted by the political leaders among security prisoners.

RECOMMENDATIONS

No inmate should ever be placed in a position to exercise significant authority over other prisoners. Though Human Rights Watch advocates the employment of inmates in a variety of maintenance jobs in prisons, we are firmly opposed to assigning inmates positions of power over fellow prisoners. In addition Human Rights Watch recommends that:

- prison systems must provide sufficient food, clothing and other necessities to all prisoners so that they are not required to perform services for fellow prisoners in order to survive;
- prison authorities must control and take responsibility for the entire institution; no enclaves managed exclusively by inmates should ever be allowed to exist within the prisons;
- prisons should never provide preferential treatment to particular groups of prisoners because of their economic and social background;
- the institution of convict officers must be abolished.

---

[9] Asia Watch Interview, February 1993.

8
DEATH ROW

Human Rights Watch opposes the death penalty under all circumstances, primarily because of its inherent cruelty. In the course of our investigations of prison conditions worldwide, we encountered disturbing examples of additional cruelty aimed at condemned inmates prior to their executions. The length of time between the passing of a death sentence and the resulting execution varies from country to country, ranging from a few weeks or even days, as is sometimes the case in China; to several years, as in the United States; to as long as over twenty years, as has been the case in Indonesia with some prisoners accused of taking part in the attempted coup of 1965 and 1966.

Death-row prisoners are often held in isolation and under exceptional security measures. This may at times be dictated by a perception on the part of the prison staff that these inmates are the most dangerous and indeed have nothing to lose, and as such are the most menacing to the safety of others. In several cases, however, we found that cruel conditions for death row inmates are inflicted as an additional punishment.

In China the law mandates that "for those who have been sentenced to death but not yet executed, instruments of restraint shall be used."[1] The instrument in question consists of leg irons, weighing more than fifteen pounds, which are worn continuously and taken off only after the prisoner is dead.

In Jamaica where prisoners condemned to death are housed in single cells with absolutely nothing to do, we heard several reports of guards physically abusing death row inmates. As one inmate, who had spent thirteen years on death row before his conviction was reversed, told us in an interview: "Possibly the most difficult thing to take is the beatings given randomly with little or no reason. Sometimes, one or two of the

---

[1] Article 17 of the Statute of Detention House.

warders may act with a sense of human respect, but the majority beat us and deprived us of the things our families brought to us."[2]

In Russia at the Butyrskaia prison in Moscow, death row cells were kept in a silent, darkened part of the facility, where we were asked not to talk above a whisper. Inmates there are kept in isolation in cells lit only by what appears to be a thirty-watt bulb, and are allowed to see no one but their lawyer.

In South Africa death row inmates in the Pretoria Maximum Security prison live in windowless cells in which the light is kept on twenty-four-hours a day.

In the United States, the country with the highest reported death-row population in the world, death-row conditions vary from state to state. Isolation and idleness are among the most common problems. A woman in Florida, whose death sentence had been commuted by the time we interviewed her, said that while under the death sentence, she had been held in total isolation for several years because she was the only woman on death row. In addition, we found frequent examples of an attitude that could be summarized as "They are going to be killed anyway, so why bother [with proper medical care, with decent living conditions, etc.]?" Human Rights Watch also received many reports of insensitivity among the staff toward the condemned. One inmate in Tennessee said that when he returned to prison from a court hearing, a prison clergyman asked him: "So, when are they going to fry you?" An inmate in Florida told us that after his friend had been executed, he overheard a guard saying: "It's about time to get rid of some Niggers here."[3]

In Indonesia during our 1989 visit the delegation interviewed two frail men—one in his sixties, the other in his seventies—who had been arrested in 1968 and sentenced to death in 1970, in the aftermath of the 1965 coup attempt against President Sukarno. They described the constant psychological torture of not knowing when they would be executed. In February 1990 four of their fellow inmates were indeed executed, more than twenty years after their conviction on charges of trying to overthrow the government. The following month, the two men

---

[2] Americas Watch, *Prison Conditions in Jamaica* (New York: Human Rights Watch, 1990) p. 21.

[3] Human Rights Watch, *Prison Conditions in the United States* (New York: 1991), p. 57.

we saw were reportedly asked to give names of next of kin, normally a prelude to an execution. International pressure and worldwide appeals appear to have postponed the executions, but as of this writing the two elderly men we interviewed, as well as four others convicted in the same wave of political trials, continue to live under a death sentence.

RECOMMENDATIONS

Awaiting execution is, in and of itself, one of the greatest sufferings a human being can experience. Short of abolishing the death penalty altogether, countries that retain it should undertake all efforts to avoid exacerbating the suffering. In particular, Human Rights Watch recommends that:

- death-row inmates should not be held in solitary confinement;
- instruments of restraint should never be used except in emergencies for brief periods;
- death-row cells should have sources of both natural and artificial light, allowing reading and writing without injury to the eyes, with light switches inside the cell;
- inmates should be allowed to study, to work if they wish, and to practice hobby crafts;
- frequent visits with relatives and friends should be facilitated and encouraged.

DAILY ROUTINE

9
ACTIVITIES

To make time pass quickly is one of the chief concerns of most prisoners. Days unfilled by activities pass slowly. All over the world inmates told us that idleness is one of the worst features of prison life.

Some prisons and even entire prison systems go to considerable lengths to assure that time in prison is not only filled but used productively. They provide education, ranging from literacy classes for illiterate inmates to university courses for those who want to pursue a degree through correspondence courses. Human Rights Watch saw impressive libraries and sophisticated sports equipment in some institutions. But these, unfortunately, were exceptions in the course of our worldwide study. In country after country and prison after prison, we were told that idleness and boredom were the way of life for inmates.

IDLENESS AND OVERCROWDING

Lack of activity is particularly difficult to bear when there is severe overcrowding. Yet in some of the most overcrowded institutions we found that inmates were provided with nothing to do and hardly ever left their cells.

In Romanian lockups, where inmates usually spend several months, they told us that except for brief trips to the bathroom, and interrogations, they are confined to their extremely overcrowded, stuffy cells for twenty-four hours a day.

In the severely overcrowded prisons in Egypt, inmates are usually allowed out of their cells for up to a few hours a day, but such out-of-cell time does not mean time outdoors, and even when out of the cell, there is nothing for prisoners to do.

In Russia, where pre-trial detention often lasts for several years, pre-trial detainees spend twenty-three hours a day in their extremely overcrowded, stuffy cells. The only authorized activity is reading, but even this is limited to what is available in the prison library and the authorities do not permit families to include books in the packages inmates are allowed to receive. "Except for two volumes of Dickens," in

53

the prison library, inmates in the Lebedeva Street facility in Leningrad told us as late as June 1991, "everything else is propaganda."[1]

In Poland, all-day lockdowns are routine in all the male closed prisons (that is prisons whose inmates do not work in the community). Inmates usually do get out of their cells for an hour to exercise, but spend the rest of the day in their overcrowded cells, with little to do.

PUNITIVE IDLENESS

On a few occasions, we observed that idleness was imposed on inmates in a punitive fashion, as if authorities were making an effort to make their time pass as slowly as possible.

In the Florida State Prison at Starke at the time of our visit there in 1991, inmates under so called close management—all of whom are housed in solitary cells—could be banned from going outdoors for years at a time, never leaving their cells except to take a shower three times a week, and were often denied access to reading material for extended periods.

In Romanian lockups, where overcrowding is tremendous and where no activities are provided by the authorities, inmates are prohibited, for no apparent reason, from lying down on their bunks (and presumably sleeping) during the day and are punished if guards catch them doing so.

IDLENESS AND SAFETY

Keeping prisoners occupied should appeal to the prison staff as well, and for a very pragmatic reason: When there is nothing for prisoners to do, violence is likely to increase. It is probably no coincidence that among the prison systems where we conducted our research, the three with the most severe prison gang problems—Puerto Rico, South Africa and Brazil—offered few activities to their inmates. Gang life fills a vacuum that is created when inmates are left day after

---

[1] Helsinki Watch, *Prison Conditions in the Soviet Union* (New York: Human Rights Watch, 1991), p. 18.

day, month after month, year after year with nothing else to occupy them.

In Puerto Rico idleness was one of the most frequently voiced complaints. Education is available only at the most basic level in most institutions, and work is provided to only about one-third of the population, and even that usually for only a few hours a day. Recreational or cultural activities are scarce as are prison libraries. The Court Monitor wrote in one of his reports: "This situation places the mass of the population in degrading idleness, shut up in overcrowded dormitories and cells during most of the day, day in, day out, for years on end."[2]

In South Africa maximum security prisoners are considered too much of a security risk to be allowed to work outside, which is where most prisoners work, often on prison farms. And where educational and recreational activities are scarce to nonexistent, the result is that the most dangerous and violent inmates spend all their time confined, leaving their cells sometimes only for half an hour every other day, apart from mealtimes. Otherwise, they are locked up as many as forty to a cell, with no relief from boredom.

In Brazil, some prisons and especially jails (in which inmates serve sentences of up to ten years), offer practically no work, recreational or educational opportunities. Inmates spend their days in total boredom, either in their overcrowded cells or in the overcrowded patio.

RECOMMENDATIONS

Providing meaningful, structured activities for prisoners may be costly and out of reach for financial reasons in some prison systems. But no inmate, regardless of the institution's circumstances, should be deprived of the right of daily time outdoors. In addition, there are many things prison administrators can do to alleviate boredom and reduce tensions with little money or through policy changes alone:

- inmates should never be banned from reading and should always have access to periodicals and broadcast media;

---

[2] 118th Report of the Court Monitor, July 6, 1990, cited in Americas Watch, *Prison Conditions in Puerto Rico* (New York: Human Rights Watch, April 1991).

- there should be no limits on the number of letters received and mailed by prisoners;
- inmates should be allowed to have radios and TV sets in their cells;
- lockdown should be used only in exceptional situations and not as a matter of routine;
- inmates should never be banned from sitting or lying on beds during the day;
- every inmate should be able to spend a minimum of one hour a day outdoors.

10
WORK

Work in prison can play a positive role. It can make time pass more quickly for the prisoner; it can teach work habits that will be useful on the outside, along with a variety of new skills; it can provide a source of income for the inmate to be spent on amenities in the prison, sent home to the family, or saved for the period after release; and it may even provide a way to earn credit toward an early release. But prison labor can also be a means to exploit and further punish the prisoner turning him or her into a virtual slave of the state.

PRISONS AS A COMPONENT OF THE NATIONAL ECONOMY

Prison Self-financing

Some prison systems make their inmate's labor the economic basis of their existence: that is, they are supposed to generate enough income to finance themselves and not to be a burden on the national budget. In Romania the law requires that all prisons should be self-financing and all expenses other than equipment and structural repairs should be covered by income generated from the work of the prisoners. In South Africa, under the current law, the Department of Correctional Services is supposed, "as far as practicable, to be self-sufficient by the optimal application of the production means based on management according to business principles."[1]

Profit-Making Prisons

Moreover, in some countries prisons are supposed to generate income even beyond their costs.

In China, where labor constitutes an integral part of prison philosophy as well as practice and where imprisonment is often called "reform through labor" or "reeducation through labor," and certain

---

[1] Dirk van Zyl Smit, *South African Prison Law and Practice* (Durban: Butterworth, 1992), p. 42.

categories of inmates are officially referred to as "personnel," prisons are an important component of the national economy. How important is impossible to ascertain because virtually all prison-related data are a matter of strict secrecy in China, to the point that prisons are publicly disguised as "factories." Provincial Prison No. 2 in Hunan is known to the world as the "Hunan Heavy Motor Vehicle Plant," while the Longxi Prison in the same province, where prisoners work in a quarry, is officially referred to as the "Shaoyang Marble Factory."

In Russia, where the majority of sentenced prisoners are incarcerated in so-called labor colonies (better known in the past, especially in the West, as the gulag), the system continues to be considered an important part of the country's production of goods.

Imposing economic goals on prisons tends to promote abuse of prisoners and coercion whenever goals are not met or when prison administrators are judged by the economic achievements of their institutions and hence need to show "better" performance. In any case, this system can only work when there is minimal unemployment on the outside or when outside businesses cannot compete with the prison economy (as in communist countries where the economy is centrally controlled).

Prisoners Held Beyond the Length of their Sentences

In China, where prisons constitute an important source of income for the country, prison authorities forcibly retain some prisoners who have finished serving their sentences for continued employment. Under this policy, which has been in place since the early 1950s, prisoners throughout the country have been forced to remain in prison after the expiration of their sentences as so-called workers, usually for the rest of their lives. The working conditions and production quotas of these workers are virtually the same as those of prisoners.

PUNISHMENT FOR NOT MEETING PRODUCTION QUOTAS

Among the most serious problems related to work in prisons are the often onerous work requirements, or production quotas. This is particularly true in countries where prison labor is part of the national economy, either because prisons are not supported from the country's budget or because, in addition, they are expected to contribute to that budget by generating income.

Particularly harrowing accounts come from China, where failing to meet production quotas is one of the most frequently and harshly punished "offenses" within the entire prison system. Penalties range from the application of restraints to isolation, beatings and even the prolongation of an inmate's sentence.

DEMEANING OR UNSAFE WORK

In several countries, prisoners must perform work nobody else wants to do because it is too unpleasant, too dangerous, or both—work that free citizens would perform only for high compensation and which prisoners can be forced to perform at little or no cost.

During our 1989 visit to Poland, we interviewed several women inmates working in a chicken slaughterhouse near Warsaw. They all complained that the work was hard and unpleasant and that even though the plant had some free workers as well, they held different, less demanding jobs.

In Czechoslovakia, where work conditions and production quotas were the source of serious human rights concerns prior to the 1989 democratic changes (and where substantial improvements have since taken place, especially with regard to the inhuman quota and punishment system), working conditions in some prison plants continued to be unsafe as of our 1990 visit. Inmates making costume jewelry worked in extremely crowded and badly ventilated rooms, and complained about having to inhale fumes from the welding processes and from chemicals used to polish metals.

Work in Russia's labor colonies is often difficult and dangerous. The so called forest colony-settlements are among those with the harshest work conditions. Prisoners at Solikamsk (in the northern Urals) routinely work outdoors in temperatures as low as forty degrees below zero and are driven to work sites in unheated trucks two hours each way.

In China, prisoners are frequently employed in mining and in agriculture, where work is exceptionally demanding physically and accidents are frequent. Chinese law stipulates that prisoners may not be required to work more than twelve hours per day, with a day of rest once every two weeks.[2]   In practice, prisoners routinely work at least ten hours, and occasionally for as long as sixteen hours a day.

WORK AS PUNISHMENT

Work is sometimes a disciplinary measure against those who violate prison rules. In China already high production quotas are often raised to punish serious violations of prison rules. In the United States, we encountered instances in which undesirable work (such as manually emptying a human-waste pit) is used to punish rule violations.

PUNISHMENT FOR REFUSAL TO WORK

In countries that make it a requirement for prisoners to work, those who refuse are frequently punished. In China beating is a frequent punishment for a prisoner who declines to work. In Cuba, where prisoners are required to work (usually under comparatively good working conditions), those who refuse to work are punished with a variety of disciplinary measures, including loss of the right to receive visits. This was especially true for the *plantados*, long-term political prisoners, some of whom were deprived of visits for years for their refusal to work.

COMPENSATION FOR WORK

The most frequent complaints regarding work that we heard from prisoners related to pay. In some countries, such as South Africa (for all prisoners) and Poland (for prisoners employed in prison maintenance), prisoners receive no pay, only an occasional monetary "prize." When there is pay, it is almost universally very low. In several countries, prisoners are required to save part of their pay for the period after their release. But in Indonesia we received complaints that prisoners never got that money upon their release.

---

[2] Article 53 of the statute of Reform Through Labor.

RECOMMENDATIONS

On the basis of our research in several countries, it appears that most human rights violations related to work occur when prisons are assigned to fulfill income-generating goals. When it imprisons its citizens, a government assumes a variety of responsibilities for them, including an economic responsibility. Provisions must be made in the national budget for the cost of the prison system. Prisons should not be required to generate income for the national economy. In addition Human Rights Watch recommends that:

- prisons should provide meaningful work opportunities for their inmates;
- prisoners should not be required to work more than the standard weekly number of work hours in the country; if overtime is needed (during harvest time, for example), it should be voluntary and with compensation, such as extra pay, vacation from work at a later time, or eventual reduction of the sentence;
- prison labor should take place under safe conditions that are not inferior to those in the country as a whole;
- in countries where labor is obligatory for inmates, prisoners should be able to obtain medical exemptions from work;
- demeaning or excessively arduous labor should not be used as punishment;
- increased production quotas should never be used as punishment;
- prisoners should be paid for their work; and there should be a mechanism assuring that all the savings accumulated during imprisonment are paid to the inmate upon release;
- prisoners who refuse to work should never be denied the minimum amenities required by the United Nations Standard Minimum Rules but may be denied such benefits of work as pay and reduction of sentence for working.

RULE AND MISRULE

11
RULES

A standard step in any prison investigation is to examine the rules setting forth prisoners' rights and obligations and the sanctions for violating those rules. Such rules do exist in most countries and in most—though there are several notable exceptions—they generally conform to international standards. Also, on paper, most countries have a mechanism for prison oversight and a system of remedies to address inmates' grievances. The questions to ask, however, are whether prisoners are informed of the rules; whether they are made aware of the remedies; how are they supposed to learn about them; and whether there is a functioning mechanism to enforce compliance.

The provision of written rules to inmates is an absolute necessity for the observance of human rights in prisons. Unless they are informed of the rules, even those inmates who desire to conform are likely to commit acts that will be considered infractions warranting punishment. Moreover, prisoners may be readily deprived of privileges that should be available to them under the law and not know about it. When there is no general access to the rules governing day-to-day living conditions, prisoners feel (and are) dependent on the good will of the staff if they seek a specific improvement in their situation.[1] The lack of consistently applied rules engenders confusion and insecurity and gives leeway to staff arbitrariness. Finally, a grievance procedure that is unknown to prisoners is obviously a sham.

In Spain, a country with progressive prison legislation and an admirable set of prison rules, prisoners had no access to those rules at the time of a Human Rights Watch delegation visit, according to numerous interviews with inmates. The authorities assured us that every prisoner was issued a brochure outlining the rules, but when we asked to see a copy, nobody in the office of the director of the prison system could find one. (The rules were later sent by messenger to our hotel.) The Spanish prison administration banned distribution of a book prepared by a

---

[1] See Dunkel & van Zyl Smit, *Imprisonment Today and Tomorrow: International Perspectives on Prisoners' Rights and Prison Conditions* (Boston: Klewer, 1991), p. 726.

nongovernmental organization that provided information about the rules, rights and remedies available to prisoners under the law.

In Egypt many prisoners were astonished to learn from our representatives that they were supposed to be visited once a month by a special inspector charged with investigating prisoners' complaints and addressing grievances.

In some countries, prisoners who inform their fellow inmates about their rights get into trouble. In the United States all prisons by law must provide inmates with access to legal services or legal libraries.[2] Prisons are equipped with law libraries and prisoners may challenge various aspects of their imprisonment in court. Some prisoners acquire substantial legal expertise in the course of their incarceration; the term "jailhouse lawyer" has been coined to describe a prisoner who becomes a legal expert and lends his or her help to other inmates. But we have received numerous testimonies and letters complaining that jailhouse lawyers are often singled out for harassment by the staff.

In Indonesia Human Rights Watch documented a case of a security prisoner who eventually died in a prison hospital from tuberculosis. According to one source, during his incarceration he had frequently been beaten and put in an isolation cell, sometimes for months at a time. He was regarded as a troublemaker by the guards for informing other prisoners about their rights, demanding that those rights be observed, and sending letters of complaint to the head of the prison and the Director General of Corrections.

In communist Poland prison rules setting out the rights and duties of prisoners were routinely kept secret. In the aftermath of the imposition of martial law in 1981, there were also reports of prisoners who were punished for asking to consult copies of the principal international document outlining prison conditions, the U.N. Standard Minimum Rules for the Treatment of Prisoners.[3] This situation changed dramatically with the advent of democracy in Poland in 1989. When we inspected Polish prisons in 1990, prisoners showed us copies of the prison rules that were available to them in their cells.

---

[2] *Bounds v. Smith*, 430 U.S. 817, 97 S.Ct. 1491, 52 L.Ed.2d 72 (1977).

[3] Paul R. Williams, *Treatment of Detainees: Examination of Issues Relevant to Detention by the United Nations Human Rights Committee* (Geneva: Henry Dunant Institute, 1990), and *U.N. Human Rights Committee Report*, 1987 (A/42/40), p. 17.

In China, prisoners are never provided with a copy of a written set of rules but, instead, are required to memorize them. Guards check on this knowledge; not remembering all the words is a punishable infraction. Meanwhile, detailed regulations on various aspects of imprisonment are secret in China. The "Detailed Rules for the Disciplinary Work of Prisons and Labor Reform Detachments," issued in 1982, are available only in special, "internal-use-only" publications that may only be seen by officials.

It is not only important that inmates should be informed of the rules but, of course, that the rules should be observed. Unless they are enforced, their existence on paper is meaningless in assessing human rights conditions, a fact that some governments fail to appreciate. On some occasions during our prison investigations, when Human Rights Watch criticized specific aspects of prison conditions, governments would simply cite the law. In Spain many provisions of the admittedly progressive laws are seldom or never enforced by the government in practice, including the requirements that all prisoners should be housed in individual cells; that no prison should hold more than 350 inmates; and the very stipulation that prisoners should be informed about the rules and their rights under those rules.

RECOMMENDATIONS

As is obvious, the availability of the rules, and access to legal documents by all prisoners are crucial in safeguarding human rights in prisons. In order to assure this, Human Rights Watch recommends that:

- every prisoner should be issued a copy of the rules upon his or her arrival in the prison; if for technical reasons it is impossible to provide each prisoner with a personal copy, regulations should be posted in a place accessible at all times by all prisoners;
- a system should be established for illiterate prisoners to be thoroughly informed about the regulations;
- prisoners should never be required to memorize the regulations;
- prison libraries accessible to all prisoners should have copies of the country's prison-related laws and of the U.N. Standard Minimum Rules for the Treatment of Prisoners;

- each prison should be required to report annually on its compliance with the country's prison rules and reports should be available publicly;
- a grievance procedure should be established to permit complaints—without fear of reprisals—about violations of the rules and for enforcement of compliance.

12
DISCIPLINE

Disciplinary measures are punishment on top of punishment. In total institutions such as prisons, where every aspect of an inmate's life is controlled, many measures affecting the everyday life of a prisoner can be punishments and the list of punishments used in prisons all over the world is almost endless. Disturbingly, Human Rights Watch discovered that in country after country, punishments meted out within the prisons are cruel, humiliating, and frequently applied in an arbitrary fashion without the slightest vestige of due process.

Punishments may range from a verbal reprimand, or a written notation in a prisoner's record, to the denial of certain privileges—such as access to television, being allowed to smoke, the opportunity to participate in social events or purchase goods from a commissary—to forfeiture of good time (a way of gaining earlier release), transfer to a higher security institution, confinement in segregation or punishment cells, or restraint in fetters or shackles.

As Human Rights Watch investigated disciplinary measures in prisons, we examined the country's prison regulations to see what measures were legally authorized. Often, we found that there were two sets of punishments: authorized and unauthorized. Both were used. The latter usually involved physical violence.

We also studied the range of offenses—it is often revealing to discover what constitutes an infraction in a particular prison system—and the corresponding penalties. In addition, we examined the degree of due process in determining penalties, and whether prisoners were afforded any possibility of appeal.

TYPES OF OFFENSES

Disciplinary measures are necessary because inmates often violate the rules and sometimes commit serious offenses. Though penalties should be imposed when an inmate attempts to escape, destroys property, inflicts violence on his fellow prisoners or staff, smuggles drugs into the prison, or otherwise disrupts order in the institution in a serious way, the offenses for which some prison systems in fact impose penalties go far beyond such matters.

In communist Czechoslovakia it was against the rules, and thus punishable, to listen to the radio; to own a book or writing pad; to receive more than one letter from one's family; not to take off one's cap when talking to a guard; to call someone "comrade" in an ironical fashion; to finish work early; or to lie on the bed during the day; study; or write letters for illiterate fellow prisoners. At the time of our 1990 visit, following the democratic transformation in Czechoslovakia, pre-trial detainees in Slovakia were still forbidden to exercise in their cells or to wear watches, or to sit or lie on the beds during the daytime.

In China inmates may be punished for not remembering all the words of the regulations; not admitting guilt; standing by the window; speaking loudly; or not arranging one's bedroll properly.

In Romania prisoners may be punished, usually by beatings on the palms of their hands, for lying on the bed during the day or taking too long while using the bathroom. Inmates are required to stand with their faces toward the wall, usually in the cell corner or at the end of a hallway, whenever a stranger enters the area.

In Turkey prisoners are prohibited to write, draw, or put up a picture on a cell wall. It can also be an offense to fail to prevent crimes or disciplinary infractions by other prisoners or else to fail to notify the administration of such matters.

CORPORAL PUNISHMENT

The following discusses the use of physical violence as a punishment in retaliation for infractions, real or perceived. The use of random violence is discussed in the "Beatings and Restraints" chapter. See also "After a Riot" for the use of violence in the aftermath of prison rebellions.

Among the countries where we investigated prison conditions, only two authorized corporal punishment in their prison-related laws. South Africa's Correctional Services Act 8 of 1959 authorizes the use of corporal punishment "not exceeding six strokes, if the prisoner is a convicted prisoner apparently under the age of forty years." During our 1992 visit, a Human Rights Watch delegation was told that such punishment was being used less and less often. The Minister of

Correctional Services told Parliament that corporal punishment was used 120 times in 1989; 102 times in 1990 and just 44 times in 1991.[1]

Egyptian Law No. 396 of 1956 authorizes the beating of juveniles and the whipping of adult prisoners as a disciplinary penalty, in specific violation of Egypt's Constitution, which prohibits inflicting physical or mental harm on prisoners. Prisoners under seventeen years of age may be beaten ten times with a thin stick, and adults may receive up to thirty-six lashes with a specially designed whip. According to prison officials, whipping is used to punish major offenses such as striking a guard or attempting to escape.

But various forms of physical violence are used in retaliatory fashion in almost all the prison systems we investigated; moreover, violence is employed in Egypt and South Africa far in excess of what is envisioned by the law. A prisoner in Egypt was whipped for writing a letter of complaint to the country's president. Another prisoner, who had written to the president denouncing that whipping, told our delegation that a few days later he was also beaten on sensitive parts of his body by security officers and then placed in a punishment cell.

A Palestinian prisoner told us that he and some eight other prisoners went on a hunger strike in July 1991 to protest their continuing detention without charge in Egypt's Abu Za'bal prison. "We were taken out separately and beaten with sticks and with hands," he told the Human Rights Watch delegation.[2]

A Somali citizen, Mohammed Mahmud Shak, died on November 29, 1991 in an Egyptian prison after he was severely beaten following an attempted escape the previous July. About a hundred guards had taken turns beating him.

In November 1992 two prisoners in the Boniato prison in Cuba were beaten for conducting a hunger strike. The previous February another Cuban prisoner, Francisco Díaz Mesa, died from a beating he had sustained for banging on the bars of his cell to protest the denial of medical attention he needed, reportedly for pneumonia.

In China, according to one recently released political prisoner, inmates were beaten if they refused to work. Beatings in Chinese prisons

---

[1] *S.A. Barometer*, vol. 6, no. 19 (September 25, 1992).

[2] Middle East Watch *Prison Conditions in Egypt* (New York: Human Rights Watch, 1993), p. 91.

have been frequent, by all accounts. Another recently released prisoner reported that guards sometimes beat inmates simply because they did not like their physical appearance.

In Czechoslovakia in June 1990—after the Velvet Revolution—a female prisoner was beaten by some six guards for looking out the window and calling out to her boyfriend.

In Kenya, a prisoner released from a maximum security prison in 1989, offered the following testimony: "Take, for example, a case when prisoner is found with half a cigarette; when he is taken to the duty officer all the prison guards in the office will be hitting the prisoner with their batons. The most horrifying aspect of this beating is that the guards normally have as their target some of the most sensitive parts of the body, mainly the knee and hand joints, and at the end of this the prisoner can hardly walk."[3]

In a lockup in Romania we encountered a young man whose hands were swollen from beatings with a rubber truncheon for offenses such as taking too much time while in the bathroom and sleeping during the day. Many inmates reported being beaten on the palms of their hands, and several more reported witnessing such incidents.

In Puerto Rico we interviewed an inmate who described an incident in which guards kicked an inmate in his genitals in retaliation for making a complaint.

PUNITIVE SEGREGATION

Solitary Confinement

> I hold this slow and daily tampering with the mysteries
> of the brain to be immeasurably worse than any torture
> of the body; and because its ghastly signs and tokens are
> not so palpable to the eye and sense of touch as scars
> upon the flesh; because its wounds are not upon the
> surface, and it extorts few cries that human ears can
> hear; therefore I the more denounce it, as a secret

---

[3] Africa Watch *Kenya: Taking Liberties* (New York: Human Rights Watch, 1991), p. 167.

punishment which slumbering humanity is not roused up
to stay.[4]

Thus wrote Charles Dickens after visiting the Eastern
Penitentiary in Philadelphia in 1842. At the time, solitary confinement
lasted for the duration of the sentence in this prison. The cell walls were
thick; each had a small yard; and each cell had a double door—one of solid
oak, the other of iron grating. Hence, prisoners never saw each other
and their only human contact was with the guards. Typically, they had
looms in their cells, or a workbench with tools, so even work was solitary.

But Dickens could have written that passage today referring to
China. Xu Wenli, an editor of a *samizdat* magazine, was arrested in April
1981. He was placed in a solitary cell, and was put to work there,
attaching ornamental buckles to shoes. In 1985, in a document he
managed to smuggle out, he recorded:

> I have always had a north-facing cell and have been kept
> in solitary confinement throughout. Since I have been
> able to exchange a few words each day with the prison
> orderlies, however, along the lines of "Lovely weather,
> isn't it," I have not yet been reduced to losing my ability
> to speak.

That smuggled document, several hundred pages long and
detailing conditions of his imprisonment, earned Xu a transfer to a
"special regime cell" where he spent the next several years under yet
worse conditions (see below).

The duration of solitary confinement applied as punishment is
usually limited by a country's law. But law and practice are all too often
two entirely separate matters. In China, Article 62 of the *secret* "Detailed
Rules for the Disciplinary Work of Prisons and Labor Reform
Detachments" of 1982 stipulates: "Except in the case of condemned
prisoners for whom final approval of execution is still pending and also
the case of prisoners currently undergoing trial, the period of solitary
confinement is in general not to exceed a period of seven to ten days.
The maximum permissible period is fifteen days."

---

[4] Charles Dickens, *American Notes.*

In Cuba a 1988 delegation that included a representative of Human Rights Watch was told that prisoners could not be kept in a punishment cell for more than twenty-one days. But one prisoner, serving twenty years for espionage, told the delegation that he had been held in solitary confinement from 1981 to 1985.

In South Africa solitary confinement may last for up to forty-two days if authorized by a magistrate.[5] Yet Breyten Breytenbach, one of the country's foremost writers, arrested for returning to the country illegally from exile in Paris and trying to set up a mixed-race democratic organization, was held in solitary confinement for two of the seven years of his imprisonment.[6]

In Poland an inmate interviewed in a punishment cell during our 1989 visit talked to us of his fears about "losing his mind." Another said, "I get depressed very easily, and stupid thoughts come to mind, like suicide."[7] The maximum time in isolation was then six months. It was subsequently reduced to one month.

In addition to concerns over the length of time inmates spend in solitary confinement, we were also distressed by how easily this supposedly most serious of sanctions is meted out to prisoners.

In Russia almost any violation of the rules—including cursing at or showing disrespect for the guards, refusing to work, arguing with other inmates, or not meeting a production quota—can result in a term in a punishment cell.

In Cuba an inmate was punished with forty-five days in solitary confinement for writing a letter to the Nicaraguan leader, Violeta Chamorro, congratulating her on winning the presidential election.

Vaclav Havel, now the President of the Czech Republic, was put in solitary confinement once for drafting letters for an illiterate gypsy.

---

[5] Dirk van Zyl Smit, *South African Prison Law and Practice* (Durban: Butterworth, 1992).

[6] Breytenbach describes his prison experience in *The True Confessions of an Albino Terrorist* (New York: Farrar, Straus & Giroux, 1985).

[7] Helsinki Watch, *Prison Conditions in Poland* (New York: Human Rights Watch, 1991), p. 30.

Isolation in Conjunction With Other Measures

Even though isolation is usually considered the most severe disciplinary measure, in several countries Human Rights Watch found that it was applied in combination with additional sanctions.

An inmate in Poland told us, "I'm beginning to feel crazy; I get no mail, no cigarettes, no visits."[8]

In South Africa inmates in disciplinary segregation are often further punished through reduced diet. Similarly, in Cuba, prisoners in punishment cells are fed only twice a day and one of those "meals" barely qualifies as such.

In Romania inmates in isolation are required to get up at 5 A.M. and to stand in their cells until 10 P.M. During that time, beds are folded up against the wall. The light is kept on day and night.

In the United States, inmates in segregation in the women's jail in Los Angeles may be additionally punished with a special diet, consisting of fully nutritional but utterly tasteless balls of a specially-prepared blend of nutritive substances.

In Russia during solitary confinement prisoners are forbidden to have possessions with them and are denied almost all other rights, including the right to exercise.

In several countries, physical restraints are used as an additional punishment in isolation cells.

Punishment Cells

Punishment cells, in addition to separating some inmates from the rest of the prison population, are frequently designed specifically to inflict physical hardships on their occupants.

In Indonesia, a former prisoner held in Besi prison in Java, described the punishment cell there as one meter square—too small to lie down.

In Russia, punishment cells—where up to three prisoners at a time may be segregated from the rest of the population—are very small (about eleven feet by ten feet), have stucco walls (which are painful to lean against), often have no windows, and have very dirty toilets. Beds in punishment cells have no mattresses.

---

[8] Helsinki Watch, *Prison Conditions in Poland: An Update* (New York: Human Rights Watch, 1991), p. 30.

In South Africa punishment cells are bare except for a mat on the floor for a prisoner to sleep on and a sink and a toilet. We were also told of the use of so called "dark cells," with no windows and barely enough space to lie down.

In Cuba, punishment cells in the notorious "rectangle of death" in the Combinado del Este prison in Havana, where many of the most prominent political prisoners served their sentences, were about ten feet long and four feet wide. Up to two people were held in each, although there were triple concrete bunks—with no bedding—indicating that three could be housed there as well. The toilet was a hole in the floor that often becomes clogged, spilling into the cell. Every cell was separated from the hallway by two doors: a barred one, partially covered by sheet metal, and a wooden one that completely shuts out ventilation and light from the hallway and was arbitrarily opened or closed by prison guards. Just inside the wooden door was a very dim light bulb, by which one could not even see one's hands. Similar cells are used in punishment wings of three other men's prisons that we saw.

In Zaire punishment cells have no windows and no ventilation; prisoners may be held in them for up to forty-five days.

In the U.S. cells in the punishment Q-wing at the Florida State Prison had no windows and very poor ventilation.

In China, the "strict regime" cell to which Xu Wenli was transferred after publicizing the conditions of his earlier imprisonment (see above), was a windowless, damp vault in which a light bulb shone relentlessly day and night. The cell was too small to stand up straight. It crawled with insects. There was a strip of matting on the concrete floor to sleep on and a bucket placed in a corner served as a toilet. Xu spent no less than three-and-a-half years in this cell.

In a Romanian lockup, our delegation saw two windowless cells measuring two-and-a-half by two feet, approximately half the size of a telephone booth. There was no source of light and no possibility to sit comfortably. In several interviews with inmates, we were told that these cells were used frequently, often for a few hours at a time. Such cells are known as *chiquitas* in Nicaragua where they were used in pre-trial detention facilities during the Sandanista period, also for a few hours at a time.

In Brazil we documented a particularly horrific example of the use of a punishment cell. In February 1989, Military Police called to São Paulo's Police Precinct 42 in response to a disturbance that erupted in the lockup, forced fifty-one men into a cell measuring less than fifty square feet, with a heavy metal door and no windows, and held them there for more than an hour. When the door was opened, eighteen prisoners were found to have suffocated to death.

THE USE OF PHYSICAL RESTRAINTS

Chains, leg irons, fetters, and shackles are prison-related artifacts one might associate with medieval times rather than the end of the twentieth century. Yet, in several countries, Human Rights Watch found various types of physical restraints are used today to punish prisoners. We want to stress a clear distinction between the legitimate use of physical restraints employed temporarily to subdue a frenzied prisoner, or as a security precaution for particularly violent or dangerous prisoners during transfers or on similar occasions, and the punitive use of physical restraints.

Leg irons and handcuffs are commonly used as a means of punishment in Romania. During our delegation's 1991 visit, we observed numerous prisoners who were shackled in leg chains and/or handcuffs for extended periods. One prisoner told us he had spent eight months in chains in Section Two of the Poarta Alba prison. At Gehrla prison, eight prisoners who had participated in the August 1990 revolt at this prison were still in leg irons and handcuffs when our delegation visited in October of the following year. We spoke to one prisoner who had been sentenced to an extra three years in prison for participation in that revolt. In addition he had been kept in restraints for fourteen months. He was unable to lift his arms above his chest and had calluses where the handcuffs rubbed his wrists.

Nor had things changed much in Romania the following year (1992) when our next delegation received repeated reports of the use of chains, handcuffs (including handcuffing an inmate to the wall in one case) and leg irons as punishment in the lockups.

In China prison rules, which all cadres and inmates are supposed to learn by heart, authorize the use of chains and fetters for those who violate the regulations "in more serious cases."[9] A wide variety of

---

[9] Asia Watch, *Anthems of Defeat: Crackdown in Hunan Province 1989-1992* (New York: Human Rights Watch, 1992), p. 77.

implements are in use, including handcuffs, ankle fetters, and chains. Under the law, the time limit for the use of physical restraints (with the exception of prisoners condemned to death, a matter we discuss in the "Life on Death Row" chapter) is fifteen days; in practice, however, such time limits are ignored.

In South Africa restraints are used as an additional means to punish those in isolation. During a 1993 visit by a Human Rights Watch delegation, we saw one inmate in an isolation cell with a chain about a foot-and-a-half long around his ankles.

In India physical restraints—fetters, shackles and handcuffs—are employed more commonly than punishment cells to deal with those who commit infractions. The use of these restraints is prescribed by the Jail Manuals, which spell out in great detail the specific manner in which prisoners should be treated. The Punjab Jail Manual, for example, provides for three kinds of handcuffs. An iron bar variety may not weigh more than twenty-one pounds. As for the leg fetters, one variety that is specified and whose use in practice was reported to us in interviews, has a bar that holds the legs apart. Though the manual says that the bar may be no more than sixteen inches in length, a former inmate gave us a description of a much longer bar that holds the legs apart in such a manner as to cause great pain after the legs have been kept in this position for an extended period. The manual allows the sixteen-inch bar to be used for up to ten days at a time, and other leg fetters may be used for up to three months at a time.

In Zaire, leg chains and metal spans are used in many prisons, mostly in the interior of the country. The restraints often cause severe burns to the skin and require a hacksaw to be removed.

PUNISHMENTS RELATED TO CONTACTS WITH RELATIVES

Reduced contacts with relatives are often used as a disciplinary measure and are a matter of serious concern. Any such measure to penalize a prisoner for some infraction also penalizes his or her family.

In some countries inmates who commit infractions are transferred to a different institution as a punishment. This often makes family visits more difficult or impossible. It is a particularly serious problem in countries that span great distances.

In Puerto Rico inmates "who cause trouble" are sometimes transferred to a prison in the continental United States. This usually ends visits because air travel is both time-consuming and expensive.

In Spain inmates are sometimes transferred from one end of the country to another as punishment. This measure is used particularly against riot leaders, real or suspected.

In the United Kingdom we were told of a practice nicknamed "ghosting," for particularly disruptive prisoners. This consists of moving such an inmate frequently throughout the prison system, presumably to make it impossible to establish ties within any prison population. It also makes it difficult for relatives to visit such a prisoner. One prisoner reported he had been held in more than thirty institutions during a four-year period.

In addition, as mentioned earlier, a ban on correspondence and visits is frequently used in conjunction with punitive segregation.

UNUSUAL FORMS OF PUNISHMENT

Prison administrations are inventive not only in defining offenses but in designing punishments. In addition to the sanctions described above which are used in many prison systems, Human Rights Watch encountered a few that are peculiar to a single system.

In China prisoners reported that guards would sometimes make an inmate stand naked in the middle of his cell for such offenses as talking to a neighbor during the night.[10] Also in China, inmates are sometimes made to sit motionless for hours every day, staring at a wall, so that they "repent their sins."[11]

In Egypt an inmate's clothes may be shredded as a punishment in addition to placement in a punishment cell.

In the U.S., 1990 court records describe a punishment called "strip status."[12] An inmate was stripped of all clothing, bedding and

---

[10] Human Rights Watch interview, December 1992.

[11] Asia Watch, *Anthems of Defeat*, p. 94.

[12] *Honed v. Maass*, 745 F. Supp. 623 (D.Or. 1990), cited in Human Rights Watch, *Prison Conditions in the United States* (New York: 1991), p. 47.

personal possessions. He was then expected to "earn" back items piece-
by-piece through good behavior. The Oregon correctional authorities,
under whose jurisdiction this practice was applied, claim this punishment
is no longer in use.

A prisoner in Indonesia was punished for playing music by a
requirement to walk stooped for two hours. Another form of punishment
in Indonesia was to force an inmate to kick rocks with his feet. And a
particularly cruel form of punishment for political prisoners in Cuba has
been the denial of medical attention.

The Punitive Use of a "Privilege" System

In South African prisons, almost everything that is not prohibited
is declared to be a "privilege": possessions, letters, visits, access to reading
material, permission to write literary pieces, authorization to have a TV
set in one's cell and more. Inmates are divided into "privilege" groups A,
B, C, and D, regardless of their security classification and the type of
institution they are in. All prisoners start in group C; their classification
is reviewed at half-year intervals, by an "Institutional Committee"
(composed of prison staff members), which upgrades or downgrades
prisoners according to their behavior.   Under this system a prisoner has
to gain the most basic rights—such as contact visits with relatives—through
a spotless disciplinary record. Even then, it takes at least one year to
move from the entry, or C level, to A group, the only one permitted
contact visits.

COLLECTIVE PUNISHMENT

In several countries, we heard complaints that prisoners are often
punished as a group without respect to whether they were individually
involved in committing an infraction. Collective punishment is, of course,
a serious violation of due process; it also adds to a prisoner's feeling that
he or she has lost individuality and become a pawn in a large system.

When we visited the Barbetron maximum security prison in
South Africa, we found that one whole section was then deprived of access
to sports and recreation as punishment for a gang fight several weeks
earlier.

In the U.S., at the time of our visit to the Immigration and
Naturalization Service (INS) detention center at Krome, Florida (where

illegal aliens were held), we were told that all the women in the institution were being punished for a protest by some of them that consisted of messing up the bathroom.

Collective punishment is most frequent in the aftermath of prison protests and disturbances. We discuss this further in the chapter titled "After a Riot."

DUE PROCESS IN DISCIPLINARY PROCEDURE

Every prison should have a disciplinary procedure and prisoners should be informed of the offenses for which they are punished and the extent of that punishment. They should also be given an opportunity to defend themselves and to appeal. Even though such a procedure usually exists on the books in most countries Human Rights Watch visited, more often than not it was violated in practice.

In particular, we are concerned that in most countries, punishments are meted out arbitrarily by prison officials without external oversight and that there is no effective mechanism for appeal. This often leads to the application of sanctions that are disproportionately harsh for the offenses committed, and affords the staff opportunities to exercise undue pressure or to avenge personal grievances.

UNDECLARED PUNISHMENT

In countries where law is respected and where disciplinary sanctions in prisons require due process, a problem nevertheless arises when measures are taken that are declared not to be punishment but, in fact, are punitive. Such measures may be imposed arbitrarily by the prison staff, without the possibility of an appeal, and with no time limit on their duration.

In England and Wales, under Prison Rule 43, the prison director may decide to separate some prisoners from the general population for the maintenance of the "good order and discipline" of the institution. Prisoners in England and Wales are generally entitled to a disciplinary hearing if they are charged with a disciplinary offense, but the invocation of Rule 43 circumvents this right. No specific offense is needed to mark a prisoner for segregation and Rule 43 does not specify duration.[13]

In the United States, many prison systems—including the federal, more than thirty state systems and some local jails—have recently designated separate institutions or parts of institutions for the confinement of prisoners under particularly harsh conditions and exceptionally strict security. Such assignment often amounts to solitary confinement for years on end. In the Florida State Prison at Starke, some inmates are held in windowless cells from which they are allowed out only three times a week, for ten minutes, to shower. Otherwise, they are alone in the cell. Such confinement may last for extended periods; some of the inmates Human Rights Watch interviewed in that prison had not been outdoors for several years. In the Maximum Control Complex in Westville, Indiana, inmates are locked in their cells for between twenty-two-and-a-half and twenty-four hours a day, never see anyone except their guards, and are often punished through the loss of access to reading materials, among other measures.

In Marion, Illinois, the harshest prison within the U.S. federal system and the model for these particularly punitive prisons, where an average stay lasts three years, prisoners are locked in their cells around the clock, except for recreation (between seven and eleven hours a week, depending on classification). Yet placement there is technically not considered a disciplinary measure; it is administrative, and as such is not preceded by a hearing. As a result an inmate is afforded no possibility of appeal, and this sanction is open-ended. The decision to confine an inmate in such an institution is made by prison administrators alone and is often based on the mere prediction that an inmate will be dangerous or predatory rather than on any actual infraction.

In Israel conditions in the modern ultra-maximum security wing of Nitzan prison are the strictest in the system and are the cause of grave concern. According to officials, prisoners are assigned to the wing on the grounds that they pose a physical danger to guards or other prisoners.

---

[13] Prison Rule 43 states: "Where it appears desirable, for the maintenance of the good order and discipline or in his own interests, that a prisoner should not associate with other prisoners, either generally or for particular purposes, the prison director may arrange for the prisoner's removal from association accordingly." Helsinki Watch, *Prison Conditions in the United Kingdom* (New York: Human Rights Watch, 1992), p. 17.

However, assignment to Nitzan is clearly used as a means of punishment, particularly against Islamists whose original crimes are considered exceptionally heinous or whom the authorities wish to punish for other reasons. Inmates, all of them Palestinians from Israel or the occupied territories, are confined to their one-man cells twenty-three hours a day, and may never go out unless handcuffed. They must wear legcuffs during visits by relatives and lawyers. Conditions at Nitzan's Ward Eight are harsher than at other facilities in ways that have little to do with protecting others. The cells are partly below street level and have poor ventilation and little natural light; access to reading materials is more restricted than at other prisons; and beatings by guards are reported to be more common than at other facilities of the Israeli Prison Service.

RECOMMENDATIONS

Sanctions for violating the rules are necessary in prisons, as they are in any society or community if it is to function properly. But, as the examples cited in this chapter demonstrate, a fundamental right—freedom from cruel and unusual punishment—is often ignored when it comes to punishing prisoners. To eradicate cruelty inflicted on prisoners by prison staff is not a matter of huge investments. What is needed most of all is a policy decision at the central level of the country's prison administration and the will to enforce this policy. Human Rights Watch believes that disciplinary measures, whether authorized or not, should be closely scrutinized by all those monitoring prison conditions: official prison inspectors, judges, nongovernmental organizations, and international bodies. In addition Human Rights Watch specifically recommends that:

- disciplinary measures should be standardized countrywide and set at the central administration level;
- prisons should keep a log of all punishments meted out;
- every prison system should have a means of monitoring the use of disciplinary measures in prisons, independent of the penal administration; the results of such monitoring should be a matter of public record;
- prison officials who employ extralegal disciplinary measures should themselves be disciplined;

- a disciplinary sanction may only be applied when the offense for which it is meted out has been specified in advance and the prisoner has been informed that such conduct is prohibited;
- upon their arrival in an institution, prisoners must be informed what constitutes an offense and the corresponding penalty;
- prisoners must be given an opportunity to appeal a disciplinary sanction to an independent decision-maker;
- no disciplinary sanction may be imposed indefinitely (i.e. "pending review");
- corporal punishment may never be imposed;
- denial of medical care may never be imposed as punishment;
- deprivation of food or deliberately distasteful food should never be used as punishment;
- deprivation of bedding and clothing should never be used as punishment;
- physical restraints may never be used for disciplinary purposes. When used to restrain a distraught or violent prisoner, they may only be used temporarily, and care must be taken not to cause physical injuries;
- prisoners should not be required to "gain" their basic rights with good behavior; punishments consisting of loss of privileges should be clearly defined and limited in time;
- collective punishment may never be imposed;
- disciplinary measures restricting contacts with relatives should be used as punishment solely for infractions related to those contacts (smuggling contraband, for example). Punitive transfer to distant institutions should never be imposed;
- solitary confinement should be used sparingly and never for longer than a few days;
- punishment cells, whether solitary or collective, should have toilet facilities and such basic furniture as a bed with bedding as well as proper light and ventilation. Cells that are intended to cause physical hardship (because they are too small, very stuffy or dark, for example) should never be used.

13
BEATINGS AND RESTRAINTS

Many of the human rights abuses that occur in prisons involve the violation of perhaps the most fundamental right of all: the right to physical integrity. Frequently, prisoners are deliberately subjected to a high degree of violence and physical abuse intended either as retaliation or summary punishment (see chapter titled "Disciplinary Measures") or to achieve a particular goal, such as obtaining a confession, breaking a prisoner's morale, extorting a bribe or simply intimidating the inmate. In some cases, the goal may also be sexual.

The most frequent reports of torture, beatings and other physical abuses come from police stations and take place during the investigatory stages of imprisonment. In some countries, torture is routinely used to extract a confession or information, in political and criminal cases alike. In a few instances, torture and other forms of police brutality function as a form of summary punishment, usually with tacit official sanction and explicit—especially in the cases of criminal rather than political suspects—public approval.[1] By and large, Human Rights Watch has considered torture separately from the general problem of prison conditions. We have published numerous reports on torture including some devoted almost exclusively to this question.[2] Here, we focus on physical abuses against prisoners that, for the most part, are not related to the investigation as such.

Sentenced prisoners or prisoners in whose cases investigation has been completed are far from being free from official physical abuse. New arrivals to a prison are frequently beaten by guards to intimidate them. At some prisons, random bursts of violence, or violent searches, are reported to take place without apparent provocation by prisoners, and are presumably intended to maintain a constant level of fear. There are also reports of sexual abuse by the staff, usually with respect to women.

---

[1] See Americas Watch, *Police Abuse in Brazil: Summary Executions and Torture in São Paulo and Rio de Janeiro* (New York: Human Rights Watch, 1987).

[2] For a complete listing see bibliography.

TORTURE TO EXTORT BRIBES

In India and in Indonesia police routinely beat virtually all criminal suspects. In both countries bribes—by the detainee or by the family—are reportedly paid to avoid torture. This system can only work if those who cannot pay are indeed tortured and the reputation of the police is such that those who can pay will not hesitate to do so quickly. Though the extortion of bribes appears to be the main purpose for the physical abuse of detainees in India, an important contributing factor is widespread public endorsement of summary punishment against those believed to have engaged in crime.

BEATINGS AND HUMILIATION OF NEW ARRIVALS

In several countries newly arriving prisoners are subjected to particularly brutal and demeaning treatment, meant, apparently, to intimidate them. In country after country, we received testimonies about "Let's get acquainted" beatings.

One former prisoner provided this detailed testimony describing a gruesome rite of initiation in Kenya:

> When we first got in there, we were told to take all our clothes off. They make you jump up and down to prove that nothing is being carried in your body. Then you are made to bend over naked and they search your anus with a cane. They do it like torture. Then they make you sit squatting—still naked—for long hours at a time, and tell you they will "initiate" you. They told us "you people are going to see." You are left squatting naked in the cell, in the dark, and suddenly they burst in and beat you thoroughly with sticks and batons. They attack you particularly on the joints, on your shoulders, head, knees, and elbows. You will be beaten like that for some time—over a period of days. After three days, our names

were then read out for what kind of work we would be doing and our 'initiation' ceremony would be finished.[3]

Accounts from Egypt echo this one from Kenya. A former security detainee described to us his treatment when he arrived at the Tora Istikbal prison in March 1991, after eighteen days of detention and torture. Upon his arrival in the prison, his head was shaved, after which he was brought to a holding area where there was a line of security force soldiers. He and the other detainees were forced to walk down the line, past the soldiers. "Each one takes a punch at you," he told us. A trade unionist, imprisoned in 1989 in the same institution, also got a special "reception." He and the other detainees who arrived with him were made to cross a gauntlet of security forces soldiers. Another prisoner, a U.S. citizen, witnessed similar beatings of newly arrived prisoners in the al-Khalifa prison in Cairo. He said that he saw a "long bull whip, black or brown," on the booking table. Though he was not beaten, the other new arrivals at the same time were whipped and beaten with sticks.[4] In Turkey, similarly, according to interviews we conducted with former political prisoners, non-political newcomers are often beaten.

In the Agua Santa prison in Rio de Janeiro we also received reports about "initiation" torture sessions. An official report by the Ministry of Justice revealed the existence of a room the inmates called the "maracana," where inmates were allegedly beaten and asphyxiated with smoke from burning paper.

RANDOM BURSTS OF VIOLENCE

Violence Against the Physical Integrity of Inmates

Violence in prisons is often completely random; prisoners are not able to anticipate the moment or guess the occasion for these sudden eruptions. In some countries, prisoners insisted to us that the guards must derive some perverse pleasure from such abuse. Whether or not

---

[3] Africa Watch, *Kenya: Taking Liberties* (New York: Human Rights Watch, 1991), p. 167.

[4] Middle East Watch, *Prison Conditions in Egypt* (New York: Human Rights Watch, 1993), pp. 92, 96.

tormenting prisoners does serve some such needs of their keepers, it serves another purpose well. It sows terror and maintains anxiety among inmates. And this, as one former prisoner in China put it, "simply makes it easier for the staff to 'maintain order.'" Violence in Chinese prisons is indeed frequent and comes in many different forms, including beatings; whipping a prisoner who has been ordered to drop his pants; assaults with electric batons; and more.[5]

In Jamaica we received numerous reports of violence from death row inmates. Guards frequently beat the condemned and took away whatever private possessions they might have accumulated. This is particularly cruel because death row inmates, even without such random bursts of violence, live in constant anxiety. The general prison population is also not free from such abuse. Former prisoners interviewed by the Jamaican Council on Human Rights reported random beatings, usually with sticks, sometimes with boards or straps. Frequently three or four warders would beat one prisoner; in fact it was rare for just one guard to beat a prisoner.

In Kenya, according to former prisoners, strip searches, anal searches, beatings, psychological humiliation and gruelling physical exercises are an integral part of the prison system.

In Romania, in the course of our 1991 visit, we were told that: "On occasion the guards take the prisoners out of their cells and make them lie on the floor in the halls. Then they walk on them and polish their shoes with their clothes. This happened to us about four months ago."[6]

We also heard testimonies of unprovoked, random violence against prisoners in Brazil and Egypt.

Violent Cell Searches

A cell is the only place where a prisoner can create some private space for himself, the place where he or she stores such private belongings—usually very few—as may be permitted. Violent cell searches,

---

[5] For detailed descriptions of various forms of physical abuse see Asia Watch, *Anthems of Defeat: Crackdown in Hunan Province 1989-1992* (New York: Human Rights Watch, 1992), pp. 74-75, 80.

[6] Helsinki Watch, *Prison Conditions in Romania* (New York: Human Rights Watch, 1992), p. 20.

which we discovered in many prison systems, are usually marked by the destruction of these few possessions. Prisoners told us that the resulting pain is not simply a consequence of that loss, but involves a sense of physical violation as well. Indeed, violent, random cell searches seem intended less to capture prohibited objects or substances, but rather to instill precisely this sense of physical violation and the concomitant increase in the sense of insecurity.

In Brazil, we heard of frequent "blitzes," assaults during which guards usually did not beat prisoners but broke everything in the cell. "The guards burst in without notice, with dogs," one inmate told us in a typical account, "and get us out of the cell. Those who won't go, get hit. They then break all our possessions, step on and smash the little furniture and other things we make [inmates often make miniature objects of matches or other pieces of wood], and break the radios and TV's we get from our families."[7]

In Czechoslovakia, we were told that, a few weeks prior to our 1990 visit to the Plzen-Bory prison, guards had entered a cell block and "smashed everything."[8]

In China's Hunan province, the raids are ostensibly carried out to inspect cells and ascertain that no forbidden goods are concealed. They have gained the metaphorical name, "Saochai descending from the mountain top." *Saochai*, meaning "those who sweep the firewood," is prison slang for officers of the People's Armed Police, who patrol the prison perimeter. The phrase "descending from the mountain top" refers to the occasions on which the officers are ordered down from their watch towers to conduct the raids on the cells.[9]

In Turkey we also compiled reports of guards bursting into cells and tearing up everything in sight—books, bedding, or clothing. In Jamaica death row cells are the frequent target of such raids. In Egypt violent searches are sometimes accompanied by violence against the

---

[7] Americas Watch *Prison Conditions in Brazil* (New York: Human Rights Watch, 1989), pp. 25-26.

[8] Helsinki Watch, *Prison Conditions in Czechoslovakia: An Update* (New York: Human Rights Watch, 1991), p. 14.

[9] Asia Watch, *Anthems of Defeat*, pp. 81-82.

prisoners. In one prison, for example, prisoners had a chemical sprayed into their eyes during a cell search.

SEXUAL ABUSE

Sexual abuse, usually against women, is frequently used during investigation as a means of intimidation or torture. Human Rights Watch has documented such practices in several of its reports, including *Double Jeopardy: Police Abuse of Women in Pakistan*. At times, rape is evidently used merely as a means of domination.

In the Spanish Town lockup in Jamaica, several women whispered to one member of our mission that the guards took them out of the cell at night and forced them to have sexual relations. In India we received numerous reports of rapes in police custody that seemed to serve one purpose only: the pleasure of the constables. A former inmate interviewed in Puerto Rico said that on her third day at the Vega Alta women's prison, she heard another inmate screaming in her cell. At the time there was a general lock down. The screaming inmate subsequently told her that she had been raped by male guards. In the late 1980s there was a wave of reported sexual assaults by male guards at the California Institution for Women.

Men are not entirely spared sexual abuse by guards. In Kenya former prisoners reported a practice dubbed "terror" in the prison slang. Every morning, prisoners were required to take off their clothes, come out of their wards and squat. This was ostensibly done as part of a search but, as one former prisoner insisted, "The guards carrying out the search are more interested in the nakedness of the prisoners than in the search."[10]

In more than one country, we have also received reports of prison guards deliberately placing vulnerable prisoners in cells in which they would be raped by their fellow inmates.

---

[10] Africa Watch, *Kenya*, p. 168.

VIOLENCE AGAINST PARTICULARLY VULNERABLE INMATES

Violence Against Women
Women are especially vulnerable to violence while in custody and in some countries we encountered instances of particular cruelty against them. In Kenyan prisons beatings are the most common form of physical abuse against women.

The Bombay Lawyers Committee reported after interviewing all the women held in the Bombay Central Jail in 1987 that more than 50 percent complained about violence and abuse. (It is worth noting that Indian law makes extrajudicial confessions inadmissible at trial, so obtaining a confession could not have been the goal.) Women in Bombay complained of being whipped with belts, especially on the thigh and upper leg, or of being hung with a pole around the back of the neck and arms, or of having their hair yanked by two policemen from either side—all this, usually, with threats of worse to come.

Violence in Punishment Cells
In South Africa we received reports of beatings of prisoners confined to punishment cells and thus *de facto* held incommunicado. We heard similar reports in Egypt. In Cuba prisoners told us they were beaten as they were taken to punishment cells.

RECOMMENDATIONS

Violence by those charged with law enforcement—that is police and prison staff—is a serious and troubling phenomenon and reflects a low regard for the rule of law. But in contrast to some other aspects of prison conditions, violence and cruelty perpetrated by the prison staff can be decreased by changes in policy and attitude. Simple policy changes do not necessarily require huge investments. Our observations in Poland and Czechoslovakia, in whose prisons physical abuses had been rampant under communism and where they have been largely eliminated since the democratic transformation of 1989, prove that improvements are possible. Governments must make it a priority to eradicate violence from their places of confinement. In particular Human Rights Watch recommends that:

- prison guards guilty of physical abuses should be disciplined and, in serious cases, prosecuted for assault, rape or other criminal offenses;
- prisoners should have access to legal information so they can be aware which practices by the staff are illegal under the country's laws, and they should be afforded a way to file confidential complaints;
- so as to allow identification of assailants and thus decrease the possibility of assault, prison staff should always wear identification badges. The failure to wear such a badge should be considered a disciplinary infraction;
- in countries where practices of physical abuse are reported by the press or by domestic or international human rights monitors, independent investigative commissions should be established to examine these accusations, identify those responsible for such abuses and to take the disciplinary measures required to eliminate such behavior and provide the information to law enforcement agencies required to initiate prosecutions.

14
AFTER A RIOT

The handling of prison riots is a specialized and highly sophisticated field that Human Rights Watch has not studied in depth. Prison riots often involve violence by both sides, severe destruction of property and, in many cases matters of life and death (especially when hostages are taken). On the other hand, we did investigate a number of situations in which, in the immediate aftermath of a prison uprising, the authorities engaged in great violence—often far more than was committed on either side while the riot was underway. We encountered several instances in which there was summary corporal punishment, either targeted at perceived riot leaders or more broadly against prisoners generally in the prison or the wing of the prison where the riot took place. The level of violence ranged from beatings to extrajudicial executions; in addition, we found blatant disregard for due process in subsequent disciplinary proceedings.

While the use of force is sometimes legitimate and even necessary to subdue the riots—though attempts should always be made to minimize casualties—the frequent employment of violence *after* prisoners have surrendered is neither legitimate nor necessary, it is sheer revenge in the form of summary punishment.

EXTRAJUDICIAL EXECUTIONS

The bloodiest known episode in the history of prison riots occurred in 1986 when rebellions broke out simultaneously in three Peruvian prisons (El Frontón, Lurigancho and Santa Barbara) holding inmates associated with the terrorist Shining Path or *Sendero Luminoso* movement. Though the exact total of the dead may never be known, at least 248 people lost their lives in the ensuing violence, 244 of them prisoners. Many undoubtedly died during the exchange of fire between the army and the prisoners (some prisoners were armed), but many inmates were executed after they surrendered. The official Parliamentary Commission that investigated the events concluded that in the Lurigancho prison, where all 124 rebellious prisoners died, no fewer than ninety were victims of extrajudicial executions. In El Frontón prison, where 118 prisoners died, the commission determined a *possibility* that some were victims of extrajudicial executions. The part of the prison where the rebellion occurred, the Blue Pavilion, was completely destroyed by military shelling at the end of the riot. It is unclear whether prisoners had tried to give themselves up before the building collapsed. But, as the commission pointed out, "The very destruction of the building, whether intentional or not, constitutes a crime against life." Furthermore, the military did not allow doctors access to the survivors, possibly increasing the number of fatalities.[1]

The October 1992 riot in the Casa de Detenção in Brazil left at least 111 inmates dead (eighty-four of whom were still awaiting trial). There were no fatalities on the side of the military police force that stormed the prison. It is unclear how many prisoners died during the incident and how many perished in the subsequent hours. Human Rights Watch interviewed survivors of the massacre and individuals who visited the prison immediately after the police withdrew. According to several of the testimonies we were able to collect, many prisoners died after they surrendered. Some bodies were discovered with their arms behind their necks, clearly indicating submission; many had been killed while naked, further evidence supporting the allegation of executions.   (As is customary in such situations, after the institution was recaptured, prisoners were ordered to strip, to ensure that they did not retain any concealed weapons.) We observed automatic bullet marks in the bottoms of inmates' bunks (suggesting that police fired up at prisoners cowering in their corners). We saw a little stool with which someone had apparently tried to protect his head; it was covered with blood and had two bullet holes showing through it. We collected testimony regarding at least two executions of inmates who had been ordered to carry bodies of the dead, only to share their fate later.

This 1992 massacre, though the bloodiest in Brazilian prison history, was not an isolated incident. In 1989, Military Police called to São Paulo's Police Precinct 42 in response to a disturbance that erupted in the lockup, forced fifty-one men into a cell less than fifty square feet,

---

[1] Comisión Investigadora del Congreso Sobre los Sucesos de los Penales del 18 y 19 de Junio de 1986, Report, p. 300. Americas Watch, *Human Rights in Peru after President's García's First Year* (New York: Human Rights Watch, 1986), pp. 99-112.

with a heavy metal door and no windows, and held them there for more than an hour. When the door was opened, eighteen men were found to have suffocated to death.

In November 1992, during an attempted coup d'etat in Venezuela, a riot combined with an attempted escape, took place in the Reten de Catia prison in Caracas. At least sixty-three prisoners were killed. Testimonies and reports gathered by Human Rights Watch in the weeks following the events indicate that many prisoners were shot while in their locked cells, and some twenty were killed in a ravine outside the prison, discrediting claims that force was used appropriately by the police and the national guard.

In 1991, six prisoners died in the Barbetron prison in South Africa during a riot, which took place at the time of a hunger strike for the release of political prisoners. According to the authorities, the deaths were caused either by smoke inhalation or by burns when cells were set alight. But prisoners and former prisoners interviewed by Human Rights Watch in 1993 said the victims had been beaten to death by guards. Local human rights activists are currently gathering information about the riot and plan to push for an official inquiry.

BEATINGS

In May 1990, inmates in Gallery 4 of the "Modelo" prison in Barcelona, Spain, started a disturbance consisting of throwing objects out of the windows of their cells and shouting obscenities. The ruckus occurred after the guards brutally subdued a mentally unstable inmate who had destroyed a television set with a pole. The director of the institution ordered the use of riot gear and the seizure of eighteen inmates identified as those who had been throwing the objects. The inmates were ordered to undress and were subjected to truncheon beatings by guards who stood in two rows while the inmates were forced to walk between them. This "walk" was repeated three times during the night. All the inmates sustained injuries, including several severe head contusions.

In late 1989 a wave of violent prison riots swept Poland. Seven inmates died during these riots and about four hundred were wounded, as were several dozen prison guards. After these riots had been quelled, mass beatings of inmates by prison guards took place. The beatings continued even after riot participants had been transferred to different locations. These beatings were extremely brutal and there was evidence that some of those involved in the abuses were under the influence of alcohol.

Participants in an August 1990 riot in one of the jails on New York City's Rikers Island (a jail complex that holds more than 22,000 detainees) were quickly overpowered by the guards, who then proceeded to beat inmates in retaliation. The incident left 120 inmates in need of medical attention, eighty-one of them with injuries to their heads, and some of those in need of immediate hospitalization because they were either unconscious or suffering from seizures. Human Rights Watch was able to interview some of the victims, who described the systematic beatings. Many of those who were beaten were subsequently placed in solitary confinement. A court eventually dismissed all the charges against the prisoners. The riot gear worn by the guards made it impossible for the prisoners to identify those who displayed particular brutality: the bullet proof vests covered the identification badges normally worn by all staff and helmets covered their faces. Following the 1990 riots, the New York City Department of Corrections introduced a new regulation requiring that vests be marked in a clear way, making identification possible.

RECOMMENDATIONS

The time right after a prison disturbance has been quelled is often the moment when the most extreme human rights violations are likely to occur. The level of tension is usually extremely high, events tend to occur very fast, and those who normally run the prison are not necessarily in full control, especially after emergency forces have been deployed. When there are casualties on the side of the government, troops often seek revenge. Riot gear frequently makes future identification impossible and, thereby increases the likelihood of abuse. To minimize violence and other forms of summary punishment, Human Rights Watch recommends that:

• members of forces that may be deployed in subduing prison uprisings must be given thorough training as to when and what type of force may be used;

- use of violence against individuals who have surrendered must be banned;
- prison guards or police who violate the rules regarding the use of force must be disciplined and, in those cases where they violate the penal law, they must be criminally prosecuted;
- automatic weapons should never be used in quelling prison rebellions;
- disciplinary proceedings against prison riot participants should be conducted with full respect for due process;
- collective punishment is always impermissible and should not be applied in the aftermath of prison riots;
- any prison disturbance that results in serious injury or death, or in which a shot is fired, should be the subject of an independent inquiry, and the findings should be disclosed publicly.

ISOLATION AND
TRANSPARENCY

15
CONTACTS WITH OUTSIDERS

Prisons are, by definition, closed institutions. Moreover, in many countries the bricks and mortar that surround the institutions are reinforced by a wall of secrecy. Yet as in all other areas of human rights, an unimpeded flow of information is vital to curb abuses.

Countries that severely limit information about their prisons tend to suffer from particularly severe human rights violations in those institutions. While the possibility of communicating with the outside world does not guarantee freedom from abuses, prohibitions on communication are almost always conducive to abuses.

The experience of Human Rights Watch in securing access to prisons in various countries of the world has been mixed. We discuss this subject in more detail in the chapter titled "Monitoring Prison Conditions." Here, we note only that of the countries where we conducted prison investigations, we were denied access to prisons in China, Spain, Turkey and India.

The openness of a prison system is measured by its practices with respect to correspondence, visits, the availability of phones, contacts with lawyers, access by prisoners to media and books, access by the media to prisons and prisoners, and access by human rights and prisoners' rights organizations.

INCOMMUNICADO DETENTION

A crucial consideration is whether there is ever a period of incommunicado detention at any stage of incarceration. This is most frequent at the outset of incarceration when, not coincidentally, most systematic physical abuses, such as torture, also take place. These are usually at the hands of police or the investigating authority. Such abuse is frequently used to obtain a confession and often also to break the morale of the prisoner. It may also be used as a means of summary punishment or to extract bribes from a prisoner's family to forego torture.

101

In some countries, incommunicado detention is authorized by law. In Spain the law allows up to five days of incommunicado detention following an arrest; in addition, a judge may order a second period of incommunicado detention, no longer than three days, at any time during the inmate's incarceration.   Under Mexican law, an inmate must be brought before a judge within three days of arrest or released; in practice, however, this is not observed, and during our two investigations we encountered many inmates who had spent a week or more under incommunicado detention in police lockups.   In Turkey suspects in political cases may be detained for up to thirty days before they are brought before a judge; common crime suspects may be detained for up to eight days prior to arraignment. In Israel and the occupied territories, the incommunicado detention period for security detainees is fourteen days.   In Egypt, there is an initial thirty-day period of so called "quarantine" during which new prisoners are not allowed family visits, although they are permitted to see a lawyer.

Incommunicado detention not only makes inmates vulnerable to torture, but prolonged incommunicado detention protects their keepers as it allows the most obvious physical marks of torture to heal.

NOTIFICATION OF KIN

A separate though related problem is the notification of the next of kin about a person's arrest.   A detention may amount to incommunicado detention when relatives have no knowledge of an arrest; thereby preventing them from visiting or arranging for a lawyer's visit. Moreover, failure to notify relatives of an arrest not only inflicts a hardship on the inmate but also victimizes his or her next of kin by causing the anguish they suffer when their loved one simply disappears.

In Romania the law requires the arresting authorities to notify relatives within twenty-four hours of an arrest.   In practice, however, according to prisoners interviewed by Human Rights Watch, such notification frequently does not occur for days, and outside Bucharest, for weeks. One inmate, a foreign national, told us that his wife had not been notified of his arrest for three months, and he was prohibited from writing to her himself.

In interviews with recently released political prisoners from China, we were repeatedly told that relatives were not notified about the arrest. Instead, they had to guess and then approach a proper authority and obtain a confirmation that, indeed, a particular individual had been detained.

CORRESPONDENCE

Mail to and from prisoners is opened almost everywhere, allegedly to check for contraband, and in most countries, it is also censored. Such intrusiveness makes inmates reluctant to report abuses in their letters for fear of retaliation. In addition, some countries, notably Cuba and China, restrict the number of letters prisoners may mail and receive. Romania, Turkey and China have gone further in assuring that conditions of imprisonment stay secret: they specifically prohibit discussion of prison conditions in inmates' correspondence. The 1988 prison regulations in Romania, still in effect at this writing, state that in correspondence with family, an inmate should "not refer to problems regarding his activities in prison." In China, "Letters to and from inmates are checked, and those which have contents hindering the reform of prisoners or exposing the reform organs will be detained."[1]

Until 1992 South African law prohibited both the discussion of prison conditions in private correspondence by prisoners and any publication describing prison life except with official confirmation. The country's Prison Act of 1959 stated that "any person who published or caused to be published in any manner whatsoever any false information concerning the behavior or experience in prison of any prisoner or ex-prisoner or concerning the administration of any prison . . . without taking reasonable steps to verify such information, was guilty of an offense." "Publication" was given a wide interpretation, such that conveying information even to one other person could be an offense.[2]

---

[1] According to Guoling Zhao, a professor at the Law College at Beijing University who contributed the chapter on the People's Republic of China. Dirk van Zyl Smit and Frieder Duenkel, eds., *Imprisonment Today and Tomorrow: International Perspectives on Prisoners' Rights and Prison Conditions* (Boston: Kluwer Law and Taxation Publishers, 1991), p. 437.

[2] See Dirk van Zyl Smit, *South African Prison Law and Practice* (Durban: Butterworth, 1992), p. 342.

As a result, not only were prisoners themselves not likely to discuss conditions of their confinement in their private correspondence, but media reporting on prison issues in South Africa was virtually obliterated as well, due to the fear of long and costly law suits in which the burden of proof lay with the accused. That provision of the law was repealed in 1992. But raising prison-related matters during family visits is still banned in South Africa. During a 1993 visit to the Brandvlei maximum security prison we observed a sign in the visiting area listing visiting rules. Item number 2 provided: "No discussions on prison administrations [sic] will be allowed."

ACCESS TO INFORMATION

In the course of our research, we encountered efforts by prison administrators to isolate prisoners further by restricting the flow of information from the outside world into the prison. This was especially true in repressive countries such as then communist Poland, the former USSR, Czechoslovakia, or South Africa, where inmates' access to newspapers, magazines, and broadcast news was carefully controlled. Prisoners were denied knowledge of significant events and were frequently amazed by the changes they discovered upon their release. Due to political changes in these countries, such isolation no longer prevails. However, according to our interviews with recently released Chinese political prisoners, their access to news is severely limited especially during pre-trail detention. A few former inmates mentioned an occasional newspaper furtively read at a guard's desk as the main source of information about outside events.

VISITS

Contacts with relatives are obviously of crucial importance to prisoners' well-being and to their chances of successful reintegration into society after their release. Usually prisoners who maintain regular contact with their loved ones while in prison are more likely to stay away from crime upon their release than people who have no outside support when they are released. The frequency and type of contacts allowed by a particular prison system plays a decisive role.

Some countries whose prisons we investigated had generous policies, allowing relatives to visit up to a few times a week, for several hours at a time, sometimes offering play areas for children, and often affording arrangements for conjugal visits. Long and frequent visits, as well as conjugal visits are characteristic in Mexico and Brazil.

On the other hand, many countries are stingy about granting visits. In Spain, although most prisoners may receive occasional "vis-a-vis" visits, which consist of either conjugal or family encounters in private rooms, "regular" visits are often as brief as twenty minutes and are conducted through a glass panel. In Jamaica most contacts with visitors occur through a glass partition and are sometimes as short as five minutes; moreover, Jamaica's prison authorities prohibit visits by children. In Israel prisoners held in the custody of the Israeli Prison Service are entitled to at least one half-hour visit every two months. In practice, as a privilege, most inmates receive more frequent visits.

In South Africa, most prisoners may only receive no-contact visits, due to a "privilege" system that allows contact visits only to the highest "privilege" group. It takes at least a year, and in most cases much longer, to advance from the entry-level "privilege" group to that allowing contact.

A big obstacle in maintaining regular contact is the physical distance relatives have to travel in order to visit. In most countries that we examined, the authorities attempt to confine inmates as close to their homes as possible. Elsewhere, prisons were located far away, or overcrowding in some areas forced transfers to distant institutions.

Prisoners in Indonesia, a country of thousands of islands—a factor that makes travel difficult—are sometimes transferred to a remote prison because of overcrowding in certain institutions, making it almost impossible to receive visits. Similarly in South Africa we repeatedly heard complaints about a lack of visits to prisoners confined as far as eighteen hours by car from their homes.

In Russia, sentenced prisoners are usually confined in so called labor colonies, or camps, located in remote and sparsely populated areas of the country. As a result, virtually all prisoners serve their sentences far from their homes and almost never receive visits.

In some countries, we came across cases in which prisoners were *deliberately* assigned to prisons far from their homes. Such transfers to distant prisons are sometimes punitive, as in Spain. Similarly in Puerto Rico we were told by prison authorities that transfers to the continental United States (several hours flight away) were occasionally used as a disciplinary measure for inmates who "cause difficulties with an institution."[3]

A separate concern arose in the case of Palestinian security prisoners from the West Bank and the Gaza Strip held in Israel proper (a practice that violates the Fourth Geneva Convention, which prohibits transfers from an occupied territory to the occupying power). Due to the fact that many residents of the territories are routinely denied the permission they must obtain from Israeli authorities to enter Israel, it is difficult and sometimes impossible for the families and lawyers of prisoners to visit them. During the first three years after the opening of the large detention camp at Ketsiot (an institution in Israel's Negev desert region), virtually no family visits took place.

Visiting can be unpleasant and even humiliating to some relatives. We were told by male prisoners in South Africa that prison guards occasionally harassed their wives and girlfriends, or else demanded payments to allow family members into the visiting area. In China, families of some political prisoners were blackmailed into making statements, promising that they would not believe anything they heard about the conditions of imprisonment, as a price for seeing their relative in prison.[4] In Indonesia prisoners told us that relatives often had to bribe guards to assure that packages they brought would reach their destination. In Puerto Rico, where we interviewed relatives of a number of inmates, all reported humiliating body searches to which female visitors, including minors, were subjected. Male visitors, we were told, were not searched.

In addition, in many countries we heard complaints about the long waits visiting relatives had to endure. In some cases, no facilities were provided for those waiting; they were just forced to wait outside the prison, regardless of the weather conditions. In others, the waiting areas were filthy and grim.

---

[3] Americas Watch, "Prison Conditions in Puerto Rico," *A Human Rights Watch Short Report*, vol. 3, no. 6, (May 1991).

[4] Committee to End the Chinese Gulag, "Update on Liu Gang" (New York: January 1993).

THE TELEPHONE

The telephone can be an important means for prisoners to maintain contact with relatives and friends. For this to be possible, obviously, a country has to have a developed network of private phones. In the United States most inmates are allowed to make phone calls. In the United Kingdom phones have just been installed in prisons all over the country. In South Africa most inmates are allowed to substitute a visit for an up-to-ten-minute phone call; the highest "privilege" group inmates are additionally allowed to make twelve more phone calls per year. In Israel, criminal prisoners have access to telephones, but Palestinian security prisoners, who account for more than half of the country's prison population, do not.

RECOMMENDATIONS

Human Rights Watch believes that contacts with the outside world are among the most important aspects of prison conditions, both as a means of preventing abuses and as a way to help an inmate stay out of prison after he or she is released. This is also one of the areas of prison conditions where a lot can be achieved through policy changes and without a great financial cost. Consequently, we call on prison administrations to undertake all efforts to facilitate contacts by prisoners with the outside. In particular Human Rights Watch recommends that:

- because of the history of abuse, incommunicado detention should be prohibited;
- the next of kin must be notified of an arrest within twenty-four hours;
- prisoners in pre-trial detention should have contact privileges (visits, mail, access to newspapers and broadcasts) that are at least as broad as those for sentenced prisoners;
- prison administrations must notify prisoners' next of kin about a transfer, serious illness or death of a prisoner within twenty-four hours. The same should apply to notification of a prisoner about a close relative's death or serious illness;

- prisoners' mail should not be read by the authorities, except where justified by urgent security needs. Letters to lawyers, when properly marked as such, must not be opened;
- every prison administration should provide a system under which inmates may send sealed letters expressing their grievances to an appropriate authority;
- there should never be limits on the number or length of letters prisoners may send or receive;
- prisoners should have access to radio and television broadcasts and be allowed to subscribe to periodicals and receive them;
- all visits should routinely be contact visits. A ban on contact visits should be used only as a disciplinary measure, for violations of prison rules related to the visits. Such a ban should never be imposed except under an appropriate disciplinary procedure and then only for a strictly specified period;
- all sorts of contacts with relatives should be encouraged and facilitated, including a system of conjugal visits for inmates without furloughs;
- relatives should be treated with dignity. Efforts should be made to eliminate long waiting periods and to provide clean and pleasant waiting areas;
- searches of relatives, when mandated by security precautions, should be conducted in a polite manner and always by persons of the same sex as the relative. Under no circumstances should a special group of relatives (for example, of a certain gender or age) be singled out for searches;
- transfers to facilities distant from a prisoner's home should never be used as a disciplinary measure;
- visits should always be allowed for at least an hour. Prisoners should have an option of lengthening the duration of visits in exchange for less frequent visits, a system that would enable relatives travelling from afar to take fuller advantage of a visit;
- children should be allowed to visit their parents in prison;
- in countries with well developed telephone networks, inmates should be allowed access to the telephone, under appropriate rules. A telephone conversation should not count as a visit;
- members of the media and organizations concerned with the rights of prisoners should be allowed to visit prisons, under reasonable rules governing duration and frequency of such visits.

16
NONGOVERNMENTAL MONITORS

As noted previously, a prisoner's contact with the outside world is among the chief safeguards for preventing or minimizing human rights abuses inside prisons. In addition to a prisoner's capacity to communicate and visit with relatives or lawyers (discussed in the chapter titled "Pre-Trial Detention"), regular access to prisons by monitoring organizations—the International Committee of the Red Cross, national and international human rights groups, prisoner aid, intergovernmental and media organizations—can play an immensely positive role in preventing or stopping abuse. Much abuse occurs because prisons are closed institutions, removed from public scrutiny. Particularly in countries without internal prison inspection systems, even the central government may not be aware of the extent of human rights problems within its prisons. Those who run prisons are likely to be less inclined to commit or tolerate abuses if they know that outsiders will inspect the facilities and that abuses will be publicized and denounced.

Unannounced, periodic visits are obviously the most effective, but even an announced inspection by outsiders has its value. Of course, the staff can spruce up a prison for the benefit of the visitors; they may give prisoners better clothes and more food for a while, and they may have the walls painted. (A Human Rights Watch representative got paint on his clothes when he leaned against a wall of a prison in Cuba that he visited on several days notice.) Trained observers, however, will pick up many details that are impossible to conceal or improve just temporarily; interviews with prisoners—or even casual exchanges when formal interviews might endanger the inmates—will reveal how different the prison is on the day of the visit from the routine; and, anyway, the fresh paint will remain after the visit.

THE ROLE OF HUMAN RIGHTS ORGANIZATIONS

National human rights organizations within each country are obviously in the best position to monitor human rights conditions within their country's prisons. They can conduct ongoing monitoring, react quickly to emergencies, and work with local media and officials to promote change. In the course of its work on prison conditions on five continents, Human Rights Watch was greatly helped by its counterparts in domestic human rights groups. Often, our research would have gone nowhere or, at best, would have been immensely difficult, if it were not for local monitors. Frequently, however, the local groups are not allowed to visit prisons or can obtain only limited access to prisons and prisoners. In several of the countries where Human Rights Watch was able to visit prisons, our local counterparts had never been allowed inside prisons and jails.

Though visits by international human rights organizations often help to focus attention within the country on the problem of prison conditions and, externally, place the issue on the international human rights agenda, it is local groups that bear most of the burden of promoting changes.

PUBLICIZING THE FINDINGS

For prison visits and scrutiny to be effective (see below for a discussion of the unique role of the International Committee of the Red Cross) the findings must be publicized. It is embarrassing and shameful for governments to be denounced as human rights violators. This shame, and the public pressure it generates, are the most powerful tools that have been devised internationally to bring about human rights improvements. When the findings of prison visits are disclosed solely to the authorities, the usefulness of such visits is extremely limited. Occasionally the central government may learn something it had not known previously and act to correct the situation; on the whole, however, confidentiality is more often a disincentive than an incentive to make improvements.

The Role of the Media

In countries with a free press, the media can play an enormous role in informing the public about human rights and their violation in prisons, and in mobilizing public pressure to curb abuses. The press should insist on access to prisons and the right to interview inmates of their choice. Local human rights organizations are frequently effective in using media as their allies, alerting them to prison-related stories and notifying them of emergencies.

The Role of the International Committee of the Red Cross (ICRC)

The one exception to the rule regarding the publication of findings is the International Committee of the Red Cross, which conducts visits to prisons worldwide and shares its findings only with the host government. There are significant differences between the ICRC and other groups conducting visits to prisons. The ICRC requests prison visits only in countries where there are significant numbers of security prisoners. Its representatives conduct regular visits over a period of months and often years. They interview prisoners in the course of long, confidential conversations and subsequently return to check that no reprisals have taken place for providing information to ICRC delegates. The ICRC's long-term presence and ongoing access to prisoners is in itself an important deterrent of torture. In addition, ICRC representatives conduct detailed surveys of the overall conditions in each institution they visit and provide specific recommendations for improvements to the government. Occasionally, the ICRC offers technical advice and assistance to a government so as to achieve its recommended changes.

The ICRC often gains access to a country's most politically sensitive and most vulnerable prisoners, and confidentiality is the price for this access. Although the ICRC rarely denounces governments, it is able to promote improvements through means that are not available to other prison-visiting organizations. Its ongoing presence often helps to stop or minimize torture and other abuses. No other organization plays an analogous role.

Consequences of Secrecy in Prison Visits

Failure to publicize the findings from prison visits may not only negate their value but could provide the authorities with a kind of smoke screen. When a government routinely excludes monitoring organizations from its prisons and then makes an exception for a single delegation to inspect them knowing that the findings will remain unavailable to the public, the effect is to help the government fend off criticisms of running a "closed" prison system. When we asked the Spanish government to allow us to see prisons in 1991, the letter turning us down cited the fact that a delegation from the European Committee for the Prevention of

Torture (APF), established under the European Convention Against Torture and Inhuman or Degrading Treatment or Punishment, had visited the Spanish prisons shortly before and was preparing a report.[1] But the results of the visits by the APF are confidential, unless the government under scrutiny decides to publish the APF report.[2] The Spanish government has not published the report as of this writing and the report's existence did nothing to break the official secretiveness surrounding the Spanish prisons.

PRISON VISITS BY HUMAN RIGHTS WATCH

When Human Rights Watch decides to undertake a study of prison conditions in a particular country, as a first step we send a letter to the authorities in charge of the country's prisons requesting permission to inspect the prisons and specifying the institutions to be visited. This is done to prevent a government's suggestion of its best or "model" prisons for a visit. We usually designate a mix of different types of institutions (police lockups, pre-trial facilities, and prisons for sentenced prisoners), male and female institutions, and those with "good" and "bad" reputations within the system. In addition, in our initial letter, Human Rights Watch informs the government that we wish to see the entire premises of each institution—again, to avoid being shown only the more presentable parts. We also ask to interview inmates of our choice privately.

Such prison visits are an important but by no means the sole basis for conducting research on prison conditions in a particular country. We also seek advice and information from local human rights organizations;

---

[1] May 14, 1991 letter from Antoni Asuncíon Hernández, the Secretary General of Penitentiary Affairs of Spain.

[2] Article 10 (2) of the European Convention for the Prevention of Torture provides that if a Party to the Convention "fails to cooperate or refuses to improve the situation in the light of the Committee's recommendations, the Committee may decide, after the Party has had an opportunity to make known its views, by a majority of two thirds of its members to make a public statement on the matter." To date, however, the APF has issued only one such public statement, with respect to Turkey.

we interview former prisoners, prisoners on furloughs and relatives of prisoners; and we obtain information from members of the clergy who regularly visit prisons, lawyers who have information about conditions through their clients, and prison officials. Human Rights Watch also studies the existing documentary material as well as the prison-related laws. Sometimes, even when we conduct prison visits, it is impossible or may be too dangerous for the prisoners to talk to us freely as they may suffer reprisals afterwards. In such cases, no formal interviews with prisoners are conducted and testimony is gathered through the other means described above. In some cases, we must rely exclusively on outside sources because the government denies Human Rights Watch access to prisons.

In the majority of cases, Human Rights Watch has been able to visit prisons we requested to see, but there were a few notable exceptions. Prior to the democratic changes in Eastern Europe, the governments of Poland and Czechoslovakia simply ignored requests to visit their prisons, and our first reports on these institutions were based solely on the "outside" material. In both countries, Human Rights Watch was subsequently invited to come back and conduct prison visits.

The governments of Turkey, India, Spain, China and the prison administration of Puerto Rico denied permission for Human Rights Watch to visit their prisons. In Spain, where Human Rights Watch was invited to visit one prison by a judge with jurisdiction over that institution, the government subsequently attempted to retaliate against the judge (see the chapter on Spain). In Egypt the government denied access to its prisons at the time of a 1990 visit by a delegation from Human Rights Watch, but it did allow a series of thorough visits in 1992.

RECOMMENDATIONS

Human Rights Watch believes that for a prison system to function properly and to minimize abuses, a system for access by independent human rights organizations as well as by the media must be established. Exclusion of such visits usually means but one thing: the government has something to hide. Human Rights Watch calls on all governments to:

- provide a system for ongoing access to prisons by local human rights organizations and for access by international groups that demonstrate a continuing concern with prison conditions;
- establish a policy for providing access to prisons by members of all media (including broadcast), and for confidential interviews with all prisoners;
- make the results of prison inspections a matter of public record except to the degree that the confidences of inmates may be violated or in the special circumstances of investigations by the International Committee of the Red Cross.

17
THE UNITED NATIONS

The United Nations has established that prison conditions are human rights issues and that they are a matter of international concern. Both the Universal Declaration of Human Rights and the International Covenant on Civil and Political Rights (the covenant) affirm the proposition that human rights extend to those who are incarcerated. Furthermore, the U.N. has adopted the Standard Minimum Rules for the Treatment of Prisoners and a number of mechanisms that are supposed to monitor prisons and implement those standards. Unfortunately, though these efforts by the U.N. reveal an ostensible concern for the plight of the imprisoned, they have been largely ineffectual in exposing abuses by member states or in improving the conditions under which prisoners live. At best, the U.N. has succeeded in establishing a useful standard by which to judge the failures of prison systems worldwide.

THE STANDARD MINIMUM RULES FOR THE TREATMENT OF PRISONERS

The Standard Minimum Rules for the Treatment of Prisoners (the rules are reprinted in full as an appendix) are the most comprehensive international agreement designed to establish standards for prison conditions and to monitor and enforce adherence to those standards. While the rules have proven to be useful as guidelines in the evaluation—and in the implementation—of prison policies, they have not been effective as part of a system for the enforcement of a minimum standard by the international community.

The rules were adopted in 1955 by the First United Nations Congress on the Prevention of Crime and the Treatment of Offenders. They describe in Preliminary Observations (1), "what is generally accepted as being good principle and practice in the treatment of prisoners and the management of institutions."

Compared to other U.N. documents addressing the conditions under which prisoners may be held, such as the International Covenant on Civil and Political Rights, which devotes four short paragraphs in very general language to the conditions of punishment and imprisonment, the rules are very specific. They set out guidelines regarding such topics as "Clothing and Bedding," "Exercise and Sport," "Instruments of Restraint," "Retention of Prisoners' Property" and other categories that are peculiar to systems of incarceration. The rules have succeeded to the extent that they are recognized as a standard by governments and prison officials in a great many countries. Indeed most countries claim to adhere to the standards set forth in the rules in their responses to the quinquennial surveys conducted by the secretary general.[1] In reality, however, many of these same countries fall far short of applying and enforcing the standards.

The rules do not have the legally binding effect of treaties and are thus merely recommendations put forth by the U.N. Their authority is further diminished by the reservation contained in rule 2, which states "In view of the great variety of legal, social, economic and geographical conditions of the world, it is evident that not all of the rules are capable of application in all places at all times." The rules thus license departures from the standards they themselves set.

The Secretary General's Survey on the Rules

Since the rules' inception, the U.N. has attempted to monitor their implementation by conducting quinquennial surveys of the member states on the extent to which the rules are followed in their prison systems. Most countries simply ignore the survey. Many others report adherence to the rules when even a superficial examination of their prisons reveals the contrary. Unfortunately, the discrepancies are difficult to prove since the specific answers of individual countries are not public. It can hardly be expected, in any case, that all governments replying to the survey will do so in good faith.

The results of the most recent survey of the member states are typical. The most obvious failure is the fact that only one-third of member states replied. Many of the worst offenders simply declined to respond rather than lie or admit violations. Furthermore, twenty-seven countries that had replied to the previous survey failed to reply to the

---

[1] *Report of the Secretary-General on the Implementation of the Standard Minimum Rules for the Treatment of Prisoners, 1990.* See also Paul R. Williams, *Treatment of Detainees* (Geneva: Henry Dunant Institute, 1990), p. 41.

most recent one.   Thus, the usefulness of the survey as an index of change in various systems has been defeated.

On its face, the survey suggests conditions in the world's prisons that do not reflect actual practice. For example, 41 out of 46 countries report full (34) or partial (7) implementation of rule 31, which forbids corporal punishment, punishment by confinement in a dark cell, and cruel, inhuman or degrading punishments. Our own research has shown that beatings as an extra-legal punishment (and less often as a legal one) are endemic in prisons worldwide and many other punishments found all over the world qualify as cruel, inhuman and degrading. And it is certainly not the case that the world community as a whole has an 89 percent rate of implementation of this rule.

The effectiveness of the surveys is further diminished by the fact that neither the U.N. Congresses on the Prevention of Crime and the Treatment of Offenders nor the Commission that does the preparatory work for the Congresses "has the necessary time and resources to properly examine, evaluate and follow-up, by way of recommendations, the surveys presented to them by the Secretariat."[2]

The Effectiveness of the Rules

Despite the ineffectiveness of the U.N. in enforcing the rules, they remain an important document. They function as a code of practice for prison officials and as a standard by which to judge conditions in prison systems. They have been invoked in setting penal policies and prison regulations in a number of countries including the U.S., Poland and South Africa. Furthermore, the rules have been enacted into law in a number of countries including the United States (in California, Connecticut and several other states) and judicial holdings have cited them as authority in the United States and elsewhere. In addition, the rules are used in the interpretation of binding documents of international law and they appear to be inching toward the status of customary international law.

A great asset of the rules is that they speak the language of the penal profession. As such, they have been particularly useful as practical guides to the maintenance of prisons. States that do respond to the U.N.

---

[2] Kurt Neudek, "The United Nations," *Imprisonment Today and Tomorrow, International Perspectives on Prisoners' Rights and Prison Conditions* (Boston: Kluwer, 1991).

surveys categorically assert that they apply the rules in their own prison systems. And a number of countries, including Afghanistan, Egypt, Ecuador and El Salvador, claim to use the rules in training courses for police and detention authorities. About 25 percent of countries responding, including Rwanda, Ukraine (as Soviet Republic) and the United Kingdom, report that they provide access to the rules to all detainees.[3] While conditions in these countries' prisons vary greatly, the emphasis on the rules is a promising sign.

The rules' greatest potential strength lies in the possibility that they will begin to be recognized as customary international law. As such, they can be used as guidance in interpreting general rules of international law. For example, the European Commission of Human Rights used the classifications contained in the rules to interpret the European Convention on Human Rights in settling a case involving conditions of detention in a Greek jail.[4]

The rules can provide similar guidance in interpreting the International Covenant on Civil and Political Rights. The covenant contains a general rule against "cruel, inhuman, or degrading treatment or punishment." The rules, on the other hand, more specifically forbid, among other things, placing the prisoner in a dark cell, the unhealthy reduction of diet, and the use of instruments of restraint as forms of punishment. The rules can thus serve as guides to the application of the more general binding international agreement.

DATA GATHERING

In addition to the secretary general's surveys regarding implementation of the standard minimum rules, the European Commission of Human Rights also conducts a quinquennial effort to obtain data on the prison populations of all member states. After sophisticated statistical analysis and processing, these data ultimately form the basis for a global report published by the commission, which details demographic and other trends in the world's prisons.

---

[3] Williams, *Treatment of Detainees*, pp. 41, 42.

[4] Nigel Rodley, *The Treatment of Prisoners Under International Law* (Oxford: Clarendon Press, 1987), p. 223.

The U.N. Service of Crime Trends conducts the survey through each country's criminal justice agencies and national statistical offices. The service makes detailed requests regarding the nature of the prison population in each country surveyed. Ninety-five countries, or slightly more than half of the U.N. member states, responded to the last survey which was conducted in 1986, and the commission anticipates a similar response to the current survey. Of those, some responded only to some of the questions. Fewer than fifty countries provided data regarding the overall number of prisoners in the country, and the commission regularly fails to, receive data from some of the world's largest and most abusive countries, including China. Since most countries keep the relevant statistics for their own purposes, responding to the surveys should be a simple matter and data should be more readily available. On the other hand, a failure to keep records regarding prison population is by itself a violation of the rules and an indication of a serious problem within a prison system.

The commission attempts to validate the responses in two ways. First, it consults the country in question through official channels regarding inconsistencies or questionable responses. Second, it looks at sources of data and evidence available through other means. The final report reflects the conclusions made during the validation process. Unfortunately, the information is not available on a timely basis. The report for the period 1986-1990 will be available in January 1995.

RECENT GENERAL ASSEMBLY RESOLUTIONS

In recent years, the General Assembly has adopted resolutions aimed at affirming and protecting the rights of prisoners. Among these are the "Body of Principles for the Protection of All Persons Under Any Form of Detention or Imprisonment" and the "Basic Principles for the Treatment of Prisoners." The body of principles, adopted in 1988, defines a number of terms and states thirty-nine principles that should be followed in administering systems of detention and imprisonment. It contains much of the language of the standard minimum rules and the International Covenant on Civil and Political Rights. The basic principles, adopted in 1990, affirm the proposition that prisoners should be accorded the rights due to others, taking into account the necessary restrictions on freedom of movement. To date, these resolutions have not enhanced the effectiveness of the U.N. in monitoring the conditions of the world's prisons.

THE INTERNATIONAL COVENANT ON CIVIL AND POLITICAL RIGHTS

The International Covenant on Civil and Political Rights and its Optional Protocol constitute a binding body of law, which can be used to address the rights of prisoners and the conditions of their incarceration. Its scope is limited to the 117 countries that have ratified the covenant and the sixty-eight that have become parties to the Optional Protocol. Pursuant to the covenant, the United Nations Human Rights Committee is empowered to implement and enforce it through a variety of operations. The most important are receiving and processing State Reports and rendering decisions on complaints.[5]

Under article 40 of the covenant, states are required to submit reports on their own laws and compliance in practice under each article of the covenant. Their responses regarding prison conditions are often merely lists of constitutional and legislative provisions that pay lip service to the rights enumerated in the covenant. References to specific practices are often divorced from reality. At best, this reporting process, like the surveys on the standard minimum rules, promotes the principle that states should pay attention to the rights of prisoners, even though the states themselves deny their own failings.

Decisions on violations of this and other articles of the covenant are made by the United Nations Human Rights Committee. Though the committee is empowered by the covenant to hear complaints by one state against another, no such complaint has ever been made. Under the Optional Protocol, the committee may consider complaints received from individuals who claim that their rights under the covenant have been violated. The committee then renders a consensus decision. Though the absence of an enforcement mechanism limits the significance of these decisions, they are an important means of registering international condemnation.

The United Nations Human Rights Committee has found violations of prisoners' rights on a number of occasions. These cases have

---

[5] Williams, *Treatment of Detainees*, p. 15.

involved violations of article 7 (prohibiting "torture or cruel, inhuman or degrading treatment or punishment") and article 10 (requiring that "all persons deprived of their liberty shall be treated with humanity and with respect for the inherent dignity of the human person.") A number of successful cases were brought regarding the conditions at Uruguay's inaptly named Libertad Prison.[6] In those cases, the prisoners' were subjected to isolation, malnutrition, lack of sunshine and exercise, unsanitary conditions and excesses of cold and heat.[7] As mentioned above, the standard minimum rules can be useful as a guide in determining violations of the covenant's prohibitions.

The U.N. recognizes that the there is room for improvement in implementation of the standard minimum rules. It has thus made some attempts to put procedures in motion that would lead to greater adherence to the rules by member countries. In its resolution of May 12, 1976, the Economic and Social Council (ECOSOC) requested the Committee on Crime Prevention and Control to formulate a set of procedures for the implementation of the rules.[8] On the recommendation of the committee, ECOSOC adopted the "Procedures for the effective implementation of the Standard Minimum Rules for the Treatment of Prisoners" in 1984.

The procedures set forth a number of measures which, if followed, would result in stricter adherence to the standard minimum rules. Among these are: enactment of the rules as national legislation; broad dissemination of the rules to prisoners and prison personnel; more effective and efficient use of the periodic reports to the secretary general;

---

[6] Uruguay had been a liberal democracy of the sort that accepted the Optional Protocol. In 1973, it suffered a military coup and a harsh dictatorship that held power for a dozen years. Accordingly, its ratification of the protocol at an earlier stage in its history made this an important means for dealing with abuses during the dozen years of severe repression.

[7] Rodley, *The Treatment of Prisoners Under International Law*, p. 229.

[8] The Committee on Crime Prevention and Control was recently made a commission and renamed The Commission on Crime Prevention and Criminal Justice. The change transformed the group from fifteen individual experts on crime to representatives of forty nations, with some of the world's worst offenders regarding prison conditions among them.

and closer interaction between the U.N., the committee and member states in the development and running of their correctional systems.

In addition, the report by the secretary general on the most recent survey of the implementation of the standard minimum rules contained a number of suggestions by member states to improve the methods of implementing the rules. Among these suggestions, it was proposed to create an international body to inspect prisons and offer advice on implementation of the Rules.[9]

RECOMMENDATIONS

Human Rights Watch believes that creating a United Nations body with a mandate for inspecting prisons is the key to more effective implementation of the standard minimum rules. We believe that a permanent working group on prison conditions, along the lines of the Working Group on Disappearances, would play an important part in improvement of human rights conditions in prisons worldwide. Such a working group should undertake prison inspections, hold hearings and publish its findings in reports for general distribution. Using information reported by the working group as well as other U.N. agencies, the secretary general should publish an annual report on prison conditions. In addition, we call on the secretary general to undertake annual demographic surveys of prisons worldwide, in place of the current quinquennial surveys, and to publish the findings within the year following the year to which the surveys refer.

We also call on the U.N. to sponsor periodic international conferences on prison conditions. These conferences would be effective in stigmatizing the world's worst violators before the eyes of the international community.

Finally, since the conditions, trends and methods of incarceration undergo constant change, the U.N. should undertake periodic examinations of the rules for the purpose of revising them to keep pace with these changes.

---

[9] *Report of the Secretary General, 1990* (New York: United Nations, 1990).

THE NUMBERS

18
THE NUMBERS

It is impossible to state with any reasonable degree of precision how many people are incarcerated worldwide at any given moment. Though some countries publish detailed statistics regarding their prison population, many release none whatsoever, either as a matter of secrecy or because collecting statistical data in that country is so haphazard.

The most systematic data gathering in the area of criminal justice is conducted by the United Nations' Crime Prevention and Criminal Justice Branch and the results are made public as "Crime Data Surveys" every five years and cover a period that goes back more than five years. In the latest edition of this international report, which deals with the years 1980 to 1986, data on prison population is supplied for fewer than fifty of the 181 countries currently in the U.N.

In public perception, imprisonment has long been regarded as marginal, affecting only a small portion of the population, and implicitly requiring only marginal public attention. Some recent studies suggest, however, that in certain countries, and especially, with respect to particular groups within the country's population, imprisonment is a substantial factor in everyday life.

A study in the United States revealed a few years ago that African-American men between twenty and twenty-nine years of age have statistically a higher chance of going to prison than going to college.[1] Of course, the United States has a very high rate of incarceration: With 455 prisoners per 100,000 citizens the U.S. has both one of the highest prisoner-to-population ratios in the world and the highest reported absolute number as well.[2]

---

[1] The Sentencing Project, "Young Black Men and the Criminal Justice System: A Growing National Problem" (Washington, D.C., 1990).

[2] The Sentencing Project, "Americans Behind Bars: One Year Later" (Washington, D.C., 1992). China's total number of prisoners is certainly higher than that of the United States, but comprehensive statistical information on that country is not available.

But an examination of the available U.N. and country incarceration statistics confirms that in other countries, or in some cases, for racial, ethnic or religious groups within countries, imprisonment is also a significant fact of life.

The prisoner-to-population rate (measured in number of prisoners per 100,000 citizens) for some of the countries for which we have 1986 data reveal the extent of imprisonment and the great disparity among countries.

COUNTRY	1986 RATE (prisoners per 100,000 citizens)
Dominica	714
Bermuda	445
Ghana	442
Cayman Islands	382
United States	336
Hungary	223
Kuwait	189
Singapore	144
Austria	83
Peru	72
Denmark	49
Cyprus	29
Indonesia	22
Burundi	18

Full understanding of the impact of imprisonment cannot be gained from this list because we lack reports on the two largest countries in the world, The People's Republic of China and India.

We have only partial data on China, but Human Rights Watch researchers estimate the number of prisoners there to be well in excess of 1.1 million (the official Chinese statistics for 1991 for the number of inmates in prisons and reform-through-labor institutions; no statistics are available regarding the number of inmates in administrative detention and in reeducation-through-labor institutions), and accordingly the ratio exceeds 100 per 100,000. From the available data on India, we estimate a rate of 34 per 100,000.

Of course, imprisonment rates have changed since 1986. For example, the U.S. has increased from 336 per 100,000 in 1986 to 455 per 100,000 as of early 1992. We have no evidence that worldwide imprisonment rates are on the decline.

Even if the rates given above were correct—and we believe that understatement for political reasons is more likely than overstatement—imprisonment affects people at a much higher rate. The number of prisoners at a given moment does not equal the number who spend at least part of the year in a prison or jail. A look at the number of prisoners in a given country compared with the number of admissions to prisons and jails during that year shows that the latter is almost invariably at least twice, and frequently as much as *ten times* the number of prisoners on any particular day of that year in that country. In the United States, the number of all admissions, both to prisons and to jails, in 1986 was close to 8.5 million, with an admission ratio of 3,483 per 100,000 people.[3] Not only do long sentences expire and new sentences begin, but also much larger numbers are incarcerated for periods such as 30 days, 60 days, or 180 days at a time. This means that the proportion of people who experience imprisonment in any given year is much higher than the prisoner-to-population ratio usually given in reports.

The fragmentary data for 1986 shows that the average prisoner to population ratio for all regions then stood roughly at 106. With the world population at the time approximating 5 billion people, that would mean the imprisonment of 5,300,000 people at any given time, and several times as many at some time during the year.

With the current lack of available statistical information, Human Rights Watch is not attempting to project how many people worldwide are likely to experience imprisonment in the course of their lives. But examining the numbers that are available makes it clear that imprisonment directly affects millions of individuals at any given time and tens of millions in the course of any given year. Over the course of a lifetime the numbers are far greater yet, rising into the scores of millions and perhaps even the hundreds of millions. In addition, of course, the effects of the experience and reality of imprisonment go far beyond the individual prisoner because close family members are inevitably affected. All this suggest that imprisonment is far from a

---

[3] Helsinki Institute for Crime Prevention and Control, *Criminal Justice Systems in Europe and North America* (Helsinki, 1990), p. 77.

marginal issue. It needs to be thoroughly examined as a human rights issue and should be of importance to the general public.

COUNTRY SECTIONS

BRAZIL

Human Rights Watch visited Brazilian prisons and jails on four separate occasions. In October 1988 we visited fourteen penal institutions in São Paulo and Rio de Janeiro states and published our findings in Prison Conditions in Brazil. *In February 1989 a representative travelled to São Paulo to visit the scene of a massacre of eighteen prisoners who suffocated to death in one of the city's police precincts, and wrote a short report titled "Brazil: Notorious Jail Operating Again in São Paulo." In October 1989 we conducted a follow-up visit to one of São Paulo's jails. In October 1992 in the aftermath of the massacre of at least 111 inmates in the Casa de Detenção prison in São Paulo we collected testimonies from the survivors and released "Brazil: Prison Massacre in São Paulo."*

Phenomenal overcrowding and occasional violent incidents of near-apocalyptic proportions are two of the features that first come to mind when describing Brazilian prisons. According to statistics released in the fall of 1992, the country held 124,000 prisoners in institutions designed for a maximum of 51,638 people. In the fall of 1992 Brazil experienced its bloodiest prison massacre to date: at least 111 inmates in São Paulo's Casa de Detenção were killed by the Military Police in the course and the aftermath of a prison disturbance (eighty-four of those killed were still awaiting trial).

Less than a year earlier, in Rio de Janeiro, thirty-one prisoners died of burns when guards threw an incendiary device into a cell at the Agua Santa prison after discovering an escape plot.

In 1989, Military Police called to São Paulo's Police Precinct 42 in response to a disturbance that erupted in the lockup, forced fifty-one men into a cell less than fifty square feet, with a heavy metal door and no windows, and held them there for more than an hour, at the end of which eighteen of them were found to have suffocated to death.

THE SYSTEM

Brazil has twenty-five state prison systems and one in the Federal District, encompassing the capital, Brasília, and its environs. The overall prisoner-to-population ratio is 82 per 100,000. In São Paulo and Rio de Janeiro, however, the states surrounding Brazil's two largest and economically most important cities, it is 168 and 45 prisoners, respectively, per 100,000 citizens. Female inmates account for about 2 percent of the prison population in São Paulo and 6 percent in Rio de Janeiro.

PHYSICAL CONDITIONS

Brazil holds more than twice the number of prisoners it has space to accommodate, and as a result, most institutions are severely overcrowded. In addition, because of the shortage of prison space, many prisoners are serving their sentences in local jails meant only for short-term stays that lack even minimal essential infrastructure. Prisoners often sleep in terribly overcrowded cells, sometimes with no furniture whatsoever, with only blankets or mats on the cement floor. Personal belongings often hang from clotheslines crisscrossing the cell, further limiting the available space. Many facilities—though not all—are filthy and smelly. We observed rats and giant cockroaches in some cells; inmates routinely showed us insects they had collected in their cells and displayed the bites on their bodies. Most cells we visited had a hole-in-the-floor toilet with a faucet directly above it for washing and drinking. We heard many complaints about the temperature: very hot and stuffy during the summer, cold and damp in the winter. In one prison we observed puddles of water on the floor of several cells; regarding one of these, an inmate commented simply: "We call it our swimming pool."[1]

PHYSICAL ABUSES

Criminal suspects are frequently tortured during interrogation by police seeking confessions. Some of our interviewees provided graphic descriptions of the types of torture they had been subjected to while in police custody. On at least two occasions, inmates in lockups showed us

---

[1] Americas Watch, *Prison Conditions in Brazil* (New York: Human Rights Watch, 1989), p. 7.

extensive hematomas and told us that they had recently been inflicted in the course of their interrogations.

Physical abuses do not end when an inmate is confined to a prison. Human Rights Watch received reports of beatings by the staff in almost all the institutions included in our studies. Beatings occur both as extra-official punishment for disciplinary infractions—ranging from arguing with a guard to attempted escape—as well as a means of intimidating and controlling prisoners.

PRISONER-MIXING

There is little segregation of different categories of prisoners. Many prisoners serve their sentences in local jails due to the overcrowding of the prison systems. First-time offenders are often housed with those convicted of the most serious crimes; pre-trial detainees live alongside those serving time for murder. Among the 111 known fatalities of the 1992 massacre in São Paulo, eighty-four were pre-trial, while the rest were serving sentences ranging from two to thirty years. All were housed together.

INMATE-ON-INMATE VIOLENCE

The pandemic overcrowding and idleness of Brazilian prisons produce serious strains and tensions among prisoners that often erupt in violence. Not surprisingly, given the extent of mixing of hardened criminals with first-time or vulnerable offenders, we were told of frequent incidents of violent inmates abusing and exploiting the younger. Beatings, knifings and rape are routine. Inmates in the Guarulhos jail told us "Every cell has a chief and homosexuality" is rampant. A former inmate, interviewed in Rio said: "There are fights over food, over cigarettes. There is a lot of homosexual rape of younger prisoners. Young people are sold by guards who then place them in the same cells as the buyers. There are many rapes and sales."[2]

---

[2] Americas Watch, *Prison Conditions in Brazil* (New York: Human Rights Watch, 1989), pp. 15-16.

In recent years Brazilian prisons have experienced bizarre waves of inmate-on-inmate killings perpetrated apparently to call attention to prison conditions or as a protest against some other prison-related matters. In the mid-1980s, at least seventeen inmates were killed in Belo Horizonte as an act of protest by the prisoners against what inmates described as subhuman prison conditions. The victims were chosen by a lottery.

Nineteen prisoners died in Rio prisons in 1988, killed by their fellow inmates who were members of a powerful prison gang, apparently after they had refused to join a hunger strike to protest the imprisonment of gang leaders in the maximum security modern facility in Bangu, near Rio.

ACTIVITIES AND WORK

In jails, where many prisoners serve their entire sentences—sometimes for as long as ten years—there are no facilities for recreation and there is hardly any opportunity for work (except for the limited number of jobs in maintenance).

In prisons, facilities in theory designed for long-term confinement, the situation is only marginally better. A few prisons visited by our delegation offered work opportunities, and some had limited educational programs. The majority however, offered neither, and among the most frequent complaints we heard concerned boredom and idleness. Sports and other recreational facilities were scarce. In the majority of institutions we visited, inmates spent most of the time locked in their cells, although in several they were allowed out into a large patio for several hours a day.

PRISONER MASSACRES

The three recent incidents mentioned at the beginning of this chapter, in which a total of at least 147 prisoners lost their lives, all occurred in response to either a disturbance or an attempted escape. In two of the cases, the perpetrators of the killings were members of the Military Police who had been called to the scene to subdue the commotion; in the third, the deaths were caused by the prison staff. In none of the three incidents were there fatalities on the side of law enforcement. In each of the cases, the government expressed its shock and promised to investigate the matter thoroughly and to punish those responsible. As of this writing, not a single member of the police or prison staff has been criminally prosecuted for the killings.

RECORD KEEPING

Another distinctive feature of Brazilian prisons that caught our attention was the apparent deficiency of prison record keeping. One of the frequent complaints Human Rights Watch heard in Brazilian prisons was that inmates are not released immediately upon completion of their sentences. No national statistics are available, but estimates provided by lawyers who have attempted to eliminate such cases ranged from anywhere between 2 and 10 percent. And, as one grim proof that the problem was indeed real and serious, we discovered that one of the inmates who suffocated in Police Precinct 42 should have been released previously because the police had dropped theft charges against him. Similarly, one of the prisoners seriously injured in the 1992 massacre at the Casa de Detenção had completed his sentence three weeks prior to the incident.

Further evidence of the fact that prison administrators were unable to determine quickly whom they were holding was the slowness in providing lists of survivors in the aftermath of the Agua Santa and the Casa de Detenção massacres. As a result, in each case, anguished relatives gathered in front of the prison buildings for days, trying to find out whether their loved ones were dead or alive.[3]

CONTACTS WITH THE OUTSIDE WORLD

Human Rights Watch found that Brazilian prisons and jails had a generous visiting policy. Inmates were entitled to several visits a month, for a few hours each. Conjugal visits were generally available to

---

[3] "2 Guards Held in Fire Killing 24 at Rio Jail," *Washington Post*, October 30, 1991; Americas Watch, "Brazil: Prison Massacre in São Paulo," *A Human Rights Watch Short Report*, vol. 4, no. 10, (October 21, 1992).

inmates as well, though in an institution such as the Casa de Detenção in São Paulo, no separate facilities were provided and such makeshift arrangements as were possible afforded little or no privacy. Mail is generally unrestricted and we heard no complaints on this subject.

But we did hear repeated complaints about guards mistreating visitors. In at least one prison, the director confirmed to us that guards illegally forced visitors to pay for visits. We also heard reports that male guards sometimes proposition female visitors in exchange for letting them enter the facility.

In the aftermath of the October 1992 massacre in São Paulo, prison authorities failed to fulfill one of their most basic obligations, which is the notification of the next of kin about a prisoner's death. All the government did to inform relatives was to post a list of the dead on the prison wall two days after the massacre. The relatives not only were never notified directly about the deaths, but after finding a name on the list, it became their responsibility to tour city morgues so as to locate the body and avoid having their loved one buried as an unknown.

CHINA

Information about prison conditions came from several sources including interviews with released prisoners. Some of them had been held in detention centers; others in prisons, police lockups and labor camps. The former prisoners came from several Chinese provinces and more often than not were held in more than one type of facility, which aided in widening the scope. In addition to these first-person accounts, information also came from documents smuggled out of prisons. A request to the Ministry of Justice for on-site inspection of prison facilities by the Human Rights Watch Prison Project has, to date, been ignored.

China's basic principle of criminal reform, set forth in an August 1992 white paper, is to "turn offenders into [people] who abide by the law and support themselves with their own labor. . . ."[1] To accomplish this end, "China does not simply punish criminals; instead it emphasizes reform and change for the better" through "physical labor in addition to legal, moral, cultural and technical education." The system in its entirety is known as *lao gai* or "reform through labor." Despite its stated goals, former prisoners have repeatedly confirmed the routine harshness and injustice of the Chinese prison system, the world's largest.[2]

Its worst abuses result from three features of the justice system: lengthy incommunicado detention; a system of administrative justice that includes indefinite detention by the Public Security Bureau (police)

---

[1] Information Office of the State Council, *White Paper on Criminal Reform*, August 11, 1992.

[2] According to statistics in the *White Paper on Criminal Reform*, China's population is 1.1 billion and "[a]bout 400,000 criminal cases are brought to trial every year in China. The country's crime incidence among the population is about two per thousand per year." Another white paper, Information Office of the State Council, *Human Rights in China* (November 1991), states there are 680 prisons and reform-through-labor institutions in China, holding 1.1 million criminals. All such statistics are highly problematic and vastly understate the population in detention by eliminating those held or sentenced administratively, those in criminal detention and those in prisons not under the jurisdiction of the Ministry of Justice.

without any independent judicial supervision, and administrative sentencing outside the Criminal Procedure Code; and reliance on a suspect's confession for evidence and as an indication of a properly repentant attitude. The white paper explicitly states that "the legal and moral education of criminals emphasizes the need to plead guilty." Taken together, these three features support an extensive structure of violence and corruption.

A TWO-TRACK SYSTEM

With important exceptions, Chinese prisons are under the jurisdiction of the Ministry of Justice. However, according to China's Criminal Procedure Code, Public Security Bureaus are responsible for detaining and arresting suspects and for pre-trial custody. Arrests must be approved by a people's procuracy or decided by a people's court. Families or work units must be notified within twenty-four hours after detention or arrest unless it is believed that such notification would hinder investigation.

When a suspect enters the judicial system, he or she normally stays for a few days at the local branch of the Public Security Bureau, in essence a police station. From there, he goes to a detention center, under direct control of a public security organ that usually corresponds with the level of court (for example, basic or intermediate), which most probably will hear his case in the first instance.[3] At this point, a suspect follows one of two routes. He may enter a criminal track, in which case he must be formally arrested within ten days from the time he was first detained. The Criminal Procedure Code, although it sets limits (approximately six months) on the time that may elapse between the issuance of an arrest warrant and a trial, has enough loopholes to keep a detainee in custody indefinitely while the state collects evidence.[4]

---

[3] China's court system is hierarchically organized, with the Supreme People's Court at the apex. Higher level courts oversee the administration of justice by courts at lower levels.

[4] See, for example, the 1984 Supplementary Provisions of the Standing Committee of the National People's Congress Regarding the Time Limits for Handling Criminal Cases.

Alternately, suspects may be administratively detained. They usually remain at the detention center housed together with those in criminal detention, until the next step in the process is reached. According to published regulations, the legal limit on administrative detention is three months and it applies to limited classes of suspects.[5] In practice, under a system, known as *shourong shencha* or "shelter and investigation," suspects other than those to whom the regulations apply are detained and limits on how long a suspect may be held are ignored. Suspects have been held for as long as four years before being charged or released.

The shelter and investigation system gives the state an opportunity to build its case while the suspect is detained before having to issue an arrest warrant. If there is no case, a suspect can be released without ever being charged, eliminating potential embarrassment to the authorities. If there is a strong case, a suspect may be switched to the criminal track and formally arrested, his case investigated further by the police, procuracy and court, and a pro-forma trial held.[6] Or, without benefit of formal arrest, trial or access to counsel, a suspect may be administratively sentenced to *lao jiao* or "reeducation through labor" for a period of up to three years, renewable for a fourth year for "failure to reform." Such a sentence is determined by a Reeducation Through Labor Management Committee made up of representatives from the Public Security Bureau and the Personnel and Civil Affairs Committees. In practice, the police make sentencing decisions.[7]

---

[5] The main legal document covering shelter and investigation confinement is the "1980 Notification Regarding the Merger of the Two Measures of Forced Labor and Shelter for Investigation into Reeducation and Rehabilitation Through Labor." It is a published State Council document. A 1985 document, "Notification of the Ministry of Public Security Regarding Strict Control of Using the Means of Shelter and Investigation," may limit somewhat the scope of the older regulations.

[6] Complicated cases have been tried in court in less than half a day.

[7] There are several sets of regulations relating to reeducation through labor, including most importantly the 1957 Decision of the State Council on the Question of Reeducation and Rehabilitation Through Labor and the 1979 Supplementary Provisions. The 1982 Provisional Measures prescribe types of offenders who may be sent for reeducation.

Another administrative sanction, *xingzheng juliu*, which Public Security Bureaus have the right to employ in accordance with the Security Administration Punishment Regulations, can result in detention for a maximum of fifteen days.

PRE-TRIAL DETENTION

The facts of a case and the issue of guilt are agreed upon during pre-trial investigation rather than during the trial itself, and when they choose, Party political-legal committees at all municipal levels may predetermine outcomes.[8]   A common Chinese adage (pace Lewis Carroll) relates to this process, "verdict first, trial second" (*xian pan hou shen*). Under the Criminal Procedure Code, once a trial is scheduled, a suspect must be notified of his or her right to retain a lawyer no later than seven days before the actual proceeding. Even this minimal period to prepare a defense may be shortened under a 1983 decision of the "Standing Committee of the National People's Congress [(NPC), China's legislature] Regarding the Procedure for Rapid Adjudication of Cases Involving Criminal Elements Who Seriously Endanger Public Security." Lawyers might not learn about their cases until a few hours before they are heard. The inadequacy of the time permitted to prepare a defense denies the primary importance of the pre-trial period in the Chinese legal system.

During the entire investigatory period, a suspect is held incommunicado. This lack of recourse to anyone outside the prison system, including family members, makes possible the routine beating, extensive use of electric batons, abuse of restraints, extended isolation and systematic torture, which are the system's hallmarks. Some suspects escape abuse for a number of possible reasons: the social status of the prisoner, his knowledge of the law, the personality of the guard and, in the case of political prisoners, a guard's sympathy with the goals of activists (though many of the latter are abused grievously).

---

[8] Supreme People's Court President Ren Jianxin in his March 1993 report to the National People's Congress said that fewer than one in 200 of the almost 2.5 million criminal suspects brought before Chinese courts in the last five years were found innocent (Reuters, March 22, 1993). Of those sentenced, one third received sentences ranging between five years of imprisonment and the death penalty.

Methods of collecting evidence include extensive interrogation of suspects by police agents. Questioning can go on for days, with interruptions only for meals and some sleep. According to former prisoners' accounts, interrogation teams use threats, tricks, and sometimes physical abuse and restraints to "persuade" suspects to confess their crimes and to implicate others. A report from the Beijing Municipal Lawyers' Association Research Department suggests that "different treatment should be given to those who have confessed and those who have not; those who have pleaded guilty and those who are obstinate. . . ."[9] Another phrase sums up this Chinese credo, "leniency for those who confess, severity for those who resist" (*tanbai congkuan, kangju songyan*). In some facilities, recalcitrant prisoners are sent to isolation cells to "reconsider" their refusals to cooperate.

A statement by Liu Fuzhi, then chief of the Supreme People's Procuratorate, recognizes that abuse of suspects and prisoners does occur.[10] In his March 1993 report to the NPC, he conceded that since 1988, some 1,687 cases of alleged torture by officials had been placed on file for investigation, and that his office was working hard to end such abuse.[11] Whatever the validity of Liu's figures, there is ample evidence from interviews with former prisoners to suggest that torturers generally go unpunished.[12]

---

[9] "Give Full Play to the Defense Functions of Lawyers During the Trial of Cases Related to the Turmoil and the Counterrevolutionary Rebellion," *Shanghai Lawyer*, no. 427, (January 1990).

[10] The procuratorate is both the prosecutorial organ of the criminal justice system and the administrative unit that oversees the entire system. Decisions on whether to prosecute rest with procuracies; courts are responsible for trying cases.

[11] Reuters, March 22, 1993.

[12] See, for example, House of Representatives, *Hearing before the Subcommittee on Human Rights and International Organizations and on International Economic Policy and Trade of the Committee on Foreign Affairs* (Washington, D.C.: Government Printing Office, September 25 and December 5, 1991); and Asia Watch, "China: Political Prisoners Abused in Liaoning Province as Official Whitewash of Labor Reform System Continues," *A Human Rights Watch Short Report*, vol. 4, no. 23 (September 1, 1992).

"CELL BOSSES"

In detention centers where as many as thirty suspects, political prisoners and common criminals alike may be crowded into one cell, a fellow inmate or "cell boss" keeps order. Some such systems are formalized while others are not. All are sanctioned by prison authorities in the interests of keeping order; and prisoners and prison guards collaborate in their operation. The boss, in an informal system, is "more or less" chosen by the guards on the basis of a prior reputation for toughness and for a certain authority among thugs. No open assignment is made. Prisoners simply note that one of their cell mates is called out for a chat by a guard, given a cigarette and, in general, treated well. Each cell boss chooses his own henchmen. He may know them from the outside, from prior incarcerations, by reputation or through mutual friends. In any case, they are people he trusts and whom he takes care of.

Newcomers immediately learn the existing hierarchy. They can decide to exhibit their own strengths and attempt to fight their way into the inner circle, or they can fight to be left alone. In the latter case, if they prevail, they may be spared unauthorized beatings and torture; loss of personal possessions such as clothes, soap and toothpaste; payment of bribes; hunger; demeaning services to the boss and his henchmen such as washing their clothes, swatting their mosquitos and giving them massages; and humiliations such as crawling on the floor.

The cell boss apportions the food, decides who sleeps near the toilet, who keeps the cell clean and, when suspects are engaged in labor, acts as production manager. He may decide on his own that a prisoner needs to be "brought into line"; or he will punish at the suggestion of a guard. In the latter case, no order is given; the guard may call the cell boss out of his cell and imply that a cell mate needs to be taught a lesson. As one former prisoner put it, "a cell boss is a good running dog." When a cell boss himself decides a prisoner has an uncooperative attitude or that he represents a threat to the existing hierarchy, the boss and his henchmen may administer a thorough beating. A quilt sometimes muffles the screams.

Although detention center rules, such as "no whispering," "no loud singing," "no cursing," "no chess playing" are painted on cell walls, their enforcement is arbitrary and dependent on prisoner/guard, prisoner/cell boss relationships or connections. Punishments for rule-breaking are diverse. A prisoner may be made to stand for eight hours for a minor infraction such as whispering. He may be handcuffed with his hands behind his back for several weeks for picking up a guard's discarded cigarette butt. To eat, the cuffed prisoner lies on his stomach and "laps his food like a dog."[13] Other prisoners are forbidden to help him on pain of similar punishment. One suspect was made to lie on his back with his hands and feet shackled to a board for eleven days for loud singing and disrespect to guards. A bedpan beneath a hole in the board substituted for a toilet. Prisoners are punished for standing by a window or for knocking loudly at the cell door in cases of illness or bathroom emergencies.

PLACEMENT OF PRISONERS

Once sentenced, prisoners are sent to prisons or to labor reform camps that may be factories, farms or mines. The only exceptions are those sentenced to less than one-year terms and those who have received the death penalty. They remain in detention centers. It is unclear if they are under the jurisdiction of the Ministry of Justice or the Public Security Bureau.

Those sentenced to be executed are placed in restraints, sometimes in special cells and sometimes with prisoners still in pre-trial detention, until their sentences are carried out, sometimes within three days of the verdicts. A round-the-clock suicide watch is manned by prisoners. Those with sentences of ten years or longer and all foreigners usually go to prisons. Those with lesser sentences go to "reform through labor" camps. Prisoners with sentences of less than ten years who are educated or have particular skills are assigned to factories. The others are sent to farms and mines where conditions are the most arduous. The differences between prisons and labor reform camps are not completely clear. Prisoners in prisons also work, often in on-site factories. One difference is that security is more stringent in prisons because the more sensitive cases are housed there.

---

[13] For extensive lists of punishments employed respectively by guards and cell bosses see Asia Watch, *Anthems of Defeat: Crackdown in Hunan Province 1989-1992* (New York: Human Rights Watch, 1992), pp. 74-91.

The disposition of political prisoners is less clear. In some provinces, all political prisoners who are criminally sentenced go to prison regardless of the length of their terms. In other provinces, there appears to be a caste system in that important political prisoners are held in prisons, often in isolation; others, less well known, go to camps.[14]

All prisoners receiving administrative sentences of three years or less, go to reeducation through labor camps, in theory, if not always in practice, separate from labor reform camps, and under the jurisdiction of a separate bureau.

When prisoners arrive at prisons or labor camps, they are assigned to "orientation" units for one to two months to begin ideological retraining. The first requirement is that they memorize a lengthy list, some fifty-six articles, of prison rules, which forces them to admit who they are (criminals) and where they are (in prison). Rules forbid prisoners to exchange information about their cases; they are required to "uphold the socialist system"; and they must admit to their criminality. Political study continues throughout their imprisonment in accordance with the state's twin goals of punishment and reform.[15]

WORK AND PAROLE POINTS

According to the *White Paper on Criminal Reform*, China's law stipulates that all able-bodied criminals must work; some 90 percent of criminals do so. *The Law on Reform Through Labor* (1987) stipulates that production is under the specific direction of the ministry responsible for similar non-prison production, for example, the ministries of Agriculture, Irrigation or Industry.

For some, particularly high-level political prisoners, there is only isolation and sporadic monotonous work, such as snipping threads off prison-sewn garments, performed within the confines of individual cells. For others, according to *The Law on Reform Through Labor*, Article 53,

---

[14] Despite a highly centralized system, the management and condition of Chinese lockups, prisons and labor camps vary extensively from province to province and from one locality to the next.

[15] Information Office of the State Council, *White Paper on Criminal Reform*, section I.

work is mandatory for nine to ten hours a day with one day off every two weeks, as prisons are expected to contribute positively to China's overall economic performance and are part of its national production plan.[16] If seasonal production so requires, prisoners are expected to work twelve hours a day. Even this rigorous schedule has been exceeded when, for example, a factory has a large order to complete in a limited period.

Prisoners work at such tasks as breaking stone, fashioning tools, manufacturing toys and garments, sewing fishing nets, assembling motor vehicles, mining graphite and farming. They are not paid and must meet quotas.

In some places, pre-trial suspects are given work and work quotas, but it appears that they are not necessarily officially penalized for refusing to work. They may, however, be punished by cell bosses or fellow inmates. In one detention center each cell was given a quota of matchboxes to complete in a month. For every 10,000 above the quota, the cell was entitled to extra food worth two *renminbi*, approximately thirty-five cents. On average, each cell received one extra dish a month.

One difference between prisoners sentenced criminally to reform through labor and those sentenced administratively to reeducation through labor, is that the latter are purportedly paid. They are charged for their meals, however, and in the one instance where figures were available, a prisoner's base rate of pay could not cover food costs.

THOUGHT REFORM AND PAROLE POINTS

Laboring "well" after sentencing is one of two ways an inmate can signal his transformation into a productive socialist citizen. The other is ideological reform. Both good work and thought reform earn "parole points" which theoretically lead to sentence reduction. Points are deducted for breaches of discipline. The system, however, is as subject to manipulation through prisoner relationships or connections and bribery as is just about everything that routinely affects a prisoner's well-being.

During the first stage in the process, one prisoner in each unit acts as a recorder, noting exemplary work performance or instances of

---

[16] According to the white paper *Human Rights in China*, prisoners work only eight hours a day and have time off during holidays and festivals.

ideological improvement, as well as rule violations. There is ample opportunity for him to ignore breaches of discipline as well as examples of productivity. His account goes to the unit chief, another prisoner, who has discretion in what he recommends to the relevant guard. The latter, in turn, makes choices about what he reports to prison authorities. Finally, the prison head makes a written recommendation to the court for review of a prisoner's case. Judgment is rendered without interviewing the prisoner. Sentences may be prolonged on the basis of similar written reports. Former prisoners report that there may be as much as a six-month lag between the time a prisoner should be released through the sentence reduction program and the actual release, effectively wiping out gains made through good behavior. Other inmates were released before their reduced sentences expired.

Earning parole points by ideological reform, is, if anything, even less straightforward. The twin measures of rectification are overt acknowledgment by the prisoner of his or her ideological misunderstanding, which must include confession of crimes, and denunciation of fellow criminals. Inmates must be alert to the prevailing party line, parroting it in study meetings and in any written material they are required to submit. Measurement is subjective.

PHYSICAL CONDITIONS

As in most countries, the worst conditions prevail in pre-trial facilities. In many, an uncovered bucket substitutes for a toilet; in others, prisoners are permitted to leave their cells twice a day for a few minutes to defecate on schedule. Interviews turned up no instances of hot water in men's facilities; and in most cases, the available cold water was insufficient for personal hygiene and laundry. In some institutions, regulations prohibited hanging up wet clothes; such rules were routinely violated. Cells were said to be freezing in winter and stifling in summer, so much so that, in some prisons, inmates strip to their undershorts. Cell mates sleep communally on a raised platform or on the floor. Some cells do not have enough room for all prisoners to lie down at once; many are so crowded that there is less than one square meter per prisoner. There is no furniture; lights are on twenty-four hours a day, but are too dim for reading. Lice, mosquitos and flies are endemic; scabies is prevalent. And there is, more often than not, absolutely nothing to do, further exacerbating the tensions among prisoners living in such close quarters. In some institutions, suspects must sit silently at attention most of the day. As a result, many prisoners develop calluses or running sores on their buttocks. Prisoners are subjected to constant surveillance from catwalks above cells and through peepholes in solid cell doors. In practice, however, there are lapses in surveillance.

Conditions in prisons and labor camps, with the exception of those built very recently, are not much better, although in some, prisoners have their own bunk beds and toilet facilities are less rudimentary. Hunger can be alleviated through the prison store or packages from home.

Inmates are required to supply their own bedding, towels, toothpaste, soap and other daily necessities. Women supply their own sanitary napkins. In most cases, families supply the articles; some are purchased by prisoners; others are borrowed. From the time they are detained until they are tried, suspects use cards supplied by the facility—in some cases, pre-printed—to request a list of items from home. After sentencing, a prisoner lists his necessities in the letters he is permitted to send home. If prisoners' families cannot send or bring the necessary articles, those already sentenced may use the minimal allowance provided each month to buy the articles from stores run by guards charging exorbitant prices. Other possible purchases include cigarettes, food such as dry noodles, and candy. Stocks vary; detention centers have no such facilities and no allowances. New prisoners whose families do not know where they are or for other reasons cannot supply the essentials, must borrow or do without. Although it is possible after sentencing to secure prison uniforms, by and large prisoners supply their own clothing to which prison stripes are affixed. After sentencing, all male prisoners routinely have their heads shaved.

PUNISHMENT

Sentenced inmates are subjected to serious physical and psychological abuse and humiliation by unit chiefs and by guards for petty infractions of prison rules, for working poorly and for "failure to reform." Beatings are frequent; electric batons, despite regulations restricting their use, are routinely employed to discipline prisoners through electric shocks. Strict regime units isolate recalcitrant prisoners in tiny cells by night and demand that inmates sit at attention on low stools in excess of eight hours a day.

CONTACTS WITH THE OUTSIDE

Pre-trial detainees are permitted neither visitors nor mail; packages may include only daily necessities. Once sentenced, prisoners may receive monthly family visits lasting from twenty minutes to an hour, depending on the facility. In one known case, visits were permitted only once every two months. The Law on Criminal Reform stipulates two visits a month, each of thirty minutes duration.

All mail is read and censored; prisoners are not permitted to discuss their cases nor to describe prison conditions. Political discussions are taboo. The quantity of permissible mail appears to vary, but no facility permits unlimited packages and letters. No radios are permitted, although some prisons let inmates watch television, as a form of political indoctrination, on a fairly regular schedule. Some prisons have loudspeaker systems broadcasting news and music. Telephones are never available to prisoners. Local newspapers are available in detention centers and are passed from cell to cell.[17] Once sentenced, a prisoner may subscribe to approved papers and receive approved books and magazines.

Regulations permitting home visits when family members are seriously ill or dying are frequently disregarded.

ACTIVITIES

Pre-trial centers have no recreation facilities. Where exercise is permitted, it is usually limited to brief, infrequent strolls in tiny enclosed exercise yards. Prisons and labor camps often have more adequate facilities, including rudimentary basketball and volleyball courts, and more access to fresh air.

Prisons have sufficient educational facilities for only a fraction of their populations. A serious effort to upgrade prisoners' basic skills and technical ability appears to be underway selectively. In some cases, much

---

[17] Newspapers in China are organs of the state or one of its specialized agencies.

of the effort relates to economic advantages, such as tax breaks, that
accrue to enterprises of prisons whose educational facilities meet certain
standards.

One feature of the educational system works to the disadvantage
of prisoners most in need. Because parole points can be earned through
educational accomplishment, the limited number of places within
classrooms are quickly filled by the better educated. Conversely, the
work is too hard for those with little schooling.

WOMEN

The proportion of women prisoners in China, as in virtually
every country, is small and their situation varies by locale and type of
facility, but they appear to be better treated than men. Women are less
subject to beatings and electric shocks. However, though the extent of
sexual abuse is not known, there are indications that sexual harassment
does occur. Some of the newest model prisons about which Human
Rights Watch has information are for women. Dormitories are relatively
spacious and have storage space for personal possessions. Bunk beds
have matching quilts. Hot water and plentiful food are available. In
return, certain women are required to perform in song and dance shows
for visitors.

"RETAINED" LABORERS

After completing their sentences, some prisoners continue to
work at prison factories, some compulsorily, some voluntarily. If, for
example, a former prisoner's old unit or *danwei*[18] does not want him
back or he has no unit to which he can return, he may choose to remain
at his work, living in on-site factory housing. In one instance, the only
separation between former prisoners' homes and inmates' quarters was
a single gate. The son or daughter of a former prisoner, upon the latter's

---

[18] A *danwei*, is more than a work unit. It is responsible for and has control
over many aspects of its members' lives including housing, medical benefits and
social services.

retirement, can inherit his prison-factory job, an important consideration in a nation of chronic unemployment and underemployment.

The system is not totally voluntary and the extent to which former prisoners can be administratively detained, under what circumstances and with what potential benefits, is unclear. It appears that a former prisoner who cannot show he has anything to go back to, neither job nor family, may be forced to stay on. With China's new emphasis on individual entrepreneurship, however, this may be changing. A newly-released inmate may be able to start his own small business, thus qualifying as "someone who has something to go back to."

There have been reports that the practice of retaining laborers is widely employed to hold recalcitrant prisoners—those who have "failed to reform themselves well." Despite completing their sentences, these former prisoners are separated from their families except for brief holidays, and lead lives that do not differ substantially from those they led in prison.

CUBA

In 1988 several groups were permitted to conduct independent prison investigations. These included the Bar Association of the City of New York and the Institute for Policy Studies. With the knowledge of Cuban authorities, several representatives of Human Rights Watch were permitted to take part in these investigations but we were never allowed to visit Cuba under our own auspices. Since then, so far as we are aware, no independent monitoring organization, including the United Nations Human Rights Commission's Special Rapporteur on Cuba, has been granted access to prisons. The International Committee of the Red Cross provided humanitarian services to Cuban prisoners starting in 1988 but was barred from the prisons in 1989 and has not been allowed to return.

Monitoring prison conditions in Cuba is a difficult task. Government officials do not respond to inquiries and statistics are extremely hard to obtain. Prison inspections by domestic nongovernmental organizations are not permitted. International nongovernmental organizations have been barred from conducting independent prison investigations for several years. The following information, therefore, is based on prison inspections undertaken in past years, as well as on reports from current and former prisoners, relatives of prisoners, and human rights monitors.

At the time that representatives of Human Rights Watch were allowed to visit Cuban prisons in 1988, there were approximately 35,000 inmates, or some 350 prisoners per 100,000 citizens, a relatively high incarceration rate. This figure did not include military prisons, which confined those serving sentences for infractions in service and, also, draft resisters. We did not see such institutions and were unable to obtain figures on them. Cuba's exceptionally long sentences may in part account for the high incarceration rate.

In general, at the time of our visits in 1988, conditions for prisoners who went along with the authorities—that is, manifested their support for the regime, accepted "reeducation" by work and participation in educational programs and demonstrated respect for the guards—were generally better than those we encountered elsewhere in countries with comparable economic conditions. Opportunities for contact with families and others outside the prison were poor, but the physical facilities, some of which had been newly refurbished immediately before our visits, were fairly good. Food was adequate and employment and educational opportunities were far better than in most other countries. Medical facilities ranged from adequate to excellent, although the lack of medicines and supplies today renders these potentially excellent facilities virtually useless.

On the other hand, political prisoners and other inmates who manifested any form of opposition or protest were treated very harshly. Their opportunities for contact with those outside the prison were further reduced and, as punishment for any form of defiance or disrespect to the authorities, they would be confined, sometimes for as long as several years, in tiny, dark punishment cells where they slept on concrete slabs, received a reduced diet, and were often not permitted to go outdoors.

Prison conditions were at their worst in the years following the revolution in 1959 that brought Fidel Castro to power, then began to improve beginning in 1984.[1] Today, however, conditions remain less than adequate and, according to reports from released prisoners, have deteriorated again—a condition that parallels the sharp decline of the Cuban economy.

In 1992 the scarcity of food and medicine, denial of medical care, unhealthy conditions and physical mistreatment worsened particularly in provincial prisons such as Kilo 7 prison in Camagüey, Cinco y Medio prison in Pinar del Río, Agüica prison in Matanzas, Boniato prison in Santiago de Cuba and Alambrada de Manacas prison in Villa Clara.[2]

Some of the problems in the prisons reflect the extreme shortages and economic deterioration of the country generally, exacerbated by the collapse since 1989 of its principal external benefactor, the former Soviet Union and that country's diminished commitment to Cuba. Throughout

[1] For a full account of prison life during this period, see Jorge Valls and Americas Watch, *Twenty Years and Forty Days: Life in a Cuban Prison* (New York: Human Rights Watch, 1986).

[2] "Report on the Situation of Human Rights in Cuba Submitted by U.N. Special Rapporteur on Cuba, Mr. Carl-Johan Groth, to the U.N. Economic and Social Council Commission on Human Rights," February 4, 1993; Americas Watch, "[Cuba] Perfecting the System of Control: Human Rights Violations in Castro's 34th Year," *A Human Rights Watch Short Report*, vol. 5, no. 1 (February 25, 1993).

the country, there is a crisis of supply in everything from food to gasoline and technical parts to medical supplies. The standard of living in Cuba has severely deteriorated, and blackouts, caused by a lack of fuel for electric power, are frequent. Public services such as transportation have come to a virtual standstill.

Recently there have been complaints of overcrowding, poor hygienic conditions, and insufficient time outdoors. Shortages include medicine, soap, toothpaste and razor blades for shaving.

The prison diet consists of lemonade or orangeade for breakfast, and small portions of broth with rice or casava or a few spoonfuls of plain white rice for lunch and dinner. Relatives may bring food, but family visits are not frequent enough to provide an adequate diet, and, furthermore, not all prisoners benefit.

POLITICAL PRISONERS

The number of prisoners held for peaceful protest and other politically-motivated offenses is extremely difficult to ascertain: current estimates range from five hundred to two thousand people. One reason for this range is that those who attempt "illegal exit" from the country are not classified by the Cuban government as political prisoners, and the number of attempted illegal exits is thought to be extremely high.

There are reports that some political prisoners have been transferred to prison facilities far from their families. This makes family visits difficult or in some cases prevents them entirely, due to the country's lack of fuel and spare parts for public transport. In addition to the psychological burdens created by the lack of such visits, inmates are thereby deprived of practical assistance from family members, such as food, medicine and other necessities. The practice also amounts to a form of extrajudicial reprisal against family members.

Political prisoners are often mixed with those convicted of common crimes. This has led to concern for their safety: violence against political prisoners by other inmates is reportedly instigated and even condoned by guards.

PRE-TRIAL DETENTION

Prisoners may be held in pre-trial detention centers up to 180 days. During this period, they are often not allowed to consult with lawyers until just before their trial, and are not given any reading material. The prosecutor may request, through the State Security Chamber of the Provincial Court, an additional thirty-day detention, thereby extending pre-trial detention to 210 days.

Because prosecutors in political cases rely heavily on confessions, the detention period is often geared to extract a confession. The charge of "enemy propaganda" may be brought against anyone who "incites against social order, international solidarity or the socialist State" by producing, distributing, or possessing oral, written or other "propaganda" according to Article 103 of the criminal code. Obviously, material evidence is not always available to support charges such as these, and thus confessions are extremely important. Detainees may be interrogated daily.

The abuses reported in pre-trial detention include being forced to stand motionless for hours, irregular meals, sleep deprivation and being woken at irregular hours for interrogation.[3]

CONTACT WITH THE OUTSIDE WORLD

The number of visits permitted to the majority of prisoners has recently increased from once every three weeks to once every fifteen days. On the other hand, family visits are sometimes denied or postponed, as in the case of political prisoner Sebastián Arcos, leader of a human rights group; his family visits have been gradually reduced to once every two months. Also, in the case of well-known political prisoners, reports indicate that body searches of visitors are more extensive and aggressive then the searches of visitors to common prisoners. Female visitors to such political prisoners are sometimes subjected to vaginal searches conducted in a humiliating way.

---

[3] Americas Watch, *Human Rights in Cuba: The Need to Sustain the Pressure* (New York: Human Rights Watch, 1989), p. 76; and Amnesty International, "Cuba: Silencing the Voices of Dissent" (London: Amnesty, December 1992).

In 1988 many prisoners were permitted to send only one letter every three months. That year the rules changed to allow one letter every thirty days. Reports indicate that mail privileges are suspended or increased as punishment or reward.[4]

Letters from family members and international organizations are not always delivered to prisoners. Yndamiro Restano, incarcerated in Boniato prison, never received several letters of support sent by humanitarian organizations.

In another case, former political prisoner Hubert Jerez who is confined in Kilo 7 prison, was forbidden contact with the outside world after he circulated a newsletter within the prison denouncing conditions there. With a pencil smuggled in by a common prisoner, he wrote a letter to President Violeta Chamorro of Nicaragua, elected in 1989, congratulating her on her political success. The letter was intercepted by authorities, and he was held in solitary confinement for forty-five days as punishment.

Prisoners are permitted nonpolitical reading material, provided and/or screened by the government, and may read the official newspaper, *Granma*. Due to paper shortages, however, copies of *Granma* are increasingly difficult to come by, even for the civilian population. According to one report, visitors are allowed to bring up to three books with them.[5]

ILL-TREATMENT

Violence by guards against prisoners continues to be a problem. Numerous beatings have been reported, usually as an unofficial form of punishment or discipline. In 1991 Human Rights Watch received reports of at least five inmates killed by guards in various prisons, and at least three detainees who died in police custody. In 1992 there were

---

[4] Aryeh Neier, "In Cuban Prisons," *New York Review of Books* (June 30, 1988). Neier, executive director of Human Rights Watch, visited six Cuban prisons with an Institute for Policy Studies (IPS) fact-finding delegation in February and March of 1988.

[5] Based on a Human Rights Watch interview with a representative of Coordinadora de Organizaciones de los Derechos Humanos in Cuba (CODEHU).

unconfirmed reports of at least three deaths in detention. In at least two of the cases the bodies showed signs of battering. One death was termed a suicide; another an epileptic attack.

PUNISHMENT

Beatings, denial of medical attention, confinement in harsh punishment and isolation cells, sometimes with reduced food and water rations, suspension of family visits, violent and arbitrary searches and confiscation of belongings, are used to punish even mild infractions of prison rules.

An example of the harsh response to nonviolent protest is the January 1991 case of thirteen political prisoners in Combinado del Este prison who refused to wear their prison uniforms, demanding political change and respect for human rights.[6] They were transferred to other prisons. Three who were taken to Kilo 7 prison in Camagüey went on a hunger strike and continued to refuse to wear uniforms. According to reports, they were held for over seventeen days with arms outstretched, chained to the iron bars of their cells. Reportedly, they were also denied drinking water for several days. Two were reportedly beaten by guards at least three times while in chains.[7]

Prisoners may be transferred to punishment cells for numerous offenses, including nonviolent protest. A notorious punishment area is "the rectangle of death" in Combinado del Este, the country's largest prison, located in Havana. Conditions similar to those in the rectangle of death were also seen by Human Rights Watch representatives in punishment areas at Boniato Prison in Santiago de Cuba, Kilo 7 in Camagüey, and Nieves Morejon in Sancti Spiritus, during visits in 1988.

There are ninety-nine punishment cells in the punishment area of Combinado del Este, each about four feet wide by nine or ten feet long. Up to two prisoners are housed in a cell, although there are triple bunks, indicating that a third could be added. The toilet is a hole in the

---

[6] A practice associated in the past with the group of long-term prisoners known as "historic *plantados*."

[7] Amnesty International, "Cuba: Silencing the Voices of Dissent," December 1992.

floor in the back of the cell, which according to prisoners, can become clogged and spill onto the floor. Sometimes punishment is accompanied by reduced food and water rations.

Every cell is separated from the hallway by two doors. A barred door, sometimes partially covered with sheet metal, is closest to the cell. A wooden door that completely shuts out ventilation and light from the hallway is arbitrarily opened or closed by prison guards. Just inside the wooden door is a very dim light bulb, controlled by the guard from the hallway. Food is given to prisoners through a small slot. There have been reports of prisoners kept naked, and forced to sleep on the floor.[8]

In Boniato the punishment cells have a one-foot-square barred window without glass, but lack electric lights. Prisoners are able to go outside for only an hour each week, and then only in large iron cages, in which only a few steps can be taken.

Major Manuel Sánchez, second in command at Combinado del Este, told a New York City Bar Association delegation visiting in 1988 that prisoners could not be kept in a punishment cell for more than twenty-one days, although one prisoner serving twenty years on charges of espionage said he had been held virtually incommunicado in the maximum security area of Combinado del Este from 1981 to 1985. He had been left naked in a small, dark and poorly ventilated cell and had received little or no medical attention.[9] Visiting the same facility several weeks later, the Institute for Policy Studies delegation encountered a prisoner who said he had been confined in his punishment cell continuously for six years.

COMPLAINTS

The Office of the Fiscalía General (comparable to the attorney general's office in the United States) told the New York Bar Association

[8] Neier, "In Cuban Prisons"; and Alice H. Henkin, Mary Jane Camejo, Richard J. Hiller, Michael H. Posner, Stephen J. Ritchin, and Kenneth Roth, "Human Rights in Cuba," *The Record of the Association of the Bar of the City of New York*, vol. 43, no. 7 (November 1988), p. 818.

[9] Henkin et al., "Human Rights in Cuba."

delegation that there is a department for the control of legality in prisons. Officers from that department are expected to spend the better part of several days each week examining prisons for violations of prison rules. If they find evidence of abuses or crimes, the Fiscalía's office is supposed to conduct an investigation and take appropriate action. However, neither this representative nor the President of the Cuban Supreme Court were able to recall a single case in which a prison guard or policeman had been prosecuted for mistreating a prisoner. Prisoners interviewed stated that the Fiscalía visited criminal prisoners, but almost never those held for political offenses. Guards accused of beating prisoners are often simply transferred to other prisons.

PRIVILEGES

In exchange for "political and ideological training," also referred to as "reeducation," and abiding by prison discipline (such as maintaining proper personal appearance, keeping facilities clean and in order, standing at attention and showing respect to prison authorities), prisoners may receive privileges including reduced sentences, more mail and family visits and permission for their families to bring them up to twenty pounds of goods per visit. As privileges may be granted, they may also be denied to those who refuse reeducation.

WORK AND COMPENSATION

Cuban prisoners may work, continue or complete their schooling to the ninth grade, and receive technical training in practical skills. According to the Cuban government, approximately 70 percent of prisoners work.[10] Construction work and furniture-making are among their trades. Salaries are comparable to those paid to non-prisoners, but the cost of confinement is deducted. The most recent rate of deduction we know of is about 35 percent of the first 100 pesos salary each month and 50 percent of anything above that. If the sentence includes fines,

---

[10] Havana Radio Reloj Network, "Workshop on Prisons Held in Granma Province," March 10, 1993; reproduced in Foreign Broadcast Information Service (FBIS), March 11, 1993.

additional amounts are withheld. Despite the deductions, prisoners are able to send money to their families or accumulate savings. However, reports in recent years indicate that not all prisoners are paid reliably.

CONJUGAL VISITS

Conjugal visits are an apparently successful element of prison life. According to one delegation's visit, conjugal facilities tend to be reasonably attractive, particularly in the case of Nieves Morejon prison, where "the conjugal pavilion is set in a part of the prison that has a small wildlife park containing a few tame deer, a flamingo, and a number of other exotic birds."[11] Opportunities for conjugal visits have increased from once a year in 1988 to once every three months in 1993.

MEDICAL/HIV

Denial of medical attention is a common complaint; medical attention is reported to be unsatisfactory and even "alarming."[12] Though some prisoners feel that the denial of medical care is a deliberate form of reprisal for disobedience, shortages in medicines and supplies account for at least some of the many reports of inadequate medical attention.

There is concern about the health of a number of prisoners who have access only to limited medications and medical treatment or who are denied medical attention in reprisal for protests or infractions of prison rules.

Because of substandard diet and the lack of medical supplies, many prisoners suffer from anaemia, diarrhea, parasites, and/or other diseases. Some political prisoners are reportedly deliberately denied medical care for serious illnesses including diabetes, tuberculosis, and duodenal ulcers.

In recent months, several reported deaths in detention have been attributed to the denial of medical attention, physical debilitation

[11] Neier, "In Cuban Prisons."

[12] "Report of the U.N. Special Rapporteur," February 1993.

resulting from hunger strikes, and alleged mistreatment by guards. There have been a number of cases of infirm prisoners who were beaten for complaining about lack of medical attention. Francisco Díaz Mesa, twenty-four years old, died in Alambradas de Manacas Prison on February 1, 1992. Reportedly, guards beat him because he was banging on the bars of his cell to protest the denial of medical attention he needed for pneumonia.

Particularly disturbing is the treatment of HIV-positive prisoners. According to reports, several dozen prisoners held in Combinado del Este Prison either have AIDS or have tested positive for the HIV virus. These prisoners are held apart from other prisoners, which is consistent with the Cuban practice of mandatory testing and compulsory quarantine for all those who test HIV-positive, and may not be receiving adequate medical attention and diet. According to a report emanating from other prisoners in Combinado del Este Prison dated June 10, 1992, Domingo Pina Montes de Oca, a common prisoner with AIDS, was sent to a punishment cell in the "rectangle of death" maximum security area, for unknown reasons. His food quota was then cut in half and the special diet recommended by doctors was discontinued, seriously damaging his health. After three weeks, he was transferred to a hospital outside the prison where he died.

In another letter dated September 14, 1992, smuggled out of the same prison by a group of political prisoners, it was reported that a number of prisoners with AIDS rioted on August 19, 1992, demanding better food and medical attention. Guards reportedly intervened to put down the riot using rubber batons, wooden sticks and other blunt instruments. A number of prisoners were injured. Several of those involved in the riot were reportedly transferred to Destacamento 47 (the official name for the "rectangle of death") as punishment. About thirty HIV positive prisoners are held in the punishment cells in Combinado del Este prison. According to information obtained, they receive only minimal care.

In the years since Human Rights Watch was last allowed to visit, the Cuban economy has virtually collapsed. At least partly as a consequence of this, all prisoners now suffer from severe shortages in food, medicine and goods. Substandard quality and quantity of food and medical treatment, as well as sporadic beatings of inmates by guards, and repression of nonviolent protests, characterize Cuban prison conditions today.

EGYPT

Human Rights Watch conducted two investigations of prison conditions in Egypt. In 1990, a delegation including a representative of Physicians for Human Rights, visited Egypt and spent ten days interviewing defense lawyers and released prisoners, although access to prisons was denied by the authorities. In February 1992 the authorities informed us that permission to inspect prisons finally had been granted; the same month, a delegation visited six prisons—including two maximum-security facilities—that at the time housed over 27 percent of Egypt's prison population. The findings were published in a February 1993 report titled Prison Conditions in Egypt.

Some aspects of the conditions in Egyptian prisons have changed little over the past half-century. Inmates continue to suffer in overcrowded, filthy environments with appalling sanitary conditions, and many prisoners enjoy only limited time outside their cells on a daily basis. Despite the commitment to prison reform proclaimed by the successive regimes of Nasser, Sadat and Mubarak, and Egypt's ratification of international human rights accords, prison conditions remain abysmal in significant respects.

In February 1992 Egypt's thirty prisons held 35,392 inmates, yielding a prisoner-to-population ratio of 62 per 100,000. Of those, 1,441 (4 percent) were women. The prisons house sentenced prisoners, suspects under investigation, defendants charged with offenses and awaiting trial or in trial proceedings, and detainees held without charge pursuant to Egypt's long-standing Emergency Law, which has been continuously in force since October 1981. The capacity of Egypt's prisons, many of which were constructed in the late nineteenth century, is about 20,000.

ADMINISTRATION AND OVERSIGHT

The prisons are operated by the Prisons Administration, a department of Egypt's Ministry of Interior, which has long been implicated in human rights abuses such as torture and prolonged detention without trial of security detainees. This sorry record renders it virtually impossible for custodial confinement under the ministry's auspices to be free of abuses of the inmate population. The situation is only exacerbated by the weak, often nonexistent, oversight of the prison system by the Ministry of Justice (through the prosecutor general's office), and by the government's continuing unwillingness to allow Egyptian nongovernmental organizations to monitor and inspect prisons on an ongoing basis.

The right of prisoners to humane treatment without mental or physical harm is set forth in the Egyptian Constitution and Egyptian law. Theoretically, internal and external oversight mechanisms are in place to uphold these rights and provide inmates with avenues to complain about mistreatment. External oversight is the responsibility of the Ministry of Justice; ministry representatives are required by law to visit prisons on a monthly basis to monitor prisoners' treatment and take complaints. But Human Rights Watch found that this system does not function properly. The overwhelming majority of male inmates rarely if ever have had access to the inspectors; most prisoners were astonished to learn that this system of oversight existed and insisted that they never saw a representative of the ministry. (Women prisoners, in contrast, indicated that they were visited by outside inspectors on a regular basis.)

PHYSICAL CONDITIONS

Egyptian prisons are generally old and many cells are severely overcrowded, although in some of the most overcrowded facilities we found entire cells that were empty. The floors of many cells are continuously damp; prison authorities typically do not provide beds for inmates, and the vast majority of prisoners sleep on mattresses or mats supplied by their families.

Living spaces lack adequate light and ventilation; these conditions are made worse by the deliberate bricking up of windows and, in two major facilities, the construction of cinder block walls in front of cells where inmates are held for long hours daily.

Facilities that should be sanitary are filthy, sometimes inoperative, and inadequate due to severe overcrowding. In many cells—and even in hospital wards—inmates store their water supply in plastic bottles and large containers. At several prisons inmates complained that the water ran irregularly and then only for short intervals. At the Abu Za'bal facility—a large, three-prison complex near Cairo—inmates have complained since 1989 about the contamination of the drinking water, charging that the poor water quality has caused illnesses. Our February 1992 inspection of this prison confirmed that visibly dirty water ran from the taps inside cells.

Numerous inmates complained that food was of poor quality and insufficient quantity. Our inspections revealed that prisoners supplement this meager diet extensively with food supplied by their families, pool these supplies, and prepare collective meals.

Some of the most vulnerable inmates are indigent prisoners and foreigners, often men and women from other African countries, who endure particularly harsh living conditions because so few necessary items are supplied by the authorities. Unlike wealthier Egyptian inmates, the foreign nationals as well as the Egyptian poor, do not benefit from regular family visits and contributions of blankets, clothing, food, personal hygiene supplies, medicines and other items. Some are forced to "work" as servants for other prisoners in exchange for needed supplies, while others beg for donations.

DAILY LOCK-DOWN

Many prisoners in Egypt spend excessive periods continuously confined to their cells. Interviews also revealed that the time inmates are allowed outside their cells does not necessarily mean time in the fresh air and sunlight, as required by international standards. Rather, prisoners are permitted only to walk in interior atriums, not outdoors. There also are considerable variations in the hours of daily lock-down, even within the same facility. The most serious complaints about lock-down came from security prisoners. Some uncharged security detainees had not been let out of their small, tightly-packed cells for months at a time. Others noted that they were allowed outside for a mere five minutes a day, a procedure the authorities called "the picnic."

DISCIPLINARY MEASURES

Egyptian law permits the beating of juvenile prisoners and the whipping of adult prisoners as a disciplinary measure. These practices are proscribed by the Egyptian Constitution, international law, and international rules for the treatment of prisoners, which prohibit corporal punishment for disciplinary offenses.

Solitary confinement for up to fifteen days is permitted for each disciplinary offense. Inmates serve this penalty in separate punishment wings, where cell conditions are especially harsh and the daily "break" outside ranges from five to thirty minutes. Not one of the many punishment cells we inspected had a toilet or running water. Most had dirty bare floors, a few filthy blankets to serve as a mattress, and little light or ventilation. In random inspections, we found five cases of the misuse of punishment cells. A sentenced teenaged prisoner was confined to a punishment cell for "treatment" of mental illness; a teenage detainee was held in a punishment cell because he refused to confess to the criminal offense for which he was arrested; and another prisoner was held in a punishment cell for weeks beyond the legal limit of fifteen days. At Qanater women's prison one occupant of a punishment cell told us that she had been held there for five months, and a political detainee said that she had been confined to a punishment cell since her arrival at the prison seventeen days earlier and had never been let outside.

UNAUTHORIZED PHYSICAL ABUSE

Based on testimony and other evidence, systematic torture does not take place within Egypt's prison system, although many torture victims can be found among security prisoners. Security detainees as a matter of practice are tortured during interrogation prior to their arrival at prisons. Interrogations are conducted by officers and soldiers of the General Directorate for State Security Investigation (SSI), the domestic intelligence agency attached to the Ministry of Interior. Interrogations take place while detainees are held incommunicado at SSI offices and, increasingly in 1992 and 1993, in remote camps of the paramilitary Central Security Forces.[1] But there have been incidents of violent beating and whipping of security and criminal prisoners. We found

---

[1] See Middle East Watch, *Behind Closed Doors: Torture and Detention in Egypt* (New York: Human Rights Watch, 1992); Egyptian Organization for Human Rights, "Torture in Egypt: Central Security Forces Camps," (Cairo: December 1992).

substantial evidence that at least some of the beatings have been highly organized, involving large numbers of soldiers and carried out in the presence of prison officers.

MEDICAL CARE AND FACILITIES

According to our interviews, medical attention has been denied to prisoners who urgently required treatment or who had been recommended for specialized care at outside hospitals. Security inmates in particular appear to have difficulty securing permission for treatment in outside hospitals. Prisoners mentioned the names of individuals who had died in prison hospitals or in their cells allegedly because of poor or nonexistent medical care; our written requests to the Egyptian authorities for information about these cases have gone unanswered.

Many prisoners complained about the lack of medicines other than aspirin, despite the authorities' claim that all prison pharmacies are supplied with necessary medicine. Numerous inmates said that when a prescription was written for them by prison doctors, they were required to purchase the medicine with their own money or have their families bring the medicine. This system places potentially life-threatening hardships on impoverished prisoners and inmates from other countries, most typically Africans, whose families are unable to visit them or to send money.

WOMEN

Women prisoners, numbering a small percentage of the penal population, are held either in the large women's prison at Qanater, outside Cairo, or in separate women's sections of other prisons.

Women are allowed to bring their infant children to prison; inmates who give birth in prison may keep their babies until they reach two years of age. Upon reaching two years, children must be given to the inmate's family or placed in an orphanage. While Qanater prison has a nursery for prisoners with children, the infants and their mothers at the women's jail at Tanta prison were packed into the same overcrowded cells as other prisoners, sleeping in less than ten square feet each on dirty cement floors.

Sentenced women prisoners are more idle than their male counterparts. At Qanater, there were only three workshops, employing less than 4 percent or forty-three of the prison's 1,100 women, lower than the already-low rates for male prisoners. There were no recreational facilities for women at Qanater or the jail at Tanta, and women at Qanater complained about long periods of daily confinement in overcrowded cells.

INDIA

Human Rights Watch conducted a two-week investigation of prison conditions in India in October 1990. Despite extensive efforts by the participants in this investigation to obtain access to Indian prisons, they did not succeed. Moreover, even though Indian officials were apprised in several different ways of the dates and purposes of the investigation, some Indian authorities treated the participants as though they had entered India covertly and for a devious purpose. Immediately prior to leaving India, both delegation members were separately detained briefly by officers of the Bombay Police Special Branch and interrogated about the details of their stay in India. The April 1991 report, Prison Conditions in India, *was based on interviews with former prisoners; lawyers who have represented inmates; leaders of India's human rights groups; doctors associated with post mortem examinations; and scholars who have studied the prisons and the police lockups; and on documentary material.*

Though reliable nationwide figures are not available, as of 1991 India appears to have confined some 250,000 prisoners in more than 1,200 facilities around the country of which more than 800 were police lockups and most of the remainder were state prisons. There have been no significant developments reported in the past two years that would alter those numbers substantially. A significant majority are "undertrials" or prisoners who have not yet been convicted of a crime. The total number of prisoners is very low for a country of 850 million people: the rate is approximately 34 per 100,000, far less than one tenth the rate in the United States and lower than almost any reported rate in the world. Unfortunately, a concomitant of the low rate of incarceration is a high degree of summary punishment by the police.

Some of this summary punishment takes place in lockups, which are under police jurisdiction. Though Indian law requires arraignment before a magistrate within twenty-four hours, remands to police custody for periods of fourteen days at a time are standard. Torture during remand is commonplace; women held by the police frequently complain of rape and other forms of sexual abuse; and, each year, hundreds of deaths are reported in police custody nationwide. Though independent autopsies are infrequent, the available evidence suggests that the great

majority are due to torture. Recent reports indicate that many are also
due to poor medical care and unsanitary conditions inside prisons.

Indian law makes confessions out of the presence of a judge
inadmissible in evidence. Accordingly, extracting such confessions is not
a major purpose of torture; rather, the main purposes appear to be to
punish suspected malefactors and to persuade their relatives to pay bribes
to the police to spare lockup inmates from torture.

Though torture is not used widely in the prisons themselves,
physical restraints—fetters, shackles and handcuffs—are employed more
commonly than punishment cells to deal with those who commit
infractions. The use of these restraints is prescribed by the Jail Manuals,
which spell out in great detail the manner in which prisoners should be
treated and how the prisons should be administered.

The main characteristic of the prisons is their class system.
Prisoners are classified "A", "B" or "C", but not on the basis of their
crimes; rather, the higher classifications are reserved for those who,
according to one of the Jail Manuals, "by social status, education and
habit of life have been accustomed to a superior mode of living."[1] In
general, those classified A or B are provided with decent conditions in
prison, while C prisoners live in more overcrowded cells, get less and
poorer food, may correspond less frequently, are not entitled to receive
as many publications, must perform menial tasks and are subject to the
fetters and handcuffs that are not used on the higher-class prisoners.
Since some prisoners confined for politically-motivated offenses "have
been accustomed to a superior mode of living," they enjoy the benefits of
the higher classifications and, in contrast to some other countries, are
often treated less harshly than common prisoners. However, in conflict
areas, where many detainees are held for security-related offenses or for
suspected militant activity, conditions are severe.

PRE-TRIAL DETENTION

Detention in police custody is limited by law to ninety days and
may not exceed sixty days in cases in which the potential sentence is
under ten years. These requirements are suspended in the case of arrests
under the Terrorist and Disruptive Activities Act (TADA), adopted in 1985

---

[1] Punjab Jail Manual.

and subsequently extended for two years at a time. Under TADA, which is widely used not only in the conflict-ridden states of Punjab, Assam, Jammu and Kashmir, but also in Tamil Nandu and Gujarat, detainees may be held for up to a year without charge.

Remands to police custody are routine except for the minority of prisoners who can afford to retain counsel. Magistrates order remands without inquiring whether any investigative purpose would be served or whether detainees would be likely to show up for trial, in effect condoning police torture to punish detainees or extort bribes from their families. Typically, lockups are bare rooms with no furniture but with a urinal and a pot in the corner that is cleaned out occasionally. Detainees are not ordinarily provided with mats to sleep on, blankets, changes of clothing, soap or toothpaste and, in many facilities, the supply of water is intermittent. They are often overcrowded, filthy and emit a strong stench. In the most recent year for which information is available, 1991 to 1992, eighteen deaths were reported in the lockups in Tamil-Nadu and eleven in Delhi. Over the years, the highest number of such deaths have taken place in Bihar, Uttar Pradesh, Andhra Pradesh and West Bengal. Most of the deaths are of males under the age of thirty.

After the expiration of the maximum period for detention in police custody, undertrials are sent to state prisons until they are brought to trial. Though current statistics are not available, it appears that even within the prisons, the majority of inmates are awaiting trial.

THE PRISONS

Aside from the class system, the most prominent feature of the Indian prisons is the system of "convict officers." There are three grades of convict officers: watchmen, overseers and warders. They are appointed by the superintendent of the prison, typically from the ranks of the longest term prisoners: that is, those who have been convicted of the most serious crimes. Convict officers perform virtually all the duties that are performed by guards in other prison systems.

The effect of the convict officer system is to transform many Class C prisoners into personal servants for the convict officers on whom they are dependent in many ways, particularly for the quantity of food they get.

India's largest prison, Tihar Jail in Delhi, which was reported to have 7,000 inmates in October 1992, appears to be more or less typical in its conditions. In Tihar, Class A is no longer in use, but Class B prisoners—of whom there are typically between 200 and 250—get a raised platform with a mat on which to sleep, or a cot; their diet includes meat; they arrive with adequate clothing or it is provided to them; they are assigned clerical work in the prison, or they take part in studies.

Class C prisoners sleep on the floor, work in a factory for minute sums that seem to disappear when they are released, get two small loaves of bread in the morning and two in the evening with some lentils and a bit of vegetable matter. If their families can supply some money to the officers, this diet can be supplemented.

Many Class C prisoners go barefoot. Typically, shoes are not supplied. In addition to bribes, Class C prisoners can improve their treatment by providing massages to convict officers, fanning them during the hot weather, or performing sexual services for them.

Juveniles are supposed to be kept separate from adults but, typically, boys as young as eleven or twelve sleep in separate wards but mingle with adult prisoners during the day.

Women are often confined in separate sections of male prisons, but do not mingle with the men. Many of the women prisoners are held in "protective custody" and are rape victims, ostensibly confined to make sure that they are available to testify against the accused rapists at trial. It is not unusual for the rape victim to be held even when the alleged rapist has not been apprehended and, accordingly, remains free. So-called female lunatics are generally confined with female prisoners, often in circumstances in which they are provided with no services. An indication of the conditions of their confinement is provided by the report that at least ten female lunatics died in Alipore Jail in Calcutta in just two months, January and February 1990.

By and large, the prisons have poor sanitary facilities. Complaints from prisoners about the lack of medical care are widespread. Reportedly, the privileges that doctors can provide—a special diet, painkillers, or transfer to a clinic or hospital—are often available only to prisoners who pay for them.

A magisterial inquiry into the death of prisoners at Tihar jail in 1992 described appalling sanitary conditions inside the jail.

All the toilets, both inside and outside the barracks, cells, and outside cells were in deplorable condition. They were choked with the huge mounds of excreta, which had not been cleared for days. In some cases they had choked right up to the door and could not be opened. There was absolutely no facility for water.[2]

The inquiry also found that the jail's drinking water was contaminated, and that ceiling fans were not working in some cells in which temperature in the summer reached well over 100 degrees fahrenheit.[3]

Medical facilities are grossly inadequate for the prison population. Only one section of the jail has round-the-clock emergency services. In case of an emergency in any of the other sections (which function independently), the prisoner has to pass through several layers of jail security and red tape. In cases of serious illness, such delays may be genuinely life-threatening. Tihar Jail's fifteen-bed addiction treatment center cannot cope with a population of addicted prisoners that averages 600.[4]

Despite the comparatively small size of the total prison population, some prisons are severely overcrowded. A government commission of the early 1980s reported that in some states "prison barracks are so overcrowded that inmates have to sleep in shifts." There has been no reported improvement in the intervening years.

The four sections of Tihar Jail in New Delhi have a total official capacity of 2,140 prisoners. As of January 1993 the actual prison population was 7,616. Two sections were particularly overcrowded: one with a capacity of 740 had 2,871 prisoners; another with a capacity of 564

---

[2] "Five Suspended for Deaths in Tihar Jail," *Times of India*, August 14, 1992, cited in Shamona Khanna, "Tihar Jail: A Glimpse Behind Prison Walls," *The Lawyers* (Bombay: April 1993).

[3] Khanna, "Tihar Jail," *The Lawyers*, p. 6.

[4] Ibid, p. 6.

held 2507 prisoners. Ward 13 of Tihar Jail Number 3 was built to hold 106 prisoners. As of July 1992, it housed 763.[5]

Human Rights Watch was denied access to the Indian prisons and lockups. Some access is available to local human rights organizations, but as these do not operate nationally, the only nationwide inspection of the prisons is by government commissions. Every few years or so, such a commission is established—often under the leadership of a prominent member of the judiciary—and issues a scathing report. These do not seemed to have made a discernible impact on conditions within the prisons.

---

[5] Ibid., pp. 5-6.

INDONESIA

A Human Rights Watch delegation traveled to Indonesia in November and December 1989, visiting seven prisons. In addition to interviews conducted in the prisons, our representatives interviewed former prisoners, criminal justice experts, lawyers and government officials. Prison Conditions in Indonesia *was published in 1990.*

Indonesia has one of the lowest prisoner-to-population ratios in the world (about 22 per 100,000). But the relatively few who do end up being incarcerated suffer from a variety of hardships, including poor physical conditions, insufficient food, clothing and bedding, and frequently serve their sentences in distant locations. And, at the early stage of incarceration—while still in police custody—they are usually beaten.

As of 1989 Indonesia held about 40,000 prisoners in 441 prisons throughout the country. Women constituted about 5 percent of the total. These figures are for civilian detention centers and prisons only; they do not include people in military custody or those detained by the Department of Immigration. The prison system suffers from widespread political manipulation and corruption, which help determine who gets arrested and why, how suspects and inmates are treated, and how they are tried and sentenced.

DETENTION

In general, prisons and prison conditions are the responsibility of the Corrections Directorate of the Ministry of Justice. There are three main types of detention centers: police lockups where the investigation of a suspect is carried out immediately after arrest; detention houses where suspects are held after initial investigation but before trial; and prisons where sentenced prisoners serve their terms.

The Corrections Directorate maintains three classes of prisons. Class I prisons have a capacity of more than 500 and are used for maximum security cases. There are nine such prisons throughout Indonesia, located in urban centers. Class II prisons have a capacity of

250-500, and Class III prisons have a capacity of up to 250. While women are generally detained in separate sections of detention houses and prisons, there are also a few women's prisons. Only in major towns and cities are detention houses and prisons separate facilities; in many places, a single building will be designated as serving both functions, although the detainees are generally kept separate from the prisoners.

Political suspects and those charged under the Anti-Subversion Law (Presidential Decree No. 11/1963) rather than the Criminal Code are often held in military rather than police custody immediately after arrest, and in military or police headquarters rather than detention houses in the period before (and sometimes during) trial. Political suspects, particularly in East Timor, may also be subject to a form of administrative detention without trial that closely resembles the reeducation-through-labor system used in China.

The rights of suspects and detainees guaranteed by Indonesia's Criminal Procedure Code, such as the right to counsel immediately after arrest and time-limits on pre-trial detention, do not automatically apply to those detained under the Anti-Subversion Law.

PRE-TRIAL DETENTION

The Criminal Procedure Code, adopted in 1981, was considered a major advance in human rights in part because of those time-limits. Even with the limits, however, lengthy pre-trial detention is still possible.

Under the code, a person may be detained for an initial twenty days by the police; the detention order can then be renewed for up to forty days. This means that a suspect can legally be detained for up to two months in a police lockup where torture and other forms of abuse are most likely to occur. At the end of that period, the public prosecutor takes over responsibility for detention; the prosecutor's office can issue a detention order for an initial twenty days. The order can then be extended by thirty days. During this time, the suspect can either remain in the police lockup, even though the police no longer have formal custody, or he or she can be transferred to a detention house. Finally, just before trial, the district court takes over responsibility for detention from the prosecutor. The court can detain a suspect for an initial thirty-day period, renewable for another sixty days. By the time the case reaches the court, the suspect usually, but not always, has been moved to a detention house. In the most ordinary case of petty thievery, then, Indonesian law allows a suspect to be held for 200 days before trial.

In cases where suspects have been charged with a crime that carries a sentence of nine years or more, detention can be extended by a maximum of sixty days at any stage in the process: investigation, prosecution or immediately pre-trial, meaning that a suspect in such a case could legally be detained for an additional 180 days, or for more than a year in total (380 days) before a trial begins.

Persons detained under the Anti-Subversion Law can be held for an initial one-year period before trial, renewable indefinitely.

ADMINISTRATIVE DETENTION

The Indonesian armed forces frequently detain civilians for lengthy periods without charge or trial in areas where separatist movements have been active. In East Timor in 1993, some twenty-four young people suspected of supporting the independence movement there had been undergoing a form of reeducation called *tahanan pembinaan*, or "detained for guidance," for more than a year, during which they worked in rural development projects under the close supervision of the army. In Aceh, on the northern tip of Sumatra where a major counterinsurgency campaign was underway from 1989-92, civilians suspected of supporting armed rebels were held in army camps, sometimes for over a year, and then released in elaborate ceremonies marked by taking an oath of loyalty to the Indonesian government.

TORTURE AND ILL-TREATMENT

Torture is commonplace during interrogation in police lockups as well as in district and sub-district military commands where, particularly in political cases, interrogation is carried out by members of the intelligence unit (*Satgas Intel*) of Bakorstanas, the internal security agency.[1] It is used as a means of forcing confessions, as a method of

---

[1] Bakorstanas is the acronym for Badan Koordinasi Bantuan Pemantapan Stabilitas Nasional or Coordinating Agency for the Maintenance of National Stability.

extorting bribes, and as an on-the-spot punishment for offenses regarded as particularly heinous, such as rape. The Indonesian government maintains that officials found responsible for torture are disciplined, but such sanctions are rare, and complaints of torture are infrequently addressed.

As the United Nations Special Rapporteur on Torture noted after a visit to Indonesia in 1991, "The fact that the police force has complete control over the first twenty days of detention makes it an implausible agency for receiving complaints about torture. . . .The fact that most torture is allegedly practiced during irregular arrest by the military security agencies also makes the police, as part of these same armed forces, an implausible agency for receiving complaints about irregularities and abuse of power."[2]

PRISON CONDITIONS

The basic law regulating prison conditions is a Dutch colonial law, Staatsblad 1917 No. 708, which has been updated by various administrative regulations from the Ministry of Justice and Supreme Court circulars. The law addresses the process for putting a person in prison (having him or her examined by a doctor, registering his or her personal belongings); maintaining order in the prison; prison visits; classification of prisoners; food and hygiene; and prison labor.

Court rulings and other administrative decisions that have effectively updated the 1917 law have never been codified, and they cover every conceivable aspect of prison life. A Supreme Court circular issued in 1989 ruled that any prisoner hospitalized could not deduct the time spent in the hospital from his prison term, because claims of illness were so often used by well-to-do prisoners to get out of prison.

Prison conditions vary according to whether a person is a detainee or sentenced prisoner, criminal or political offender.
Detainees are allowed to wear their own clothing and work on a voluntary basis, but they are kept locked up most of the day. Sentenced prisoners wear prison uniforms and are allowed out of their cells most of the day for various activities. Political prisoners are generally kept

---

[2] "Visit by the Special Rapporteur to Indonesia and East Timor," United Nations Document E/CN.4/1992/17.

separate from criminal offenders and often receive better treatment, in part, perhaps, because they are visited regularly by the International Committee of the Red Cross.

Cells in most Indonesian prisons are fairly large rooms, housing sometimes twenty to thirty prisoners. Prisoners are issued mats to sleep on, which they roll out over a single concrete platform along the length of the cell. Mattresses or pillows can be brought in by families or obtained for a price from prison guards. Single cells are used for punishment or in some cases, for maximum security prisoners. In seven prisons visited by Human Rights Watch, most cells had one barred window for light and slats in the door for ventilation. Smaller cells had no electricity; larger rooms had one light bulb that at least in one prison was left on all night. There were occasional shortages of water for toilets.

Women are kept separate from male prisoners, although there are few prisons exclusively for women (one is the model women's prison in Tangerang, outside Jakarta, where women live in small cottages with rooms containing beds and bedding). Women may keep children up to the age of two in their cells with them. Juvenile facilities are also limited; in 1989, a Human Rights Watch mission visited one prison where a twelve-year-old boy was detained with adults.

Conditions also differ between those close to major urban centers and those in more remote areas. The latter tend to be worse, in terms of facilities available to prisoners. Overcrowding is relatively rare in Indonesian prisons, except in areas where counterinsurgency campaigns are underway or where the political situation for other reasons is tense.

Beatings and other forms of corporal punishment are common to all Indonesian prisons. In some cases, prisoners are beaten by guards for offenses such as complaining about food, fighting, and even on one occasion, an unpleasant remark about a guard's clumsiness in a prison soccer game. Prisoners are also known to beat up other prisoners as a way of establishing a dominant position in a cell.

GRIEVANCE PROCEDURES

In theory, the behavior of prison officials is governed by Regulation 30/1980 on Disciplinary Regulations for Civilian Government Employees. This applies to prison guards and administrative staff of the prison.   Individuals or their families can also bring civil suits against abusive prison staff, which sometimes happens but rarely succeeds.

Criminal investigations of military or police against whom complaints have been lodged are conducted by the Office of the Provost at Armed Forces Headquarters (police are under the authority of the Ministry of Defense and Security).   Occasionally, such an investigation will result in formal prosecution and conviction in a court-martial.

CORRUPTION

Corruption is endemic to the Indonesian prison system and takes a major emotional and economic toll on the families of prisoners.   In a case in 1992, the parents of a sentenced student in Yogyakarta had to pay the equivalent of ten U.S. dollars a visit to see their son.   The payment includes money to enter the prison, to bring food, and to actually see the prisoner.   Further payments are necessary to prolong the visit or to visit on days other than those designated as visiting days.   The corruption is such that the family of one prisoner actually gave a prison guard the equivalent of a regular salary to let in friends and family at any time.

According to one former prisoner interviewed by Human Rights Watch, "The [prison] staff would get you anything you wanted from the outside for a price, and some prisoners paid a fee of Rp.25,000 [about U.S. $12.50] a month to prison staff as a 'tax' on their trading operations inside prison."[3]

DEATH ROW

Indonesia has some two dozen inmates on death row, ranging from a Thai seaman convicted of drug-smuggling to six elderly men in prison for almost twenty-five years for their role in a coup attempt in 1965.   All of the latter are held in a special section of the L.P. Cipinang, the main prison in Jakarta, the capital.   All are subject to the constant psychological torture of not knowing if or when they will be brought

[3] Asia Watch, *Prison Conditions in Indonesia* (New York: Human Rights Watch, 1990), p. 20.

before a firing squad. In 1990, four prisoners were executed after more
than twenty-five years in prison.

ISRAEL AND THE OCCUPIED WEST BANK
AND GAZA STRIP

Human Rights Watch conducted an investigation of prisons, military-run detention centers, and police jails in Israel and the occupied territories between July 29 and August 7, 1990, which resulted in the publication of Prison Conditions in Israel and the Occupied Territories *the following year.*

The prison system in Israel and the occupied West Bank and Gaza Strip consists actually of two very different systems: the facilities run by the civilian Israel Prison Service (IPS), a semi-autonomous agency within the Ministry of Police; and the detention centers operated by the army (the Israel Defense Forces, IDF). The latter houses only one category of prisoners: male security prisoners from the West Bank and the Gaza Strip, while the former holds all types of prisoners.

The per capita rate of incarceration for Palestinian residents of the occupied territories is higher than in nearly all countries that release such statistics. With more than 12,000 persons from the West Bank and the Gaza Strip incarcerated as of April 1993, the per capita rate of incarceration was roughly 667 per 100,000 residents, down from one-and-a-half times that rate earlier in the Palestinian uprising, which broke out in December 1987. Nearly all of these are men and nearly all are held in connection with security rather than common criminal charges.

The rate of incarceration for residents of Israel proper is considerably lower: Israel had 110 prisoners per 100,000 population in 1989; for Jews, the rate was 93, for Israeli-Palestinians it was 187. There were a total of 116 women in prison in April 1990, most of them Israeli criminal offenders.

The two foremost problems relating to conditions in Israeli prisons are systemwide overcrowding and the physical mistreatment, including torture, of Palestinian security suspects from the occupied territories under interrogation during pretrial incommunicado detention. The mistreatment is inflicted for the most part by interrogators from the IDF and the General Security Service (GSS), Israel's internal intelligence-gathering agency. For most Palestinians who have undergone coercive GSS or IDF interrogations, nothing they experience while serving their sentences approaches the mistreatment they suffered during their pre-trial questioning. Fourteen Palestinians died during or shortly after interrogation since the beginning of the intifada; several of these deaths were the direct or indirect result of interrogation methods or of medical negligence by the authorities.

In contrast to the law in Israel, where suspects must be brought before a judge within forty-eight hours of arrest, Israeli military law in the West Bank and Gaza Strip allows suspects in the occupied territories to be held for up to eighteen days before being brought before a judge. In practice, Palestinians undergoing interrogation who are suspected of grave offenses are held incommunicado for two weeks or longer, usually in separate interrogation wings of IPS prisons, police jails, and IDF detention centers. It is during this stage that the most severe abuse occurs.

As mentioned above, Israel's prison system comprises two very different systems: the facilities run by the civilian Israel Prison Service (IPS), a semi-autonomous agency within the Ministry of Justice; and the detention centers operated by the IDF. This division stems from—but does not correlate exactly with—the two populations under Israeli rule. These two populations are the five million Jewish and Palestinian citizens of Israel proper and of east Jerusalem (whose annexation by Israel is not recognized by the international community), and the 1.8 million Palestinian residents of the West Bank and Gaza Strip, which Israel has occupied since 1967. Because of the differences between the two systems, they will be described separately here.

IPS-run prisons are designed for long-term incarceration and house residents of both Israel and the occupied territories. They are classified as minimum, medium, and maximum security.

IDF detention centers, which are mostly tent camps surrounded by barbed wire, house only residents of the occupied territories who are security suspects. All of the IDF detention centers are run as maximum-security facilities.

Most of the IDF camps were hastily opened to accommodate the thousands of Palestinians arrested during the first three years of the uprising. Because of their makeshift construction and design, the camps are inadequate for long-term incarceration. Nonetheless, many of the inmates have served three years or longer in these camps.

The first place of detention for most suspects after their arrest is the local police jail. In the occupied territories, suspects may initially be brought to local jails, to holding areas within military compounds or to interrogation centers.

Systemwide, citizens of Israel and Palestinians from the occupied territories are separated from one another. Prisoners from the occupied territories are segregated according to whether they are accused of security or criminal offenses. Adults and minors are also segregated from one another. There is some mixing of pre-trial and convicted inmates.

Israel has on occasion approved requests from human rights organizations, such as Human Rights Watch and the Israeli chapter of Defence for Children International, to visit detention facilities. It also allows the International Committee of the Red Cross to visit on a regular basis all Palestinian security prisoners and detainees following their fourteenth day in detention.

IPS PRISONS AND POLICE JAILS

The IPS operates twenty-one prisons, fifteen inside Israel, five in the West Bank and one in the Gaza Strip. IPS prisons hold both residents of Israel and of the occupied territories.

Jails can be found in major police stations in both Israel and the territories. They are meant to hold only those persons who have not yet been charged. Once charged, an inmate is supposed to be released or transferred to an IPS prison, but due to overcrowding in IPS prisons, many suspects remain in police jails after they are charged and some even after they have been tried and sentenced.

IPS prisons hold all Israeli-Jewish prisoners and Israeli-Palestinian prisoners, except those who remain in police jails. They also hold most Palestinians from the occupied territories who are serving sentences of five years or longer. On October 13, 1992, there were 4,100 Palestinians in IPS prisons, all but "a few hundred" of whom were security prisoners, according to the IPS spokesperson.

IPS prisons are professionally run and generally provide adequate food, clothing, outdoor time, family and lawyer visits, access to media and reading material, and flow of correspondence. There is no pattern of physical violence by guards. Exceptions to this general picture will be discussed below.

The major problem in the prison system is overcrowding. On the average, cells provide only 2.6 square meters per inmate, according to the

IPS annual report of 1989-90. These dimensions are most claustrophobic for Palestinian security prisoners, who are confined to their own wings for much of the day because they refuse to participate in prison work programs (except in jobs that directly benefit other prisoners).

The physical conditions of IPS prisons vary depending on the age of the facility, but most are acceptable. Their lay-outs range from multi-floor cell-blocks typical of larger prisons to more agreeable medium and minimum security prisons composed of bungalows or barracks surrounded by greenery. Some of the older maximum-security prisons, such as Ayalon (Ramleh), are humid, poorly ventilated and experience infestation and sewage problems.

While the physical conditions for Palestinian security prisoners and maximum-security criminal prisoners are similar, certain measures taken in the name of security greatly constrict the day-to-day life of the security prisoners. Unlike criminal prisoners, security prisoners have no telephone privileges, eat their meals in their cells, and may meet their visitors only when separated from them by a thick grill. Criminal prisoners, by contrast, receive regular access to the telephone and meet their visitors in open rooms. Convicted prisoners are able to have reasonable and confidential access to lawyers, although lawyers representing security prisoners are routinely made by the prison authorities to waste time during their visits.

Women who are arrested are taken first to police jails. If not released, they are transferred to IPS custody; the IDF does not have detention facilities for women.

The IPS runs two facilities for women: Neve Tirzeh penitentiary for criminal offenders, and a modern two-story wing of HaSharon prison for security offenders from the occupied territories. Women who are pregnant when imprisoned are permitted to keep their babies with them for two years.

IPS requires that all prisoners have family visits at least once every two months. This minimum is respected; in practice, most prisoners receive visits more frequently, a "privilege" that is sometimes revoked as a punishment. Other "privileges," such as permission to visit friends in other wings or to make purchases at canteens, are also subject to revocation as a punishment.

More severe punishments include placement in isolation cells for up to two weeks, separated by a one-week interval. Inmates in punitive isolation lose certain privileges, including outdoor time. The long-term placement in isolation cells of "dangerous" prisoners, such as at Nitzan prison, is discussed below.

There are at least two civilian-run facilities where conditions are most problematic, the main police jail in Jerusalem, and the ultra-maximum security Ward 8 of Nitzan Prison in Ramleh, which has been used to keep inmates in long-term isolation.

When Human Rights Watch visited the Russian Compound in 1990, inmates were living in woefully overcrowded and poorly ventilated dungeon-like cells that stank from the unprotected toilets in the corners of the cells. Despite modest improvements since then, overcrowding remains a serious problem; some cells are packed to nearly three times their capacity.

Conditions in the modern ultra-maximum security wing of Nitzan prison are the strictest in the IPS system and are the cause of grave concern. The approximately thirty inmates, all of whom are Palestinians from Israel and the occupied territories, are confined to their one-man cells twenty-three hours a day, and may never leave their cells unless handcuffed. Legcuffs are worn during visits by relatives and lawyers.

According to the IPS, prisoners are assigned to the wing solely on the grounds that they pose a physical danger to guards or other prisoners. However, assignment to Nitzan is clearly used as a way of punishing individuals, particularly Islamists whose crimes are considered exceptionally heinous or whom the authorities wish to punish for other reasons.

Although there have been improvements since 1992, conditions at Nitzan's Ward Eight are harsher than at other facilities in ways that have little to do with protecting others. The cells are partly below street level, and have poor ventilation and little natural light. Access to reading materials is more restricted than at other prisons. Beatings by guards are reported to be more common than at other IPS facilities. Lawyers representing clients at Nitzan are routinely treated with disrespect, made to waste time and then allowed only a brief consultation with their clients. A prison guard stands within earshot during their consultation.

The requests of Human Rights Watch to visit Nitzan were refused in 1990. The request was renewed in 1993 and was pending as this report went to press.

Similar issues arise with regard to the isolation wing at Beer Sheva prison. A pathologist from the Danish Physicians for Human Rights who visited the wing in February 1993 described the cells as 2 by

1.25 meters in size, with no light except for artificial light filtering through a ventilation shaft in the ceiling. "By standing on the bed, it was just possible to read," he wrote.[1]

IDF DETENTION CENTERS

It is now five years since the IDF detention centers assumed a major role, in tandem with the IPS, in incarcerating Palestinians. Conditions have generally improved at the IDF centers during this period. Nevertheless, the tent camps in which most of the Palestinians are confined are unsuitable for long-term incarceration.

On April 11, 1993, the IDF reported that its five principal detention centers (excluding Tulkarm) held 6,482 Palestinians, 3,976 of whom were sentenced, 526 were charged and awaiting trial, 1,654 were detained until the end of court proceedings, and 326 were administrative detainees. Another 177 were being held in short-term holding facilities.

As a class, the IDF detention centers are inferior to the IPS prisons in ways that go beyond the difference between tents and indoor cells. The guards at IPS prisons are experienced professionals who carry no weapons; in IDF camps, armed soldiers keep watch on the prisoners from the other side of the fence, and in Ketsiot, often point their loaded weapons at them. Access to reading material and media is far more limited, and provisions for lawyers' visits are poor. However, prisoners in IDF camps, as in IPS facilities, are adequately fed.

Inside the detainees' tents, there is little space that is not occupied by bedding. While the inmates are free during the day to move around the larger fenced-in open area, they are confined to their crowded tents at night, during inclement weather, and during punitive lockdowns.

Any assessment of IDF camps must give substantial weight to the largest and worst facility, Ketsiot. Located in a remote corner of the Negev desert, Ketsiot is far from both the Gaza Strip and the West Bank and thus highly inconvenient for lawyers and prisoners' families. It is subject to daytime temperatures exceeding 100 degrees fahrenheit in the summer and freezing nighttime temperatures in the winter. These conditions impose added hardships on prisoners in fragile health.

---

[1] Physicians for Human Rights Denmark, *Report on the February 21, 1993 Autopsy of Samir Muhammad Khamis Abdul Karim Salama* (Denmark: 1993).

Tension and fear among staff and inmates is higher at Ketsiot than at other IDF camps. The guards frequently fire tear gas into the prisoners' enclosures. They also are armed with rubber and live bullets, which have been used on occasion during disturbances.

THE INCARCERATION INSIDE ISRAEL OF RESIDENTS FROM THE OCCUPIED TERRITORIES

Israel violates article 76 of the Fourth Geneva Convention by incarcerating residents of the occupied Gaza Strip and West Bank in IPS and IDF facilities inside Israel. Among other hardships, this violation of international law makes it difficult and sometimes impossible for some relatives and lawyers of inmates to reach the prisons. This is due to the fact that many residents of the West Bank and the Gaza Strip are denied the permission they must obtain from Israeli authorities if they wish to enter Israel. Also, authorities frequently seal off the crossings from the West Bank and especially Gaza into Israel, thereby preventing lawyers from reaching their clients. This problem would be solved by transferring all prisoners who are from the occupied territories back to a facility in their area of origin, in compliance with international law.

HUNGER STRIKES

During 1991 and 1992, Palestinian security prisoners staged two major hunger strikes in IPS and IDF prisons. In June-July 1991, prisoners struck to protest a deterioration of conditions that followed the Gulf War. Their grievances included shrinking food rations, inadequate medical treatment and materials for personal hygiene; interference with family visits; excessive use of solitary confinement; restrictions on education; inadequate exercise time; and restrictions on communications between prisoners. The strike ended sixteen days later when the prisoners reached an agreement with Israeli authorities that addressed several of the grievances.

The 1992 strike was prompted partly by the prisoners' claim that authorities had not fulfilled their promises from the previous year's strike. The issues were much the same: health care, solitary confinement; overcrowding; harassment by guards; obstructions of lawyers' access to prisoners; restrictions on educational materials; and inadequate outdoor time. The strike ended after nearly three weeks, with the authorities agreeing to some demands, rejecting others, and agreeing to study the rest. As of March 1993, the issue of long-term confinement of Palestinian security prisoners in isolation cells remained unresolved.

JAMAICA

Human Rights Watch has conducted two investigations of conditions in prisons and lockups in Jamaica. In 1990 a delegation visited Jamaica and inspected five of the eight prisons (including all of the main penitentiaries, but omitting one farm prison and one small rehabilitation center) and six lockups. The eighth prison was closed for repairs. The mission talked with prisoners, but was not permitted to talk with detainees (although many detainees shouted their problems to the delegation through the bars). The mission also talked with government officials, former prisoners, attorneys and human rights activists about conditions in prisons and lockups. A report, Prison Conditions in Jamaica, was issued in 1990. In 1993 a delegation met with officials, human rights activists and attorneys to determine whether improvements had taken place. A short report "Human Rights in Jamaica: Death Penalty, Prison Conditions, and Police Violence" was published in April 1993.

Dreadful physical conditions, including lack of in-cell plumbing, open sewers on the prison grounds, lack of furniture and severe overcrowding in most institutions are the most prominent features of the Jamaican prison system.

In 1990, about 3,500 inmates were incarcerated in Jamaica's eight prisons, about 700 above the officially-stated capacity. About 3 percent of the inmates were women. The country's prisoner-to-population ratio is about 160 per 100,000.

Prisons and lockups are under the jurisdiction of the Ministry of National Security (until recently, prisons were under the jurisdiction of the Ministry of Justice).

PRE-TRIAL DETENTION

The Jamaican Constitution provides that detainees are to be brought without delay before a court. Police officials report that detainees are to be brought before a court within forty-eight hours of detention. A 1986 Human Rights Watch report, *Human Rights in Jamaica*, found that many detainees were held for considerably longer periods. The average time of detention for forty-five people represented by the

Jamaica Council for Human Rights in 1984 and 1985 was seventeen days before being brought before a court. A 1991 report by consultants from the United Kingdom stated that police detained people without charges and failed to bring inmates promptly before a judge as required by law.   The consultants found people detained in filthy and crowded conditions for long periods; in one example, they found a thirteen-year-old boy detained for stealing pineapples who had been held for thirteen days in an unlit and unventilated cell.

PHYSICAL CONDITIONS

Lockups in Jamaica are located in police stations and are administered by police for inmates detained before charges or before trial.   Prisons are administered by corrections officers for convicted prisoners; remand prisoners are sometimes confined in prisons as well and are kept separate from convicted prisoners.   The two chief prisons that house two-thirds of all inmates are routinely filled well over official capacity; others may not be.   Lockups vary in the degree to which they are overcrowded.

In October 1992, in a horrible example of overcrowding and police negligence, nineteen men were confined in a cell eight by seven feet at the Constant Springs lockup.   The only ventilation came from holes drilled into the solid door of the cell.   Police officers ignored the detainees' cries for air.   The men were held in the cell for forty hours. Three died of asphyxiation.   A coroner's jury found cause to believe that some police personnel were guilty of manslaughter; the matter was referred to the Director of Public Prosecutions to determine which individuals should be charged.   No action has yet been taken.

Both our missions to Jamaica found that conditions in the island's prisons and lockups were appalling and violated international standards for the proper care and confinement of inmates.   All of the institutions failed to provide the barest essentials for decent treatment, including the basic necessities for personal hygiene, a nutritionally adequate diet, and the requisite medical, dental and psychiatric care.

Sanitation in the two main penitentiaries was frightful; human excrement ran through the grounds of one prison.   An overwhelming stench pervaded the prison.   These prisons, housed in ancient buildings, lacked in-cell plumbing.   Inmates had no beds or bedding, but slept on concrete floors, often three to a cell that measured five feet by eight feet. No clothing was provided to prisoners. Prison officials told the delegation that the food provided for inmates was inadequate in amount and quality; in 1993, about fifty cents a day is budgeted to feed a prisoner. Most prisoners were provided with extra food by their families. Four prison riots between 1990 and 1992 have protested prison conditions.

Death Row, located inside of St. Catherine District Prison, housed 270 condemned men in December 1992. Following a 1992 law that reserved capital punishment for a narrower range of offenses, the sentences of about 170 convicts were commuted from death to life imprisonment. In January 1993, one hundred men remained on death row.

The conditions on death row are dreadful. Prisoners are confined to their cells for long periods with no work and no educational facilities. Sanitary conditions are terrible and medical care inadequate. Inmates complain of beatings by guards.

Visiting is severely limited in the two chief prisons. Prisoners talk to relatives from behind glass panels; a sentenced prisoner is allowed one visit a month, while a prisoner awaiting trial or appealing a conviction may receive two visits a week. Visiting in smaller prisons is more relaxed, sometimes allowing for contact visits.

Physical conditions in the island's lockups varied in 1990; one relatively new lockup was clean and almost empty. At the other extreme, the Spanish Town lockup held eight-six people crammed into ten cells that measured eight feet by ten feet. Of the eighty-six prisoners, ten were serving short sentences, sixty were awaiting trial and sixteen had not yet been charged; some of the latter had been detained for as long as five months. Although the mission's visit took place during the day, the cellblock was pitch-black and a floodlight had to be hooked up from outside the block before the delegation could enter. The stench was overpowering and there was no ventilation. Each cell held between five and ten prisoners; five women occupied one of the cells.

Inside each cell was a concrete slab upon which one or two prisoners could sleep. The others slept on the floor, which was wet and filthy. No bedding was provided. To go to the bathroom, inmates had to call for a guard and be escorted to the end of the block where two non-functioning toilets were located. The stench at the toilet area was even more acrid than in the rest of the block. A cell immediately adjacent to the toilet area housed six men. No soap, toothpaste, or toothbrushes were provided. Feces that had come from inside the building stood in a stagnant pool outside the cells. Inmates called out to the delegation about the lack of toilet facilities and the lack of air; many displayed many insect bites on their bodies. Several women whispered to one member of the mission that the guards took them out of the cell at night and forced them to have sexual relations. The Spanish Town lockup provided little medical or dental care and mentally ill prisoners received no attention at all because the local hospital refused to accept them.

ACTIVITIES AND WORK

No work or activities are provided for inmates of lockups in Jamaica. Prisons vary. At the time of the mission's visit in 1990, there were two farm prisons in which inmates did farm work for four or five hours every day. Some recreation was available. Unfortunately these prisons have the capacity for only about 500 of the approximately 3,500 to 4,000 prisoners held at any one time.

In the two chief penitentiaries, St. Catherine's District Prison and the General Penitentiary, work was provided for very few inmates. Woodworking and other shops had fallen into disrepair. Inmates complained about the lack of work possibilities. Recreation consisted only of milling around in a yard for a few hours a day. Inmates were locked in for the night from 3:00 or 3:30 P.M. (after eating their last meal of the day) until 8:30 or 9:00 the next morning.

In South Camp Rehabilitation Centre, a smaller institution that can house 305 prisoners but has sometimes held as many as 400, some inmates worked as tailors at the time of the mission's visit in 1990. Other prisoners took basic classes in reading and writing and could borrow books from the prison library. Some recreational activities, for example, dominoes, were provided.

WOMEN PRISONERS

In 1990, women prisoners were held in Fort Augusta, a fort built by the British in the early 1800s. The capacity is 200, but at the time the delegation visited, the prison held 115 women. The dormitories were relatively clean, but the toilets did not function and the women had to use slop buckets. The women wore paisley uniforms provided by the prison. The only rehabilitation program provided was a poorly equipped hairdressing shop.

An inmate is permitted to keep with her for several months a baby born while she is in prison. Inmates can visit with families in an open area in the yard; children are not permitted to visit their mothers.

DISCIPLINARY MEASURES

Inmates have alleged brutal beatings by guards in the chief penitentiaries; frequently these beatings were said to involve three or four guards beating one prisoner. The director of the women's prison acknowledged that there had been occasional instances of brutalization of prisoners by guards.

MEXICO

Human Rights Watch conducted an extended examination of prison conditions in Mexico in 1989 and 1990, which led to the publication in March 1991 of Prison Conditions in Mexico. *Since that time we have conducted follow-up prison visits and interviews with government officials and have visited two additional prison facilities. Since the release of our report, Mexico's prison system has come under heightened scrutiny from the government's National Human Rights Commission (CNDH). The CNDH has toured prison facilities in every state and has issued dozens of hard-hitting recommendations calling on states and the federal government to introduce significant reforms.*

Mexican prisons are vastly overcrowded, dilapidated and conditions are often hazardous and unsanitary. Beatings and mistreatment of inmates by the guards is also a problem. Assaults, including fatal ones, among the inmates are also frequent. Prisoners' daily life is not structured and inmates have a large degree of discretion over their daily routines. Family access is easy, including conjugal visits, and to a large extent prisoners rely on goods brought in from outside for survival.

In November 1992 officials of Mexico's Department of Prevention and Social Readaptation reported that the country's 446 federal and state prisons held 86,334 prisoners. The country's prisoner-to-population ratio stands at 97 per 100,000. Women constitute about 4 percent of the prison population. The percentage of indigenous prisoners is reported by government officials to be less than 1 percent, though nongovernmental groups claim the figure is much higher. Prison capacity is approximately 70,435. Capacity is being increased through new prison construction and renovation of some existing prisons, though the government admits that the number of planned new spaces will not alleviate a serious problem of overcrowding in Mexico's prison system.

Mexico is a federal system; approximately two-thirds of all inmates are charged with state crimes while one-third are charged with federal crimes. Nearly 70 percent of all prisoners charged with state crimes are unsentenced. As of November 1992, 51 percent of all federal prisoners were sentenced; the cases of the remaining 49 percent were still in judicial proceedings.

TYPES OF PRISONS.

Each of the country's thirty-one states and its Federal District maintains a prison system for prisoners charged with or sentenced for non-federal crimes. The federal government operates federal police lockups, two maximum security prisons in the states of Mexico and Jalisco, and a federal penal colony on the island of Islas Marias. The government is building two additional maximum security prisons to house those convicted of serious federal criminal offenses such as narcotics trafficking. But most federal prisoners are housed in state prisons.

Most state prison systems consist of police lockups and municipal jails, and one or more larger prisons. In the Federal District, the prison system consists of police lockups, three large pre-trial detention facilities, a penitentiary for male prisoners who are serving their sentences, and an institution for women.

PRE-TRIAL DETAINEES.

Mexico's constitution includes a wide range of protections for pre-trial detainees. Anyone detained by the police must, within three days of arrest, be committed by a judge to a detention facility or be released. The constitution further provides that prisoners charged with crimes carrying sentences of less than two years must be tried within four months after arrest; those charged with crimes carrying longer sentences must be tried within one year. Male and female prisoners are to be housed in separate facilities and minors are to be housed apart from adults. Unsentenced prisoners are to be housed separately from prisoners who are serving their sentences.

In practice, all of these constitutional guarantees are violated. Human Rights Watch delegations in October 1989 and January 1990 interviewed many prisoners who had spent a week or more in incommunicado police detention before being brought before a judge for the first time. The National Human Rights Commission (CNDH) has reported on cases in which the three-day rule was violated and prisoners were held in incommunicado detention, tortured, and subjected to other forms of cruel, inhuman or degrading treatment before being brought before a judge. In several detention facilities, Human Rights Watch encountered prisoners in the intake area who had been there for longer than three days without having been arraigned.

The amount of time between arrest and completion of trial often exceeds constitutional limits. We encountered many prisoners who said they had been in pre-trial detention for over a year. Some prisoners have been held in pre-trial detention for periods that exceed the allowable sentences for their alleged crimes.

Prison design and overcrowding make it difficult for officials to keep unsentenced and sentenced prisoners apart. Outside of the Federal District, the practice of mingling is so common that it was found in thirty-three prisons visited by CNDH between June 1991 and June 1992.

MISTREATMENT OF INMATES

Beatings and mistreatment in prison are widespread. The CNDH condemned beatings and mistreatment by prison officials in eleven prisons between June 1991 and June 1992.

Prisoners are often killed or injured by other prisoners. Prison gangs terrorize other inmates and have set off prison riots that have lead to deaths of inmates and prison officials. In more than seventy-five visits to prisons around the country, the CNDH has repeatedly denounced what it terms "self-government," or rogue authority structures created and run by prisoners who typically co-opt part of the prison population and buy off or intimidate custodians and officials.

PHYSICAL CONDITIONS.

Overcrowded and dilapidated, unsanitary and hazardous conditions are pervasive throughout Mexico's prison system. In many facilities prison food is nutritionally inadequate or vermin infested. Physical and mental health care services are typically substandard.

ACTIVITIES AND WORK.

Lack of jobs and vocational training is a pervasive problem. Large workshops sit empty because equipment is in need of repair or because prisons lack the means to purchase materials.

On the other hand, there are positive features of Mexican prison life. Prisoners' families are encouraged to visit and many prisoners enjoy conjugal visits and continue to play a role in parenting and day to day family decisions. In virtually all state prisons, prisoners exercise significant control over their daily routines.

CONDITIONS FOR WOMEN.

Physical conditions for women prisoners are as bad or worse than those for men, and opportunities for women to make meaningful use of the time spent in prison are even more limited. In contrast to male prisoners, many of whose wives and families visit regularly and bring them food, blankets, clothing, and other necessities not adequately supplied by prison authorities, women get much less of this type of support.

Rules regarding treatment of mothers of infants and toddlers vary: some facilities forbid even nursing women to keep their infants with them; others allow infants and toddlers to remain with their mothers and provide child care centers and segregated housing. In some prisons, school age children live inside prison walls.

Male and female prisoners are usually housed separately, but there are glaring exceptions. In 1991 and 1992, the CNDH identified three prisons where male and female inmates mingled. Human Rights Watch saw mingling of male and female prisoners in one institution, and found minors incarcerated with adults in four of the prisons we visited.

RECENT DEVELOPMENTS.

Mexico opened its first federal maximum security prison in January 1992. The newly-built prison is designed to hold the most serious criminal offenders including narcotics traffickers and those responsible for organizing prison gangs or leading prison uprisings. Unlike other prisons, prisoners here must conform to a structured daily regime. Food, clothing, and medical services are adequately supplied by the prison administration. Family visits are more restricted than at other facilities and are made more difficult for many prisoners because of the prison's location. The prison provides Mexico with the means to reduce tensions at other prisons by having a place to transfer the most violent or corrupt inmates. But opposition politicians fear that the lack of clear criteria for determining who is a dangerous prisoner could result in the facility's misuse in times of political tension to isolate political figures.

PERU

Human Rights Watch visited the Lurigancho prison in Lima in 1990; the women's prison of Santa Mónica, in Chorrillos, on three occasions (1987 and May and July, 1992); and the maximum-security facility of Canto Grande in 1987. In 1993, we attempted unsuccessfully to visit the new prison in Puno, following a public announcement by the Government of Peru that international organizations would be given access to detention centers. Since February 17, 1993, we have repeatedly asked for permission to visit several prisons. On May 12, 1993, we received a letter form the Peruvian Embassy in Washington denying us access to Peru's prisons. This marked the first time in ten years that a Peruvian government flatly refused to grant us prison access.

Peru's prisons are plagued by multiple problems: life-threatening shortages of food, medicine, water and basic supplies, like mattresses and blankets; a high incidence of communicable disease, like tuberculosis and cholera; extreme violence between guards and prisoners, including massacres, and between prisoners themselves; rampant corruption; a complete lack of legal assistance for poor and indigent prisoners; frequent reports of torture and abuse by police and guards; cruel and inhumane treatment for the mentally ill; few rehabilitation programs; and severely restricted access to exercise, family visits or medical care.

Peru has 109 functioning prisons, 35 in northern Peru, 19 in Lima, 39 in southern Peru and 16 in the central highlands and one labor camp, called El Sepa, in the department of Madre de Dios. People accused under the Treason Law are incarcerated in facilities within military bases.

According to a 1991 census by the National Penitentiary Institute (INPE), there were 17,241 prisoners in Peru. Since August 1992, at least 2,500 people have been arrested under new anti-terrorism laws, bringing the total population up to about 20,000, roughly 91 for every 100,000 inhabitants. Executive decrees promulgated after the "self-inflicted" coup of April 5, 1992, impose harsh penalties on those suspected of crimes of drug-trafficking, espionage, terrorism and treason. Eight per cent of prisoners (1,500) are female. The 1991 survey noted that 23 per cent had received a sentence. The rest were either accused or in the process of being tried. Often, the wait for a court decision is longer than the applicable sentence.

Prisons are guarded by the Security Police, a division of Peru's National Police. The INPE, part of the Ministry of Justice, maintains prisons and provides food, medical and other services. In the case of facilities used exclusively to confine those accused or convicted of membership in armed insurgencies—including Yanamayo in Puno, Las Palmas air force base in Lima and the Callao navy base—the military appears to be in charge, although the Security Police and INPE may continue to play a role.

PRE-TRIAL DETENTION

The Peruvian Constitution stipulates that the maximum time a suspect apprehended in flagrante delicto may be kept in police custody is twenty-four hours. The security forces also carry out frequent, massive sweeps and detain people not involved in the immediate commission of a crime (for instance, for failing to carry proper identification). Afterwards, the suspect must either be released or passed to the custody of a penal judge. According to law, a judge must be notified within twenty-four hours of a detention. However, in practice, detainees are often kept incommunicado and in unacknowledged detention, temporarily "disappeared." This is true for detentions carried out by both the police and the military.

Torture is common in these circumstances. Methods include severe beatings, electric shocks on the hands, face and genitals, rape, near drowning in filthy water ("the submarine"), hanging by the arms tied behind the back, sleep, food and water deprivation, death threats and threats against family.

The pre-trial detention center in Lima, Peru's capital, for those charged with crimes other than treason is located in the basement of the Palace of Justice and is known as "La Carceleta." Detainees charged with treason are remanded to military custody. Although La Carceleta has a capacity of 300 detainees, overcrowding is common. Not only recent arrestees are kept here, but also any detainee scheduled to appear in court. Prisoners report being kept for days without exercise or adequate food. Some have told Human Rights Watch that they must bribe guards to allow in extra food or clothing provided by their families.

Outside Lima, there are no similar provisional detention centers. Detainees remain in police custody until a judge orders their formal arrest or sets them free.

There have been cases where a prosecuting attorney (*fiscal*) has asked for or a judge has imposed a sentence for less time than a detainee has already been in prison awaiting trial.

LIVING CONDITIONS

Overcrowding is one of the most serious problems in Peru's prisons. An estimated 69 percent of the prison population is concentrated in 25 of the 109 functioning institutions; most are in Lima. Lurigancho Prison, with a capacity of 1,200 prisoners, contained at least 5,000 in 1991. Miguel Castro Castro (Canto Grande) Prison, built for 800 prisoners, held 2,500. An August 1992 census taken at Santa Mónica Prison for Women in Chorrillos counted 650 inmates in a facility initially built for 230.[1]

Human Rights Watch is aware of three new facilities either completed or under construction for prisoners convicted of terrorism and treason. A new cellblock was completed in mid-1992 at Santa Mónica Prison to accommodate women charged and convicted of terrorism. Also in use is a new facility for armed group leaders in the Callao navy base. Under construction is a new facility near Yanamayo Prison in Puno. We are not aware of any new facilities for common prisoners.

INMATE CLASSIFICATION

Peruvian law mandates that inmates should be separated according to the following criteria: men from women; charged from convicted; first-time offenders from repeat offenders; and minors under twenty-one years of age from adults. In practice, these provisions are frequently violated. For instance, we have documented cases in Castro Castro prison and the Ayacucho prison where men and women mix with

---

[1] This census was taken before May 1992, when several dozen Shining Path prisoners were transferred to Santa Mónica from another facility, contributing to even more serious overcrowding.

relative frequency. In Chiclayo's Picci Prison, people who are charged with crimes live in the same areas as those already convicted and repeat offenders. Minors are frequently treated as adults, and incarcerated in the same areas.

Article 233 of the Peruvian Constitution states the right "of those charged and sentenced to occupy establishments that are healthy and suitable"; however, this is usually not the case. More often, living conditions depend directly on how much cash an inmate has to bribe guards, INPE workers and other prisoners for protection, and such services and goods as extra food, an in-cell television, telephone, cook, bodyguard and other special privileges. Those without resources—peasants, petty criminals, the urban poor and the mentally ill—face life-threatening conditions.

FOOD

Severe food shortages are among the most serious problems in Peruvian prisons. In Lurigancho prison, overcrowding translates into chronic food and water shortages, and numerous deaths. Some cases in which prisoners starved to death have been reported. For many years, indigent prisoners there have lived in an open area called "La Pampa." In 1990, reporters who visited "La Pampa" discovered that inmates received as a daily ration eight grams of rice and two pieces of bread. As a supplement, they trapped animals, like dogs, and scavenged food from garbage piles.

ACTIVITIES

Peruvian prisons offer few educational or work opportunities. Most have no workshops or educational facilities. In several cases, machinery donated for workshops has "disappeared," presumably sold by prison personnel.

Human Rights Watch has reported that in Lurigancho Prison, "since 1987, guards have robbed anything transportable outside the prison for sale. Workshops that operated in the Industrial Cellblock have been dismantled." The report adds that "inmates cannot organize themselves to install workshops because they run the risk that the materials they have will be robbed by police."[2]

In some prisons, prisoners do some folk art with wood, cloth and straw, selling items through their families. In Castro Castro Prison, for instance, prisoners sell woven straw bags to visitors on visiting day. However, prisoners must often acquire materials to work with from outside. One exception is Santa Mónica Prison for Women in Chorrillos, where women can take part in a knitting workshop. Women who work can then take advantage of the "two for one" law, which allows an internee to reduce a sentence by working.

DISCIPLINARY MEASURES

Prisoners can be punished for disciplinary infractions with a range of sanctions that include an admonition; suspension of exercise or communal recreation for up to thirty days; limitations on outside communication for up to thirty days; and isolation for up to thirty days for a single offense, and forty-five days when the offense occurs while a thirty-day sentence of isolation is in progress.

The application of punishment frequently depends on a prisoner's relationship with the authorities and the ability to buy privileges. Punishment is more often applied to those without money, while those with money can purchase lenience.

OUTSIDE CONTACTS

The Peruvian Constitution prohibits the isolation of prisoners "except in the case where it is indispensable in order to clarify a crime, always according to the rules and time period established by law" and states that "the authorities are obligated to indicate without delay the place where the detained person is being kept." This provision is violated daily, in cases of both police and military detentions.

In Castro Castro prison, some prisoners are allowed to speak with their lawyers in special rooms and without time limits. Two visiting days

---

[2] Americas Watch, *In Desperate Straits: Human Rights in Peru after a Decade of Democracy and Insurgency* (New York: Human Rights Watch, 1990), p. 47.

each week are provided for family members, one for visits by women and one for men. Women visitors are only allowed in if they wear skirts. Occasionally, the authorities have suspended visits arguing that there is a threat of a riot. Most prisons do not have special areas for family visits, so they generally take place in a prisoner's cellblock and cell. Conjugal visits are allowed, but few prisons have private rooms for couples.

WOMEN

There are six prisons for women: in Lima, Chiclayo, Cuzco, Arequipa, Tacna and Puno. Other prisons have special women's cellblocks.

According to press reports, sexual harassment, abuse and rape by the Security Police are common in Peru's women's prisons. In some cases, women have also traded sexual favors for such privileges as extra food, access to a telephone and help in importing illegal liquor or drugs.

Human Rights Watch has reported the frequent use of rape as a form of torture against women in police detention. Such rape is almost impossible to prove, since the policemen involved often force their victims to eliminate evidence by changing clothes and taking a shower. Despite the frequency of reports of rape in such conditions, very few policemen are eventually prosecuted or punished.

Although the law establishes that mothers may keep children up to three years old with them, in practice rules vary from prison to prison.

SECURITY PRISONERS

A clear distinction can be made between the treatment received by common prisoners and those incarcerated under the Anti-Terrorism Law or the Treason Law. Though common prisoners suffer harsh conditions, these reflect neglect, mismanagement and corruption, but by in large are not codified in law. In contrast, harsh prison conditions are imposed by law on those accused or convicted under the Anti-Terrorism and Treason laws.

For instance, suspects in security-related crimes may be held by police in incommunicado detention up to fifteen days before being brought before a judge. If a judge agrees, police may extend such detention to thirty days. Torture in these circumstances is common. Contact with lawyers and family members during this time is strictly prohibited. At the end of their detention, suspects are often presented to the press in striped convict uniforms as "proven subversives" before they have faced a judge, been formally charged or even allowed to consult a lawyer.

Convicted prisoners are also presented to the press in striped convict's uniforms, a practice that appears designed to humiliate, since it serves no other purpose and is not used either in prison or for common prisoners. When he was first presented to the press, and again when he was transferred to the Callao naval base, Abimael Guzmán, the convicted Shining Path leader, was dressed in this garb and confined in an animal cage.

Terrorism and treason legislation mandates pre-trial detention for all suspects, regardless of the crime they are accused of, and denies the right to habeas corpus or *amparo* until the trial is completed. As a result, a new prison population has sprung up and includes a significant number of people detained on weak evidence or none. This population includes children as young as fifteen.

Those charged with or convicted of terrorism are under special restrictions. Under prison regulations, food rations usually consist of two pieces of bread and tea for breakfast, and either soup, wheat stew or rice with vegetables and a hint of meat later in the day. Gifts of food by family members, which could supplement the meager diet, are severely restricted.

According to a November 1992 Urgent Action issued by Amnesty International, women incarcerated on terrorism charges in Santa Mónica Prison and men in Castro Castro were fed only once a day and denied all access to reading and writing material or radios. For much of 1992, prisoners were kept under twenty-four-hour lockdown, and spent months locked three to a cell without a moment outside. According to press reports, at the Callao naval base the Peruvian government has constructed underground facilities that are specially designed to exclude all natural light to imprisoned guerilla leaders.

Our mission that visited Santa Mónica in May discovered that women had been prevented from receiving family visits since the prison disturbances several weeks before and had yet to receive any outside clothing, food or medications. Most had only one set of clothes. None had been allowed to speak to a lawyer.

Often, the lack of water is so acute in Castro Castro that prisoners are forced to save small amounts for several days, then wash out of a bucket in their cells.

Access to medical care is also severely restricted. One man accused of terrorism and held in Castro Castro Prison reports that he was forced to wait over two months to see a doctor for a heart condition. Afterwards, his doctor informed him that he could no longer offer treatment, since the mere fact that he attended a patient charged with terrorism put him at risk of arrest as a terrorist collaborator.

Women charged with or convicted of terrorism in Santa Mónica Prison report that they are subject to midnight searches by hooded men who yell insults, mistreat them and confiscate food and other belongings.

A different set of visiting rules applies to those charged with or convicted of terrorism and treason. In the case of terrorism, visits are allowed only by two immediate family members at a time once a month for thirty minutes. In practice, however, family members report that after they pass the Castro Castro security controls and wait for the inmates to appear, they have less than fifteen minutes to communicate. To do so, they must speak loudly so that their voices carry through the double pane of glass separating them from the room where the prisoners are brought. Two prisoners are brought to each booth, so there is no privacy.

Those charged with or convicted of treason are kept in isolation and prevented from receiving visits for one year. As yet, no prisoner has been there for a year, so it is not clear what visiting rights will be allowed subsequently.

Apparently as part of its get-tough policy with prisoners, in July 1992 the Ministry of Justice began to impose new conditions for prison access on the delegates of the International Committee of the Red Cross (ICRC) who regularly visit prisoners accused of security crimes. By September, all ICRC delegates' authorizations had expired because of these new restrictions. ICRC prison visits were not restored until March 1993, after heavy international pressure.

Human Rights Watch was granted access to Santa Mónica Prison and the Ayacucho facility in 1992, but has been refused all prison access since.

VIOLENCE

Peru was the scene of the most bloody prison rebellion on record. In 1985, Lurigancho inmates who belonged to the Shining Path staged two riots during which they took hostages and made demands for special privileges and recognition as political prisoners. These riots presaged a tragedy to come.

On June 18, 1986, Shining Path inmates staged coordinated uprisings in Lurigancho, in the island prison of El Frontón, and in the women's prison of Santa Bárbara, in Callao. The government of President Alan García reacted violently and desperately: it declared a war zone in the prisons and called in the Armed Forces to quell the riots. The army took command of the operation in Lurigancho, and the navy did the same with El Frontón. Judges and prosecutors, prison authorities and the government's own Peace Commission members were denied access to the prison as well as permission to try to negotiate a peaceful solution. Four prison guards were killed by the rioting inmates. A day later, the riots were over. In Santa Bárbara, the riot was quickly suppressed: two rioting inmates died. In Lurigancho, about twenty inmates died during the battle for control of the cellblock, and all of the survivors, more than 110, were murdered after their surrender. In El Frontón, the navy destroyed the cellblock with explosives with most inmates and hostages still inside. Some thirty inmates (of a total of around 135) were apprehended and taken to hospitals or to other prisons. Of the more than 100 dead in El Frontón, many were captured alive, some were killed on the spot and others were taken away, apparently to naval installations, never to be seen again.

The total number of inmate deaths for these tragic episodes is well over 200. A military court investigation ended in prison sentences for only a handful of army and Republican Guard officers. The navy never accounted for its actions in El Frontón. A Senatorial Commission of Inquiry chaired by opposition Senator Rolando Ames produced a detailed, devastating report, which the majority party members refused to endorse. The case of El Frontón is presently before the Inter-American Court of Human Rights, a judicial body of the Organization of American States. A hearing on the merits is scheduled to take place in July 1993.

In 1987, Human Rights Watch denounced the violence in Peru's prisons as in part the product of manipulation by police authorities, who impose a climate of terror on inmates. Security Police have been repeatedly linked to a thriving liquor, drug and prostitution business within many prisons. Time and again, prisoners have charged that police searches are accompanied by beatings, threats and thefts of personal belongings, including food.

One of the most tragic events after the April 5, 1992 coup by President Fujimori in which he seized power from the congress and the courts was the violent repression of a disturbance in Castro Castro Prison that began on May 6 and lasted four days. This maximum-security prison houses most prisoners accused or convicted of belonging to Peru's two guerrilla insurgencies: the Communist Party of Peru-Shining Path and the Túpac Amaru Revolutionary Movement (MRTA). On May 6, the security forces entered in order to transfer some women to a new facility. The women resisted, apparently with the aid of some male prisoners. In the ensuing battle, three policemen and ten prisoners were killed. Mediation by third parties was rejected by the government, which opted for a frontal assault on May 10. A total of thirty-nine prisoners died and many more were wounded.

Although the government declared that there were no excesses or abuses committed, Human Rights Watch believes there is evidence to suggest that at the very least excessive force was used and there is a strong possibility that several inmates were executed after surrendering. At the time of this writing, no internal investigation of the clash has been made public, and no outside group has been allowed to conduct an impartial investigation.

POLAND

Human Rights Watch conducted two investigations of prison conditions in Poland. In 1987, a delegation visited Poland and interviewed recently released prisoners, but we were unable to obtain access to prisons at that time. That investigation resulted in a June 1988 report, Prison Conditions in Poland. *In early 1989, we received assurances from the Polish government that we would be allowed to visit prisons of our choice. We travelled to Poland shortly before the end of communist rule and visited prisons and police stations around the country. Because • of the dramatic political transformations Poland underwent soon thereafter, we conducted a follow-up mission in the fall of 1990; the two trips resulted in the January 1991 report,* Prison Conditions in Poland: An Update.

In the last several years Polish prisons have undergone radical changes. Some have resulted directly from the political transformations related to the end of communism in that country but many actually preceded the revolution. In the late 1980s, the overall number of prisoners, and thus the overcrowding, decreased due to general amnesties; new more liberal prison rules went into effect. After the advent of democracy, prisons became more open to the media, human rights organizations and prisoner rights activists. What did not improve is the infrastructure: many prisons are still in terrible physical shape. There is also less work for inmates, and thus more idleness, due to the country's growing unemployment.

At the end of 1992, Poland held 61,409 prisoners in some 150 prisons. There were 1,370 women inmates, or 2.2 percent of the prison population. Pre-trial detainees accounted for 23.1 percent of the total. The capacity of the system is 62,676. The country's prisoner-to-population ratio is about 153 per 100,000.

Prisons and pre-trial facilities are under the jurisdiction of the Ministry of Justice.

Under the current law, police lockups can hold inmates for up to forty-eight hours. After this period, a detainee must either be charged and transferred to a pre-trial facility, or released. In practice, however, we encountered prisoners held in police lockups for as long as five days.

PRE-TRIAL DETENTION

The length of pre-trial detention is not limited by law. As a result, pre-trial detention for as long as one year is common, and in some cases can last for two or more years. In addition, inmates in pre-trial detention have fewer privileges, including seriously limited contacts with the outside world.

PHYSICAL CONDITIONS

Polish prisons and jails (pre-trial inmates are held either in separate institutions or in selected areas of prisons holding sentenced prisoners) are usually very crowded. Even when an institution is filled below or at its stated capacity, the space allotted to each inmate is small (thirty-two square feet as per the current regulations). The situation is further exacerbated by the fact that many male inmates spend twenty-three hours a day in their cells.

Lighting is insufficient in many Polish prisons and light switches are often located outside the cell and cannot be controlled by inmates. We have also received frequent complaints that the cells are too cold in the winter, too hot and stuffy in the summer. This is due to the fact that some of the prisons are centuries old or occupy buildings that were not built to be prisons.

ACTIVITIES AND WORK

Under the law, inmates are required to work. Currently, however, due to the high unemployment rate nationwide, most prisoners have no work and are forced to spend almost all day in their cells. Following an appeal from the national ombudsman's office, the head of the prison system issued a circular directing that cells should be opened during the day, except those at the highest security levels institutions, but there has been strong resistance from prison directors. In practice, lockdowns continue in many of the male institutions. According to information provided recently by the Ministry of Justice, in the majority of male prisons of the closed type (whose inmates do not work outside the prison premises) cells are locked except during the daily exercise period.

Recreational and sports facilities are scarce. Many inmates spend their days in crowded cells in total idleness except during a one-hour "walk" in a small enclosed outdoor area and occasional visits to a "day room" with a TV set and a ping-pong table.

WOMEN PRISONERS

Female inmates account for a small proportion of the population and as a result, there are only four women's prisons in the entire country. Women thus frequently serve their sentences far from home and accordingly have fewer visits. Women are allowed to have their children of up to three years of age with them in prisons.

DISCIPLINARY MEASURES

Several improvements relating to both authorized and unauthorized disciplinary measures, have occurred in the years since our first investigation.

According to our interviews, beatings by guards—a wide-spread problem prior to 1986—have been virtually eliminated. An exception in this respect were the beatings that followed the 1989 wave of prison riots in several institutions nationwide. As a result, disciplinary proceedings were initiated against 132 staff members and five officers were dismissed. A number of criminal investigations are still underway as of this writing.

Reports of beatings by the police have also decreased dramatically. During our 1990 visit, however, two out of some twenty inmates we interviewed at police stations reported they had been beaten and had lodged formal complaints with a representative of the ombudsman's office with whom we conducted these visits.

Authorized disciplinary measures range from the loss of various privileges to solitary confinement, which can last for up to one month. The notorious sanction of "hard bed"—in the past the most frequent measure—consisting of replacing one's mattress with wooden slabs for up to fourteen days, has been recently abolished. For approximately four years, this measure has no longer been applied to women.

CONTACTS WITH THE OUTSIDE

This aspect of prison conditions has been particularly affected by recent political changes in Poland. While in the past inmates were virtually sealed off from the outside world, with rare visits and very limited and controlled access to information, they are now afforded a more generous visiting policy and access to media through private TV and radio sets and press subscriptions. In addition, furloughs of up to five days are granted to many inmates. There are no longer limits on the number of letters written or received by each inmate, although correspondence in both directions is routinely read by the staff. Letters that are illegible or do not have a return address will not be delivered to inmates.

A wide range of organizations, including human rights groups, media and religious associations, now have access to prisoners and may visit regularly.

Inmates awaiting trial, however, continue to have their contacts with the outside severely restricted. They are entitled only to non-contact visits and every visit has to be authorized by the prosecutor overseeing the investigation. Correspondence, no longer limited in frequency, is also controlled by the prosecutor and, according to inmates' complaints, often delayed for weeks.

FOOD

We received many complaints regarding the quality of food. According to our interviews, food is made even less appetizing by the fact that meals are usually eaten in the midst of the smells coming from the toilets, due to the fact that most Polish prisons have neither dining halls nor toilets separate from the cells. As a result, inmates frequently end up eating all their meals in their cells, in the vicinity of unshielded toilets.

ROMANIA

Human Rights Watch conducted an investigation of prison conditions in Romania from October 17 to November 2, 1991. Two representatives visited the following prisons: Jilava Hospital, Poarta Albă, Mărgineni, Tîrgşori, Tîrgu Mureş, Gherla, Aiud, Arad and Găieşti (Reeducation School for juveniles). The investigation resulted in a June 1992 report, Prison Conditions in Romania. *Although we had obtained permission from the Ministry of Interior to conduct an investigation into conditions in police lockups during the November 1991 mission, such efforts were obstructed by Romanian government and police officials. Finally, in July 1992, we were granted access to police lockups throughout the country. The findings from that mission resulted in a report in January 1993,* Lockups in Romania.

Prison conditions in Romania reflect decades of neglect, the current economic crisis, and years of extreme repressiveness. Old habits die hard and many of the Ceausescu-era prison rules are alive and well in today's Romania.

As of December 31, 1992, there were 44,011 prisoners held in Romanian prisons and juvenile reform schools, 10,966 of them in pre-trial detention. Among the total were 1,436 female prisoners (including 130 minors) comprising approximately 3.3 percent of the total population. The country's prisoner-to-population ratio is 193 per 100,000.

There are no separate pre-trial facilities in Romania. All detainees awaiting trial are kept in police lockups until the completion of the police investigation. They are then transferred to prisons to await trial.

The prison system is under the jurisdiction of the Ministry of Justice. Police lockups are under the jurisdiction of the General Police Inspectorate, a division of the Ministry of the Interior.

PRE-TRIAL DETENTION

The duration of pre-trial detention is not limited by law. Those detainees interviewed by Human Rights Watch had been in pre-trial

detention for an average of eight to ten months, with many held much longer. Detainees held in police lockups had little access to fresh air, reading materials, or exercise.

Detainees' contacts with the outside world are severely limited during the criminal investigation. None of the detainees we interviewed were allowed to receive or send correspondence. Few were able to receive visits, although they are theoretically allowed two visits from first degree relatives per month. Although required by law, few detainees had been told that they have a right to legal counsel. No one was allowed to speak to their lawyer in private.

Once detainees are transferred to a prison facility, they are placed under a separate, and slightly more favorable, regime than convicted prisoners.

PHYSICAL CONDITIONS

Physical conditions in Romania's prisons and police lockups reflect decades of neglect, as well as the disastrous economic conditions that currently exist throughout the country. Prisons are old and in disrepair. Mattresses, blankets and prisoners' uniforms are ragged and often dirty. Toilets and showers are primitive, though usually functional. There is only minimal artificial light due to the shortage of light bulbs. Heat is completely inadequate.

The prisons are overcrowded, making it difficult to separate different categories of prisoners, or to provide each prisoner with his or her own bed. Stuffy and cramped cells, as well as the long hours inmates must spend in their cells, contribute to tensions and violence among inmates.

ACTIVITIES AND WORK

All prisoners who are physically able to work are required to do so by law. Romanian prisons have a variety of work programs, including some apprenticeship programs, as well as the opportunity to work outside the prison. However, an increasing number of prisoners have no work due to the high level of unemployment. Those prisoners who do not work are typically locked in their cells at all times during the day except

when they are allowed to exercise. All meals are eaten in the cells (except for lunch at the women's prison and in the reeducation schools).

Prisoners are given the opportunity to acquire at least a minimum of education inside prison. In addition to work and education programs, prisoners have some minimal access to newspapers and broadcast media. None of the prisons we visited had any sports facilities or equipment. The typical exercise area was a walled courtyard where prisoners could walk in a circle. Prisoners rarely get sufficient exercise. Inmates consistently reported that they average between fifteen and twenty minutes of exercise a day, and that there are many days when they do not exercise at all. Inmates who work, inmates in isolation and those who have attempted to escape are not allowed to exercise.

WOMEN PRISONERS

Because women comprise a small proportion of the prison population, they do not experience overcrowding to the same extent as male prisoners. At the time of our mission, Tîrgşori, the only women's prison in Romania, was 23 percent under capacity. Other women prisoners are housed in small sections of men's prisons.

Women prisoners generally have adequate access to gynecological care. In most cases, however, such care is provided by doctors outside the prison. There were no gynecologists on staff at the prisons. Women prisoners frequently do not have adequate sanitary supplies.

There are special regulations governing pregnant women in prisons. They may receive larger packages, additional visits, letters, and more money than other prisoners. Pregnant women appear to receive medical care during pregnancy that is comparable to the care received by other Romanian women. Any complications result in an immediate transfer to Jilava Prison Hospital, or in an emergency, to a local hospital. As a matter of course, pregnant women are transferred to Jilava Prison Hospital after their sixth month. After a woman gives birth, the directorate may interrupt the prison term for a year so that the mother may care for the new infant. This period may be extended by a court.

DISCIPLINARY MEASURES

Under Romanian law, the following disciplinary measures may be taken against a prisoner: warning; withdrawal of one, several, or all rights to receive visits, packages and to send and receive correspondence; simple isolation, up to fifteen days; severe isolation, up to ten days, only with the prison doctor's permission.

Romanian law also provides for punishment by transfer for a period of three to twelve months to a prison where a restrictive regime may be applied. However, according to the Directorate of Prisons, a directive was issued that deprivation of food could no longer be used as a means of punishment. Nevertheless, several inmates reported that they had received a restricted diet (one day bread and water, one day regular caloric intake) while in severe isolation, and several directors expressed the view that food could still be restricted as part of severe isolation.

Severe isolation appears to be the punishment of choice in Romanian prisons, and is used to punish relatively minor breaches of prison rules. Isolation cells contain no furniture other than metal beds that are folded up during the day. Prisoners reported that they are often forced to stand from 5 A.M. to 10 P.M. during their stay in isolation.

One of the most troubling aspects of the Romanian prison system is the continuing use of methods of restraint such as handcuffs and leg irons for long periods solely as a form of punishment. Other humiliating and degrading practices include the shaving of inmates' heads and the requirement that inmates stand with their faces to the wall in the presence of visitors.

CONTACTS WITH THE OUTSIDE

All communications between inmates and outsiders are closely monitored by the prison staff. Families of inmates are allowed to visit from once a month to once a week depending on whether the inmate is in pre-trial detention or is a juvenile or pregnant. Inmates may also receive food packages and personal items from their families. All visits are non-contact and take place in cubicles separated by metal grids. Occasionally, inmates may be authorized to meet visitors at a table. Such contact visits are usually a reward for good behavior, and are rarely granted.

All conversations are monitored by the guards on duty. Visits by lawyers are monitored as well. Prison officials seemed especially concerned that inmates not discuss their trials or prison life with visitors. Prison regulations set out by the directorate in 1988 and still in effect state that, in correspondence with family, the inmate should "not refer to problems regarding his activities in prison."

FOOD

Adequate and nutritious food is a problem throughout Romania. The same is true of the prisons. We received some complaints about the quality and quantity of food. Most prisoners, however, seemed resigned to the food they received.

The quantity of food each prisoner receives is rigidly determined by law. Convicted prisoners who do not work receive 2,900 calories per day. An additional 1,000 calories are added for those who work. Those awaiting trial receive 3,400 calories per day. (During the Ceausescu era, caloric allowances for Romanians who were not in prison were determined by such factors as occupation.) Prison medical staff may authorize additional calories where necessary.

Inmates are allowed to receive packages of a specified weight from their families. These packages may include foodstuffs. In addition, the directorate has recently authorized inmates to receive an additional five kilograms of fresh fruits and vegetables per month. Many inmates, however, do not receive such supplements from their families.

RUSSIAN FEDERATION AND AZERBAIJAN

Human Rights Watch conducted visits to twenty-one facilities in Russia and Azerbaijan in June, July and September 1991. Prison Conditions in the Soviet Union *was published in December 1991, on the eve of the country's breakup.*

Our 1991 report on prison conditions in Russia and Azerbaijan was published on the eve of the collapse of the Soviet Union, a country that at the time had one of the highest prisoner-to-population ratios in the world. The Soviet Union has since fragmented into fifteen nation-states, whose Soviet-based prison systems were more or less identical. While the 1991 report was limited to two republics, prison conditions in other republics most likely did not differ significantly from those in Russia and Azerbaijan. In the future, prison arrangements and conditions in each former republic will likely vary as the sovereign states change their Soviet-inherited criminal justice systems.

THE SOVIET PRISON SYSTEM

The Soviet prison system, which still exists in the Russian Federation and Azerbaijan, consists of four main types of establishments: pre-trial detention centers, labor colonies, closed prisons, and colony settlements.

Pre-trial detention centers hold detainees through trial, and also after conviction and sentencing until their appeals have been exhausted. Labor colonies were the most common form of post-trial incarceration in the Soviet Union, and continue to be so in Russia and Azerbaijan. The colonies are segregated by sex and by "regime," which depends on the convict's criminal record and the type of crime committed, and determines the level of prison security and prisoner privileges.[1]   A

---

[1] In Russian terminology, "regimes" are, in order of increasing severity, general regime, strict regime, strengthened regime, and special regime (there are no special regime women's labor colonies).   They correspond roughly to minimum security, medium security, medium-maximum security, and maximum

217

fundamental problem with this system is that it often makes nonviolent repeat offenders and violent criminals serve terms together in special regime colonies.   A labor colony (or labor camp) is bounded by a perimeter fence of barbed wire manned by armed guards.   The compound inside consists of open living barracks, one or more factories, medical facilities, a dining hall, a commissary, and other facilities.

Convicted criminals who are judged to be especially dangerous or who misbehave in labor colonies can be sent to closed prisons, where they live in locked cells (as opposed to the open barracks of the labor colonies) and are required to work, but not under the relatively open circumstances of the labor colonies.

Colony settlements, which have no armed guards and the widest inmate privileges, are the least restrictive form of incarceration, but often entail harsh living and working conditions.

PHYSICAL CONDITIONS

Conditions in pre-trial detention facilities, where detainees may be held for years awaiting trial, packed into overcrowded, airless cells with appalling living conditions for twenty-three hours per day, were typically the worst in the Soviet prison system.   All of the pre-trial centers Human Rights Watch visited in 1991 were decrepit, lacked ventilation, hot in summer, cold in winter (we were told), and smelly.   Detainees were packed into cells in which double and triple-decker bunks and a toilet take up almost all available space.   Inmates ate and used the toilet in their cells.   Although inmates were entitled to one shower per week, showers often did not work or were scarce.

Overall, conditions in pre-trial detention and administrative detention facilities in Russia remain abominable due to the continued lack of an effective bail system and, more generally, to an unreformed and sluggish criminal justice system.[2]   Our 1991 report noted that detainees languish without justification for an average of four to six months, and

---

security.

[2] Under Russian law, individuals may be detained for up to fifteen days of "administrative punishment" without trial for minor offenses upon the decision of a judge.

in many cases for much longer, in violation of Russian law and international standards. Today a large number of individuals under criminal investigation are in custody, despite the fact that by law they may be released until trial provided they sign a statement promising not to leave the city in which they reside.

More than 200,000 individuals are currently held in pre-trial detention facilities and the overall number of pre-trial detainees is rising rapidly: In February 1993 alone it rose by 8,000 persons, and similar increases in the prison population are projected for March and April 1993, due mainly to a new anti-crime campaign.

Overcrowding in pre-trial facilities is particularly acute in big cities such as Moscow, St. Petersburg, and Ekaterinburg as well as in regional capitals, where there are twice as many inmates as beds. In Moscow's pre-trial facilities inmates sleep in three separate shifts and suffer from swollen legs simply because there is nowhere to sit.

Living conditions in labor colonies compare favorably to those in pre-trial detention centers. When Human Rights Watch visited labor colony barracks in the summer of 1991, they were quite clean, had decent ventilation, and had comfortable temperatures, including in Azerbaijan, where temperatures can reach 90 degrees fahrenheit in the summer. Winter temperatures are a problem in Russian labor colonies, however. Plumbing is primitive in most colonies, although comparable in many cases to conditions in freedom. Toilets and showers are dirty and smelly.

WORK

In pre-trial facilities, inmates awaiting appeal (and, in theory, with the permission of the procurator, inmates awaiting trial) work at maintenance jobs at the prison facilities. Inmates at labor colonies are required to work, and although by Russian law the work week may not exceed forty-eight hours, local prison administrators may decide the exact number of hours inmates must work. Prison labor typically involves furniture making and finishing, lumbering, construction, and small-scale metalwork. Prisoners receive nominal salaries. Work conditions in colony factories are primitive, and although the work often involves contact with harmful chemicals or dangerous machines, few if any labor safety procedures are followed.

Work conditions in the "forest" colony settlements are among the worst in the entire prison system. Prisoners at Solikamsk (in the northern Urals) routinely work outdoors in extremely cold temperatures (as low as -40 degrees fahrenheit), and have to be driven two hours to and from the work site in unheated trucks.

The Russian Federation's system of prison labor colonies to this day is considered an important part of the country's production of goods. Formally, inmates are, as in the past, required to work. In reality, even though most prisoners reportedly want to work, a 30 percent unemployment rate is reported in Russian labor colonies. This corresponds to the growing unemployment in the Russian economy, and the chaos that has resulted from a rocky transition to a market economy.

PUNISHMENT

Pre-trial detention centers, labor colonies, and closed prisons share a similar structure of disciplinary sanctions, which ranges from informal warnings, formal reprimands and restriction of privileges, to terms in "punishment cells." Despite this graded structure, almost any violation of prison regulations—from using the informal "you" with prison guards to acts of serious violence—trigger terms of up to fifteen days in punishment cells. Physical deprivation is clearly used as a form of punishment in these cells. The cells are very small (about eleven by ten feet for a three-person cell), have stucco walls (which are painful to lean against), often have no windows, and have very dirty toilets. Beds in punishment cells have no mattresses. Prisoners are forbidden from having personal possessions with them, and are denied most other privileges as well, including exercise time. Isolation—considered a severe form of punishment—is discretionary in labor colonies, and mandatory in closed prisons. Although by law prison officials can no longer use reduced diet as a method of punishment, in 1991 Human Rights Watch found that a female inmate serving a term in a punishment cell in Azerbaijan was illegally being fed reduced rations.

CONTACTS WITH THE OUTSIDE

Prisoners in pre-trial detention may not receive visitors or send letters unless the investigator in charge of their case (or, in the case or criminal appellants, a judge) specifically allows it. Both types of inmates may receive mail, including one food package per month. More contacts with the outside are allowed in labor colonies, where inmates have the right to three short visits (usually four hours each) and two long visits (three days) per year. They may receive two packages of printed matter per year and send an unlimited number of letters. Mail is read in both directions and may be censored.

As noted above, the type of prison and the type of regime in which the inmate is serving affect inmate privileges, including contacts with the outside. In closed prisons, inmates may send only one letter per month; those serving in strict regime may send only one every two months.

UPRISINGS

Beginning in 1989 inmates in Russia staged protests, hunger strikes and riots, due in part to the unbearable conditions in Soviet prisons. This trend reached a peak in 1991, when, in a wave of prison uprisings in Tselinograd and Krasnoiarsk (the latter lasted forty days), inmates attempted to draw attention to staff abuse, inhumane conditions in punishment cells, and poor medical care. No uprisings were reported in Azerbaijan.

The dramatic wave of uprisings in labor colonies ebbed toward the end of 1991 and the beginning of 1992. This may be accounted for by the increasing humaneness within the prison system and the widening of the discretion and powers of labor colony administrations. The drop in prison uprisings coincided with a sharp drop in the number of hostage seizures, attacks on guards, and various forms of opposition activities against prison administration.

RUSSIAN FEDERATION

The Russian Federation continues to have the former Soviet Union's high prisoner-per-population ratio. Its current prison population—including convicts, those awaiting trial and those serving in other types of custody—numbers close to 500,000, or 335 prisoners per 100,000 in the Russian Federation. All figures cited in this section are as of March 1993.

Prison Structure

The Main Administration of Corrections and Punishment (Glavniy Upravleniie Ispolneniia Nakazanij, or GUIN) of the Ministry of Interior of the Russian Federation is the government agency with jurisdiction over the prison system, presiding over 744 prison facilities with a capacity of 617,000. Russia's 159 pre-trial detention facilities and jails are severely overcrowded, with a capacity for 166,000 and a current population of 209,000.

The 57 general regime labor colonies for men are operating at near capacity: 75,000 inmates live in facilities meant to hold 77,800. Strengthened regime prisons for those already serving prison sentences have a capacity of 286,000 and hold 198,000. The 104 strengthened regime labor colonies have a capacity of 144,000 and hold 102,000. There are 23 special regime labor camps for inmates who are considered especially dangerous recidivists. They have a capacity of 20,500 and currently hold 17,800. Strengthened regime facilities are always maintained separately from other facilities.

Women inmates number 16,900 in a system of 25 colonies intended for 36,500, and are placed in only two types of facilities: minimum and medium security. Prison conditions in these facilities are identical to their counterparts for men, with the exception that regular inmates and recidivists are held in separate facilities. The latter facilities can hold 2,000; currently 1,401 women are serving in them.

In certain women's facilities inmates may have their children with them. According to amendments to the criminal code, women currently serving sentences who had less than one year left to serve when the amendments were adopted may keep their children with them until they are released.

It is important to note, however, that many other government agencies and ministries are involved in detaining citizens and are not represented in the statistical update that follows. They include:

- the Public Order Administration, which supervises police lockups;
- the Special Timber Colonies of the Ministry of Internal Affairs, which has its own labor colonies and prisons, and which uses prisoners for heavy, timber-related labor;
- the Ministry of Health, which oversees special psychiatric prison hospitals;
- Alcohol-Rehabilitation Centers (where alcoholics are "cured" through labor), which are under the direct jurisdiction of the Ministry of Internal Affairs;
- the Ministry of Defense, which has its own disciplinary battalions and military detention center.

Although we do not discuss these agencies and facilities, they should be included in the future work of human rights and prisoners' rights projects because, among other reasons, they confine a large number of people.[3]

Overall Evaluation and Recent Developments

Six months after the Soviet Union's disintegration, Russia adopted a package of amendments to its criminal code, code of criminal procedure, and corrective-labor code that reflect the challenge the other new states face in improving the notorious Soviet prison systems. The amendments, adopted June 12, 1992, provided for an amnesty for certain categories of prisoners and made minor improvements in prison conditions. While welcome, these amendments have not fundamentally changed the Russian Federation's poor prison conditions, a direct legacy of the Soviet Union. The recent changes include:

---

[3] Perhaps as many as 1,600,000 in the entire former USSR. See Galinskii, *Argumenty i Fakty*, no. 41, 1991.

- vacations for inmates;[4]
- churches of various faiths were permitted to operate in prison facilities;
- inmates may now use telephones (technical problems, however, detract from this new privilege);
- special force militia detachments, known in Russian as OMON, (equivalent to riot police) and their counterparts from the Ministry of Internal Affairs that were used to put down prison disturbances or to carry out searches of prison establishments and were previously unregulated by GUIN, were placed under GUIN supervision at the end of 1992;
- prior to the June 12 legislative changes, a December 1991 Presidential Decree had granted inmates at labor colonies the right to receive their full salaries, as opposed to the 50 percent until then; previously the other half of an inmate's earnings was deducted as prisoner upkeep costs.

AZERBAIJAN

The following information relates only to the Department of Corrections (UID) of the Ministry of Justice of Azerbaijan and does not include penal establishments supervised by other state agencies. Only corrective labor colonies, parole centers, and open prison institutions fall within the jurisdiction of the UID. Pre-trial facilities and police lockups are under the jurisdiction of the Azerbaijan Ministry of Internal Affairs.

---

[4] According to information provided by the Russian government, from the time when the June 12, 1992, amendments took effect through the end of 1992, 4,300 inmates of labor colonies in the Russian Federation got vacations that included the right to leave the grounds of their respective labor colonies. In addition, about 4,000 took their vacations on the territory of the labor colonies. Many of the institutions, for example those in Cheliabinsk, have special vacation facilities for inmates. About 1,500 inmates received extended visits with relatives or friends, in special buildings located just outside the facility.

Of the 4,300 inmates who took vacations off prison grounds, 128 violated rules regarding the length of their vacation; searches are out for 38 missing inmates, 7 committed new crimes during their vacation, and 10 violated various administrative rules.

Types of Institutions under UID

Azerbaijan's 16 labor colonies have a capacity of 10,000 and a population of 5,053 inmates (or 80 inmates per 100,000 inhabitants of Azerbaijan). Among them are two minimum security colonies, four medium security colonies, three medium-to-maximum security colonies, and one women's colony (total population: 60), and one colony for juveniles (total population: 90). Between two and four square meters of living space is allotted to each inmate. Certain colonies have their own medium and medium-to-maximum security sectors.

Internal rules governing prison facilities are identical to their Russian Federation counterparts. Previous limits on visits and packages have been abolished for inmates of all categories except those serving *prison*, as opposed to labor, colony sentences. Inmates may not make phone calls.

Azerbaijan has maintained mandatory labor because the government cannot afford to absorb the entire cost of prisoner maintenance. Many prisoners currently want to work because the government has abolished all limits on the amount of money inmates may spend at labor colony stores, where food and other consumer goods are available.

Developments and Legislation

Azerbaijan was the first post-Soviet state to transfer its prison system from the Ministry of Internal Affairs (where it consisted of corrective-punitive bodies) to the jurisdiction of the Ministry of Justice. This reorganization, brought into effect by President Abulfaz Elchibey on January 9, 1993, was announced as a measure to humanize the prison system. Indeed, the preamble to President Elchibey's decree declared that these fundamental changes in the prison system were aimed at improving the system of judicial decisions and making the entire corrections process better and more humane for inmates.

In recent times, there have been no instances of prison disturbances in the Azerbaijan prison system.

SOUTH AFRICA

Human Rights Watch conducted an investigation of prison conditions in South Africa in 1992 and 1993. During the course of two separate missions to the country, the following prisons were visited: Pretoria Central, Durban Westville, Robben Island, Pollsmoor, Rooigrond (Bophuthatswana), Umtata Central and Wellington (Transkei), Brandvlei, Kroonstad, Barberton and Modderbee. A report on prison conditions in South Africa will be published in the course of 1993.

Prison conditions in South Africa have been directly affected by the political changes in the country since the beginning of 1990. Significant reforms of the system have been implemented, and conditions have improved in some respects. Nevertheless, at 355 prisoners per 100,000 citizens, South Africa continues to have one of the highest prisoner-to-population ratios in the world, and many aspects of prison life remain depressingly unchanged from the years of official apartheid.[1] In particular, South African prisons are places of extreme violence, where assaults on prisoners by warders or other prisoners are common and not infrequently fatal.

Perhaps the most important result from the political developments affecting prisons in South Africa has been the release of large numbers of security prisoners.[2] In addition, the South African government has repealed racially discriminatory legislation relating to the

---

[1] The total number of prisoners in South Africa, excluding the nominally independent homelands, passed 110,000 in October/November 1992. Population statistics in South Africa are notoriously unreliable, but the figure for the same area is estimated to be thirty-one million. The ratio from these figures is roughly 355 per 100,000. However, prison statistics for the "independent" TBVC states (Transkei, Bophuthatswana, Venda and Ciskei—together estimated to have a population of 7.5 million) are not easily obtainable, and could skew this ratio.

[2] Approximately 1,400 prisoners sentenced for security offenses were released during 1990, 1991 and 1992, under the terms of agreements between the government and the African National Congress (ANC). The independent Human Rights Commission, a South African nongovernmental organization, claims that up to 250 security prisoners may still be in custody.

prison system, and the desegregation of prisons has begun. The Prisons Service has been separated from the Department of Justice and renamed the Department of Correctional Services; a new non-custodial sentence of "correctional supervision" has been introduced; and the imposition of the death penalty has been drastically curtailed, while a moratorium on hangings is in place. However, State President F. W. de Klerk announced in March 1993 that parliament would be given the opportunity to vote on the resumption of hangings.

Meanwhile, an attempt has been made to address the question of overcrowding. Common law prisoners have benefitted from successive general amnesties explicitly aimed to address the problem of severe overcrowding of many prisons. Tens of thousands of prisoners were granted early release during 1991 and 1992, though most of them would have been released within a few months in any event. In January 1993 the government stated that the prison system then held 110,000 prisoners in accommodations designed for approximately 84,000 (an overcrowding rate of 23 percent), and that the sentences of 7,500 prisoners would be remitted. In March 1993 the early release of a further 6,000 prisoners was announced.

VIOLENCE IN PRISONS

The most striking feature of prison life in South Africa is its violence. An elaborate gang structure operates throughout the prison system, and riots between different gangs take place regularly; individual cases of assault occur on a daily basis, and sexual abuse is common. There is substantial evidence of collusion by warders in the gang system, even to the extent of instigating murder. In addition, assaults by prison warders on prisoners occur frequently. During 1991 prisoners made 1,426 complaints regarding assaults committed by warders (it is certain that many incidents are not reported); sixty-three warders were subsequently charged with assault, and twenty-four were found guilty.[3]

---

[3] Information given to Parliament by Minister of Correctional Services Adriaan Vlok, March 13, 1992. *SA Barometer*, vol. 6, no. 19 (September 25, 1992).

CLASSIFICATION OF PRISONERS

South African prisoners are classified not only according to a security assessment, but also by "privilege group." Prisoners are assigned to one designation among groups A, B, C, or D, and receive a different package of privileges according to their group. All prisoners start in group C; their classification is reviewed biannually by an "Institutional Committee," which grades individual prisoners according to their behavior. Under this system, visits, letters, access to reading material or television and many other aspects of prison life are all considered privileges.

PUNISHMENT

The threat of reclassification within the privilege system or the assigning of a different security status are the most important means of control over the individual prisoner; however, other forms of punishment are available, including the isolation of the prisoner, with or without a limited diet, and corporal punishment.[4]   Prisoners are sometimes assaulted while in solitary confinement. Groups of prisoners are often punished collectively for gang activity.

PHYSICAL CONDITIONS

South African prisons must be amongst the cleanest in the world, although prisons in the homelands tend to be more run down. Overcrowding means, however, that in some prisons cells with adequate facilities for twenty prisoners may hold forty or more. Moreover, there are significant variations between and within prisons. Many prisoners do not have beds, but sleep on mats on the floor; some prisons do not have dining halls, so prisoners are obliged to eat outdoors or in their cells.

---

[4] Minister of Correctional Services Adriaan Vlok stated to Parliament on March 16, 1992 that prisoners had been deprived of one or more meal on 27,930 occasions during 1991; and that corporal punishment, not exceeding six strokes, had been used forty-four times. Ibid.

Rural prisons, whose inmates are usually many hundreds of miles from their homes and therefore do not receive regular visits, often have the worst conditions.

RACIAL DISCRIMINATION

The most significant variations in physical conditions arise from the different treatment of white and black prisoners. Apartheid in the prison system has formally ended and whites and blacks are now held in the same prisons. Even so, whites often receive better treatment, ranging from housing in less crowded cells to greater access to training facilities and less onerous work. Some blacks held in formerly white prisons benefit from the historically better conditions afforded to whites; few whites are exposed to the worst prisons in the system, and most continue to be held in the better-equipped prisons previously reserved for "Europeans."

ACTIVITIES AND WORK

In most medium security prisons, prisoners are obliged to work. They may be employed as agricultural laborers on large prison farms; elsewhere, they may work as cleaners, gardeners, or maintenance staff on or off the prison premises. They are not paid, although those in more skilled occupations may receive a gratuity of up to the equivalent of a few dollars a month. Prisoners in maximum security prisons often do not work, and may as a consequence be confined to their cells for all but a half hour or hour-long exercise period per day. This inactivity is an important factor in the perpetuation of the gang system.

In the prisons visited by Human Rights Watch, most prisoners had access to sports at least once a week. Televisions and radios are allowed, but prisoners have to pay for them. Prisoners may study, but beyond the most basic level, must pay their own way. Job training to a quite sophisticated level is available in some prisons, usually those that formerly housed only white prisoners; in many prisons, however, there is little or no attempt to provide prisoners with training to support themselves other than by crime once they are released.

WOMEN

As in most countries, women form a small proportion of the prison population in South Africa. As a consequence, they are not subject to the same conditions of overcrowding as the male prisoners. Since there are few women's prisons, they too may be held far from their families; for those with young children this is a particular hardship. Children up to two years of age may stay with their mothers in prison.

PRE-TRIAL DETENTION

A large proportion of South African prisoners are held awaiting trial. Delay in the judicial process is one of the principal contributors to overcrowding and, while most prisoners awaiting trial are brought to court within a few months, some may remain in prison for over a year.[5] Prisoners awaiting trial receive better treatment than sentenced prisoners in some respects: they may wear their own clothes and are allowed a greater number of visits; however, the overcrowding may be worse, there are no opportunities for prisoners awaiting trial to work, and the gang system operates equally in awaiting trial cells. Pre-trial detention does not automatically count towards a prisoner's sentence, although a judge *may* order that time spent awaiting trial should be considered time served.

POLICE LOCKUPS

Many if not most prisoners are held in police lock-ups before their first appearance in court (which should be within forty-eight hours of arrest), after which they are usually transferred to prison. Prisoners

---

[5] As of December 31, 1991, 23,694 prisoners of a total prison population of 96,908 were awaiting trial. A government survey of all prisoners awaiting trial carried out on January 2, 1991, indicated that such prisoners had been held in custody as follows: one to 14 days, 25.7 percent; 14 days to one month, 30.5 percent; one to three months, 33 percent; between three and six months, 8.3 percent; longer than six months, 2.5 percent. However, in a survey of five urban prisons in February 1991, 16.29 percent of awaiting trial prisoners had been held longer than six months. Ibid.

may also be detained in lockups while awaiting trial, for periods up to several weeks, with judicial authority.

SECURITY PRISONERS

During the emergency that was in force between 1985 and 1990, many thousands were detained under the emergency regulations. Mass long-term detention of this type has ceased, although emergency-type laws still apply in "unrest areas" declared by the government in many black townships. In addition, detentions for interrogation or for preventive purposes are authorized under the Internal Security Act. Extensive amendments to the Internal Security Act adopted in 1991 have significantly improved conditions for security detainees, historically subject to extreme levels of abuse, and in most respects they are now legally subject to the same treatment as unconvicted prisoners.

JUDGMENT DEBTORS

South Africa is unusual in providing for the incarceration of judgment debtors; that is, persons against whom there is an outstanding judgment in a civil proceeding. If possible, judgment debtors are supposed to be segregated from other prisoners; however, if this is not possible because of the small number of prisoners of the same category, judgment debtors may be housed with other unsentenced prisoners. This was the case in those prisons visited by Human Rights Watch. In other respects, the conditions of their detention are similar to those for awaiting trial prisoners.

SPAIN

In 1991 Human Rights Watch wrote to the Spanish Ministry of Justice to request permission to conduct prison inspections. The Spanish government refused. We were able to visit two prisons in Cataluña, but both are managed independently from Madrid and we were not allowed to see any of those facilities we specifically requested to inspect, particularly the Modelo prison in Barcelona. We were able to inspect police lockups both in Madrid and in Barcelona, however, and our findings were published in Prison Conditions in Spain, *simultaneously released in Spanish.*

Despite the government ban, we did see one prison in Madrid. Judge Manuela Carmena, who at the time was the Penitentiary Judge in charge of the Carabanchel prison, suggested that our delegation accompany her on her routine visit to that prison. Her decision was met with resistance from the facility's director and, so as to protect him from possible repercussions, Judge Carmena wrote an affidavit stating that she assumed jurisdictional responsibility for our presence within the prison.

A few months later, at the time of the opening of the Commission on Security and Cooperation in Europe human rights meeting in Moscow in September 1991, Human Rights Watch published a twenty-page document that described aspects of prison conditions in six European countries and the United States. The document received wide publicity in Spain, with several major newspapers pointing out in their coverage that Spain and Turkey were the only two countries that had refused access to their prisons. A few days later, Antoni Asunción, the head of the Spanish Prison System, announced that he was directing a request to the General Council of the Judiciary to discipline Manuela Carmena for taking our delegation on a tour of the Carabanchel prison.

There was a wide response in Spain to the vindictiveness displayed by the Spanish prison administration in this instance. In addition to numerous press articles and coverage in broadcast media, 1,500 individuals, including several hundred lawyers, numerous intellectuals, and other personalities signed an advertisement in support of Manuela Carmena. In December, the General Council decided that Judge Carmena had committed no disciplinary infraction and closed the case. In early 1993, Judge Carmena was elected to the prestigious post of Dean of Judges in Madrid.

Severe overcrowding, violence, and idleness are the three major problems of Spanish prisons. Eighteen years after the death of Generalissimo Francisco Franco and the advent of democracy, prison conditions are among the most serious human rights concerns in Spain.

As of January 1993, Spain held approximately 42,600 inmates (up from 36,000 two years earlier) in a system consisting of 93 prisons, nine of them in the autonomous region of Cataluña (surrounding Barcelona), with a combined capacity of 25,000 spaces. Of the total prison population, 32.7 percent are pre-trial detainees. Women account for approximately 9.2 percent of prisoners. About 500 inmates nationwide are security prisoners, confined on charges of or sentenced for terrorism.

PRE-TRIAL DETENTION

Under Spanish law, pre-trial detention may last for as long as four years and, indeed, many detainees await trial for extended periods. The Ombudsman of Cataluña commented in. an interview that by the time some individuals go to trial, they have already completed their entire potential sentences.

Following an arrest, a detainee may be held in a police lockup for up to seventy-two hours, after which time he or she must be released or transferred to a prison. In prisons, pre-trial detainees are generally afforded the same conditions as sentenced prisoners and are often housed together with them. The one significant distinction is that pre-trial detainees are unable to benefit from a fairly generous system of furloughs for certain categories of sentenced prisoners.

PHYSICAL CONDITIONS

Overcrowding is one of the chief problems in the country's prisons. In male prisons, two or three prisoners are usually housed in cells designed for one (the General Penitentiary Organic Law of 1979 requires that all prisoners should be housed in individual cells; this provision, like many other stipulations of this law, is seldom observed in practice). In the one female prison we visited in Barcelona, inmates were housed in larger cells, holding up to sixteen people. In order to cope with the lack of space, some of the beds were triple-level bunks.

According to information from the Spanish Association for Human Rights, some prisons occasionally resort to the use of bunks with four levels. Cells were tidy and clean, but patios were full of trash and quite filthy.

Inmates and relatives of inmates told us in interviews that some prisons were very cold during the winter and extremely hot during the summer. In the south of Spain temperatures can get as high as 115 degrees fahrenheit, and there is no air conditioning in prisons. Conversely, some prisons in the north of the country, where it often gets below freezing, lack functioning central heating.

Cells in police stations were windowless, badly lit, and poorly ventilated; most were also filthy. The only piece of "furniture" in all four of the lockups we visited was an elevated platform serving as a bed, often for several detainees at a time. We saw some extremely dirty blankets and plastic mattresses. Cells did not have toilets or sinks. We were told that detainees "did not use showers," even though there were showers near the cells. In the Madrid station we visited, cells were empty during our visit because inmates had been transferred shortly before our arrival (transfers, we were told, are often made several times a day). In Barcelona, we observed overcrowding and people sleeping on the floor of a police lockup.

ACTIVITIES

One of the most frequently heard complaints about Spanish prisons is that prisoners have nothing to do. Most spend their entire days in the large prison patios, playing cards or guitar, drinking coffee (which can be purchased from a canteen that operates like a store, with access for inmates for several hours during the day) or occasionally playing soccer. During "patio hours" prisoners are not allowed to go back to their cells.

Some prisons offer limited educational opportunities. Only a small proportion of inmates have any kind of jobs (20 percent, as of two years ago), and of those only about a quarter have paying jobs.

DISCIPLINARY MEASURES

Inmates who disobey the rules are punished with a number of measures, ranging from a loss of privileges to segregation. Even though, under the law, segregation may not last more than fourteen days, in practice, we were told, consecutive sanctions are sometimes applied and inmates can end up spending as long as forty-five days in solitary confinement.

Inmates deemed particularly dangerous by prison authorities are placed under a special regime, known as Security Level One. As of 1991, there were almost 1,600 inmates in this category. The Level One regime is characterized by nearly total lockdown and isolation. Such inmates are allowed out of their cells for at most two hours a day; that is the only time when they are allowed to interact with anyone other than their cellmates. Communications through the window with prisoners in other cells is prohibited. In some cases, inmates are not allowed to lie down on their beds during the day. Every six months, each Level One inmate's case comes up for review by the correctional authorities.

Most inmates held under the anti-terrorist law are subject to the Level One regime. Pre-trial detainees who are deemed particularly dangerous (including all those held on charges of terrorism) are also subject to that regime.

A frequent disciplinary measure not included in the official list of sanctions is the transfer of an inmate to a different institution. Spain is a relatively large country and assignment to a prison distant from one's home constitutes a significant hardship both for the inmate and for his or her relatives. This measure is particularly applied to suspected riot leaders.

We also received reports of excessive violence by prison officials. Such incidents are especially likely to occur during riots or other acts of group disobedience.

CONTACTS WITH THE OUTSIDE WORLD

Spanish law allows incommunicado detention for up to five days following the arrest and for an additional three days at any time during the incarceration; this second period of isolation must be authorized by a judge.

All inmates are entitled to two visits per week, at least twenty minutes in length. All such visits are conducted through a partition that prevents any physical contact. In addition, prison regulations make it possible for most inmates to receive so-called vis-a-vis visits, usually once every two months. These encounters are either conjugal visits or family visits in private rooms and can last for up to three hours.

Prisoners who have completed one-fourth of their sentence, and are not classified as Level One, are entitled to furloughs. Mail is unrestricted in quantity but may be opened and is often read. Inmates are allowed to make a single phone call about once a month.

As indicated above, we received repeated complaints about the suddenness of transfers of inmates from one institution to another, often at a great distance. Relatives are not notified until after the transfer, and there have been cases in which visitors undertook a trip to visit an inmate only to discover the transfer.

Access for prisoner rights groups, which used to be quite frequent, has been restricted in recent years due to a change in the policy of the Ministry of Justice.

WOMEN INMATES

Four women's prisons in Spain house the majority of Spain's female inmates. In addition, there are several female sections attached to male institutions. These annexes are often very small, sometimes holding as few as two inmates. These small annexes usually offer very little in terms of educational or recreational opportunities. On the other hand, women housed in the few large institutions, are often held far away from their relatives and receive few visits.

TURKEY

Human Rights Watch first conducted an investigation into conditions in prisons in Turkey and issued a report, Prison Conditions in Turkey, *in 1989. Because the Turkish government refused to permit the delegation to visit prisons, the report was based on interviews with recently-released prisoners, prison experts, lawyers and human rights activists. In 1992 a mission visited detention centers in police stations with the permission and cooperation of the government and interviewed former prisoners, then published* Broken Promises: Torture and Killings Continue in Turkey. *Minister of Justice Seyfi Oktay told the 1992 mission that future visits to prisons in Turkey would be permitted.*

Most of those suspected of crimes in Turkey, either ordinary or political, are brutally tortured by police during interrogation. These suspects are detained for periods far in excess of what is permitted by the European Convention on Human Rights. Few have access to attorneys during the period of interrogation, before charges are brought. Pre-trial detainees may be detained for long periods—sometimes for years—while awaiting trial or during lengthy trials. Once in prison, some inmates are beaten—sometimes in collective punishments—and subjected to harsh punishments in overcrowded cells, often in inhumane conditions.

Turkey aspires to full membership in the European Community and describes its efforts to improve its prisons as attempting to attain "European standards." Moreover, Turkey has ratified both the United Nations and European Conventions against Torture and other Cruel, Inhuman, or Degrading Treatment or Punishment. But abuse of detainees and prisoners continues.

In December 1988, 51,897 prisoners and detainees were incarcerated in Turkey's 644 prisons and detention facilities. Additional prisons have been built since 1988. The country's prisoner-to-population ratio in 1988 was 99 per 100,000. In 1991 thousands of prisoners were released under an amnesty. Human Rights Watch does not know how many prisoners remain in Turkish prisons at present.

Prisons are run by the Ministry of Justice. Police lockups are run by the Ministry of the Interior.

PRE-TRIAL DETENTION

An unknown number of inmates are held in police custody in Turkey before being charged. Some are held in ordinary cells in police stations; some are held in interrogation centers that are part of large police stations. Most detainees, both those suspected of political crimes and those suspected of ordinary crimes, are brutally tortured—women and children as well as men—during interrogation by police. Many are convicted only on the basis of confessions elicited during the interrogation period.

Torture techniques regularly used include: suspension by the arms or wrists, which are often first tied behind the back of a naked, blindfolded victim; electric shock to the genitals and other sensitive parts of the body; *falaka* (beating the soles of the feet until they swell and bleed, sometimes making it impossible for victims to stand); rape, both vaginal and anal, sometimes using truncheons or gun barrels; shooting highly-pressurized water at victims who are sometimes restrained in rubber tires; severe beatings with sticks and truncheons; pulling victims by the hair, sometimes pulling out clumps of hair; pulling hair from victims' beards or mustaches; placing victims on blocks of ice; forcing victims' heads into excrement; or placing victims in small cells with attack dogs who attack and bite them.

After legal charges, if any, are filed, defendants are held in a prison where those awaiting trial, those on trial, and those already sentenced, are often mixed together, although the law prohibits such mixing. Because trials in Turkey can take many years and some involve hundreds of defendants, inmates often spend many years in the pre-trial or trial phase. Some defendants who serve long periods of incarceration are ultimately acquitted. Time served in pre-trial detention counts toward an ultimate sentence.

Hundreds of people suspected of belonging to Dev Sol, an extremist group that espouses violence for political purposes, were arrested in 1982. Some were released from custody in 1987, after serving five years in detention. Others remained in custody until a verdict was reached in 1991, a total of nine years.

A legal reform bill enacted in 1992 differentiates between those suspected of ordinary crimes, who are to be tried in criminal courts, and those suspected of political crimes, who are tried in State Security Courts, special courts designed to cope with acts or threats of political violence.

State Security Courts were re-established by the 1982 Constitution, following the 1980 military coup. Originally set up in 1973, the courts were held unconstitutional in 1976. The purpose of these courts is to deal with offenses against the "indivisible integrity of the State with its territory and nation, and free democratic order, or against the republic, whose characteristics are defined in the Constitution, and offenses directed against the internal and external security of the state." The eight State Security Courts currently deal for the most part with crimes covered by the Anti-Terror Act of 1989, an extremely broad statute that, among other things, permits prosecution of those criticizing the state. State Security Courts reportedly heard about 4,600 cases in 1991.

Under the new law, ordinary criminal suspects may be detained for twenty-four hours for individual crimes before being taken before a court, and may be detained for up to eight days for collective crimes (crimes committed by more than one person). Human Rights Watch does not know whether these time limits are observed.

Under the new law, political suspects can be, and are, detained for far longer—for as long as thirty days before appearing before a judge.

These eight-day and thirty-day detentions are in clear violation of the European Convention on Human Rights. In 1988 the European Court of Human Rights held that a detention period of four days and six hours violated Article 5(3) of the European Convention of Human Rights, which provides that detainees must be brought "promptly" before a judge.[1]

The 1992 legal reform bill provides that ordinary suspects may have immediate access to attorneys, but that political suspects may not. Reports from Turkey indicate that in neither case are detainees routinely permitted access to attorneys.

PRISON CONDITIONS

Prisons are divided on the basis of security—open, semi-open and closed. Special closed prisons exist for prisoners deemed to have committed particularly serious crimes.

---

[1] *Brogan v. United Kingdom* (1988).

Our 1988 mission found that prison inmates were deliberately abused. Among the abuses were brutal beatings, although the systematic beatings that took place between 1980 and 1984 appeared to have substantially decreased in frequency. Reports of some collective beatings continue in 1993, however. Our 1989 mission found excessively harsh punishments involving the deprivation of basic necessities like food and medical care; intolerable punishment cells; discrimination against political prisoners; and unusually onerous rules. The mission also found pervasive corruption among prison guards.

The mission found overcrowding in some prisons (six men in a six by ten foot cell with three double-decker bunks and a hole-in-the-floor toilet). Many cells were infested with rats, mice and insects, were filthy, had vile smells and a lack of air and water. Clean water was unavailable in some prisons. Food was disgusting. About fifty cents a day was provided to feed each inmate. Adequate medical care was unavailable.

CONDITIONS IN POLICE INTERROGATION CENTERS IN 1992

In August 1992, the Turkish government permitted a Human Rights Watch mission to visit police interrogation centers in four cities: Ankara, Istanbul, Adana and Antalya. Most of the cells in the interrogation centers were empty at the time of the visit. Our mission found clean, bare cells, often with no beds or bedding. The government has issued orders that cells in police stations are to be brought up to "European standards," with adequate light, air, space and proper sleeping facilities.

UNITED KINGDOM

Human Rights Watch conducted two investigations of prison conditions in the United Kingdom. In June 1991 a delegation visited eight prisons and published Prison Conditions in the United Kingdom *the following year. In February 1993 we visited two prisons in London as part of a follow-up investigation.*

At the time of our 1991 visit to prisons in England and Northern Ireland, British prisons had recently experienced a wave of bloody and destructive riots and had come under close scrutiny by an independent commission. Between April 1 and 9, 1990, riots took place in twenty-six prisons, leaving 220 staff members and ninety-six inmates injured. One inmate died in a fire, one was injured in a way that might have contributed to his subsequent death and one of the inmates involved in rioting committed suicide after the riot ended. Several prisons were seriously damaged, with one left in need of total rebuilding. In response to the riots, the Home Secretary appointed an independent commission, headed by Lord Justice Woolf to conduct an inquiry into how and why the disturbances took place. The findings, known as the Woolf Report, were very critical of the state of affairs in British prisons including the system's frequent failure to comply with its obligation to treat prisoners with humanity and fairness. The Woolf Report subsequently served as a blueprint for prison reform. The main problems that led to the riots—terrible overcrowding, lack of in-cell plumbing and idleness for most prisoners—were still evident when we visited. Shortly thereafter, a series of steps, including both structural and policy changes designed to reform the British prisons, were undertaken. In addition, a new law that went into effect in October 1992 contributed to a significant decrease of the number in prisoners. Our February 1993 follow-up visit to two London prisons revealed that significant changes have taken place or are under way, but it also showed that many of the earlier problems continue.

As of December 1992, the United Kingdom held approximately 47,500 prisoners (40,500 in England and Wales, 5,252 in Scotland and 1,770 in Northern Ireland) in a total of 154 prisons (130 in England and Wales, 19 in Scotland, 5 in Northern Ireland.) Women inmates constituted just under 4 percent of the prison population in England and Wales, less than 3 percent in Scotland, and 2 percent in Northern

Ireland. The prison population has decreased significantly in recent years, from 55,047 inmates as of December 1989. Still, with 82 inmates per 100,000 people, the United Kingdom continues to have one of the highest prisoner-to-population ratios in Western Europe.

In England and Wales, prisons and pre-trial facilities are under the jurisdiction of the Home Office's Prison Service Secretariat. In Northern Ireland, the prisons are administered by the Northern Ireland Office and in Scotland, the prisons are administered by the Scottish Office, but the British government is ultimately responsible for prisons in both Northern Ireland and Scotland.

PRE-TRIAL DETENTION

In England and Wales, court time limits recently have been instituted to curtail long pre-trial detention periods. According to the new limits, offenders must be dealt with by the lower court within seventy days of committal. More serious offenders that are sent to the higher court must be dealt with within an additional 112 days (if referred by a lower court first), for a maximum of 182 days on pre-trial for the most serious offenses. Although a prisoner should be released if these pre-trial limits are exceeded, prison monitoring groups within the U.K. have reported that the courts will instead approve an extension to avoid releasing a prisoner before trial. Nonetheless, those organizations have reported that the average pre-trial detention period has been reduced slightly since 1991, when the average pre-trial stay was fifty-three days.

In Northern Ireland, pre-trial periods are seldom less than twelve months, and usually about fifteen months. Time spent on remand is considered time served if a prisoner receives a custodial sentence.

PHYSICAL CONDITIONS

Access to sanitation facilities was a major problem at the time of our first visit in June 1991. Cells had no toilets and prisoners were forced to use plastic chamber-pots, usually in the presence of their cellmates, and empty the pots into the wing's toilet facilities, a process known as "slopping out." By the time of our February 1993 visit, plumbing had already been installed in many cells in prisons throughout

the country and construction was underway in others to meet the government's self-imposed deadline for achieving in-cell plumbing in all prisons by 1994.

ACTIVITIES AND WORK

In England and Wales, some prisoners spend as many as twenty-three hours each day in their cells. At prisons where work or educational programs are not widely available, only the small percentage of prisoners who are allowed to work as orderlies are out of their cells for more than an hour or two each day. At the time of our June 1991 visit, half of the prisoners at remand and local prisons were not involved in any work or educational programs. All prisoners are allowed "exercise time" for an hour each day. Exercise time in local prisons is usually spent in a small concrete yard with little or no sporting apparatus; some prisons do have gym facilities. Most inmates estimate that, on average, prisoners at local prisons spend at least twenty to twenty-one hours locked up each day. Prison officials dispute this claim. In recent months, efforts have been made to increase the out-of-cell time for all inmates. Periods of so called "association" were implemented. They consist of opening cells in one part of a prison or a floor at a time, and letting inmates spend some time with inmates other than their cellmates. During "association," prisoners may watch TV, play games, or socialize. But, because "association" is organized on a rotating basis, each individual prisoner has only a few hours a week to spend in this way.

In Northern Ireland's Belfast Remand Prison, prisoners spend an excessive amount of time locked in their cells. Prison officials report that although prisoners are entitled to at least two hours of exercise time and two hours of association, prisoners do not share out-of-cell time with prisoners affiliated with members of opposing paramilitary groups. At Maghaberry Prison, prisoners are "integrated" with members of opposing paramilitary groups and are rewarded with adequate work, educational, and recreational activities.

WOMEN PRISONERS

Women account for under 4 percent of prisoners. There are twelve women's prisons in England and Wales (as opposed to more than 100 for men), and due to this fact one of the most serious problems facing women prisoners is the distance between their homes and the prisons where they are incarcerated. The Prison Service reports that it is examining ways to keep women prisoners closer to their homes, including the creation of community prisons.

In England and Wales there are now thirty-eight places for mothers and babies in three prisons. At two of these prisons, infants may remain with their mothers for eighteen months; at the other prison, the infant may remain with his or her mother for nine months.

In Northern Ireland, Maghaberry Prison's Female Section is the only prison where women are held. There are mother-baby units where an infant may remain for one year after birth.

DISCIPLINARY MEASURES

If a prisoner is found guilty of an offense, he or she may be punished by disciplinary measures ranging from the forfeiture of privileges for a period not exceeding twenty-eight days; to stoppage of earnings for a period not exceeding twenty-eight days; to confinement in the cell for no more than three days; up to the forfeiture of remission of sentence for a period not exceeding 180 days.

Under Prison Rule 43, prisoners may also be separated from the general population for the maintenance of "good order and discipline," or at the prisoner's request. Prisoners are entitled to a disciplinary hearing if they are charged with a disciplinary offense, but are not entitled to a hearing if they are segregated for "good order and discipline" under Rule 43. A body belt may be used to subdue violent prisoners.

At the time of our 1991 visit, in England and Wales, there were reports of the unauthorized use of force against prisoners by prison officers.

In January 1993, Home Secretary Kenneth Clarke announced that a "Prisons Ombudsman" would be appointed. The ombudsman will consider complaints from prisoners who have failed to obtain satisfaction under the internal grievance system. In addition to considering individual complaints, the ombudsman will review the complaints procedures.

In Northern Ireland, a prisoner is entitled to a disciplinary hearing with the prison director for minor charges with punishments ranging from loss of remission of up to twenty-eight days to solitary confinement for up to three days. For more serious offenses, the case is referred to the Board of Visitors, an outside oversight body, and may be punished by loss of up to 180 days remission and solitary confinement for up to fifty-six days.

CONTACTS WITH THE OUTSIDE

In England and Wales, convicted prisoners may receive two visits each month, for at least one hour each. Unconvicted prisoners may receive three one-hour visits a week, whenever possible. Some visiting areas are cramped and visits are held with little privacy. In recent months, the Prison Service has expanded opportunities for contacts with the outside by allowing more prisoners to take advantage of the Home Leave program and by installing telephones throughout the prison system.

The right to send and receive mail has recently been expanded to allow prisoners, unconvicted or convicted, essentially as many letters as they wish. In some cases, however, a prison director may limit the numbers of letters mailed out or received by convicted prisoners.

In Northern Ireland, unconvicted prisoners are allowed up to three visits per week for thirty minutes each. Convicted prisoners are allowed one statutory and three "privilege" visits per month. The length and timing of visits vary from prison to prison. Some visiting areas are cramped and visits are held with little privacy.

Remand prisoners are allowed to send and receive as many letters as they desire. Convicted prisoners are allowed to send or receive one statutory letter per week; in addition, convicted prisoners are allowed one non-statutory letter per week. Except for letters relating to legal proceedings, all letters may be read by prison authorities and stopped if their contents are found to be "objectionable." As in other parts of the United Kingdom, telephones are now available to prisoners in Northern Ireland.

After twelve years, prisoners serving life sentences are allowed home leave during Christmas and in the summer.

FOOD

Throughout the United Kingdom, prisoners complained that the quality of the food was poor and that they were usually hungry in the evening due to long intervals between the last meal of the day and the first one the next morning. Supper is served in British prisons between 3 and 4 P.M. while breakfast is usually between 8 and 9 A.M. In addition, because most prisons lack dining halls, food is made additionally unappetizing because it is eaten in the presence of plastic chamber-pots (or toilets, in those prisons where remodeling has already taken place).

UNITED STATES

Over the course of a year, Human Rights Watch conducted a series of visits to various types of correctional facilities, including state and federal prisons, jails and an Immigration and Naturalization Service detention institution. We gained access to these prisons with various degrees of difficulty (it took up to several months in some states to obtain permission). In one case, that of Puerto Rico, we were refused permission to visit prisons. A report, Prison Conditions in the United States, *based on the findings of the visits and extensive supplementary research, was published in November 1991.*

With a ratio of 455 prisoners per 100,000 inhabitants and with more than a million people behind bars, the United States can claim the dubious distinction of being among the world leaders in both categories. Beyond the sheer magnitude of the problem, perhaps the most troubling aspect of the human rights situation in U.S. prisons is a trend we observed that could be labelled "Marionization." In 1983, the federal prison at Marion, Illinois, until then similar to other maximum-security penitentiaries, implemented a series of extraordinary security measures. Since then, at least thirty-six states have followed suit in creating their own super-maximum security institutions (called "maxi-maxis" in prison jargon). Conditions in these institutions are much harsher than in any other prisons in the country, and this strict regime is administered solely by prison officials without independent supervision. As a result, inmates may be sentenced twice: once by the court, to a certain period of imprisonment, and the second time by the prison administration, to particularly harsh conditions. This second sentencing is open-ended, limited only by the overall length of an inmate's sentence.

THE SYSTEM

The United States has fifty separate state prison systems, a federal prison system, the District of Columbia system, the prison system of the Commonwealth of Puerto Rico, and numerous county- and community-based jails (more than 3,300 as of 1988). On any given day, they hold more than 1,300,000 inmates.

247

PHYSICAL CONDITIONS

Jail and prison conditions vary significantly from state to state, and from jurisdiction to jurisdiction. Overcrowding, however, is a common problem in most of the United States. Indeed, as of January 1992, courts had found that in forty states, the District of Columbia, and in more than 500 local jail jurisdictions, overcrowding and related conditions violated the federal or state Constitution.[1]

Because of this overcrowding, prisons and jails have increasingly been relying on dormitory rather than cell housing. Dormitories, where as many as fifty or more inmates may sleep in a single large room, in addition to providing no privacy, produce very serious safety concerns, since prisoners are left virtually unsupervised during the night.

SAFETY

Inmate-on-inmate violence is a serious problem in U.S. prisons and assaults are frequent. About 4 percent of all deaths in state and federal prisons are assassinations by fellow inmates (the majority of deaths are from natural causes; the statistics also include suicides, accidents, and executions).

There are numerous reports of homosexual rapes, and the actual number of these incidents is certainly even higher due to the widespread underreporting of rapes by victims.

Jails, where pre-trial detainees are held, along with those serving shorter sentences, tend to be particularly violent. Due to deficient record-keeping and lack of adequate classification, persons arrested for minor offenses are frequently housed alongside dangerous and predatory criminals.

DISCIPLINARY MEASURES

Inmates who violate prison rules are punished through a variety of sanctions that range from loss of privileges to disciplinary segregation.

---

[1] Information from the National Prison Project of the American Civil Liberties Union (ACLU).

In addition, as indicated earlier, some prison systems in recent years have established separate institutions, or parts of institutions, in which conditions are particularly harsh and security is exceptionally strict. Placement in such "maxi-maxis" is technically considered an administrative rather than a disciplinary measure, and as such is not preceded by a hearing. As a result, an inmate is afforded no possibility of appeal, and this sanction's application is open-ended. The decision to place an inmate in such an institution is made by prison administrators alone and is often based on the mere estimation that an inmate is potentially dangerous or predatory rather than on any actual infraction committed by that inmate.

Conditions in these institutions can be extremely harsh and often amount to solitary confinement for years on end. In the Florida State Prison at Starke, some inmates are held in windowless cells from which they are allowed out only three times a week, for ten minutes, to shower. The rest of the time they are alone in the cell. This situation may last for a few years. Some of the inmates Human Rights Watch interviewed in that prison had not been outdoors for several years. In the Maximum Control Complex in Westville, Indiana, inmates are locked in their cells for between twenty-two-and-a-half and twenty-four hours a day, never see anyone except their guards, and are often punished with the loss of access to reading materials, among other measures. In Marion, where an average stay lasts three years, prisoners are locked in their cells round the clock, except for recreation (between seven and eleven hours a week, depending on classification group).

In addition, we have received numerous reports of unauthorized disciplinary measures, mostly beatings. Several prisoners interviewed by Human Rights Watch reported witnessing beatings, usually in retaliation for making complaints or arguing with a guard.

We also interviewed several inmates who had participated in a jail disturbance at the Otis Bantum Center on Rikers Island in New York in the Summer of 1990. Inmates reported that they were brutally beaten after the disturbance had been quelled. These allegations were later confirmed by an official commission appointed by the Mayor.[2]

---

[2] City of New York Department of Investigation, *Report to the Mayor: The Disturbance at the Rikers Island Otis Bantum Correctional Center, August 14, 1990: Its Causes and the Department of Corrections Response* (The City of New York: April 1991).

WOMEN

Women account for about 6 percent of total state inmates, with proportions varying from state to state, and for about 7 percent within the federal prison system. Since 1980, the number of female inmates has been growing at a greater rate than that of men.

Because of the relatively low numbers of women inmates, the number of female prisons is low. Consequently, many women are housed far from their homes and, as a result, receive few visits. This is a particularly serious problem for women serving sentences in the federal system, because there are only eight federal prisons in the entire country that house women convicts.

As of this writing, only New York state allows women to keep their infant babies in prison with them for a year, or slightly longer if the mother is scheduled to be released soon thereafter. In the remaining states and in the federal system, no babies are allowed, and if an inmate gives birth while serving her sentence, the baby is immediately taken away from her and placed with relatives or in foster care.

CONTACTS WITH THE OUTSIDE

Visiting rules vary from jurisdiction to jurisdiction. In most cases, inmates are allowed at least one visit per month, ranging from as little as thirty minutes to a few hours; such visits are usually conducted in visiting rooms, allowing for a degree of physical contact. Non-contact visits, where visitors and inmates are separated by a glass partition, are the rule in the maxi-maxi federal prison at Marion and for some prisoners in certain other maxi-maxi institutions (both state prisons and jails).

Conjugal visits are allowed in only a few states and only to a limited number of prisoners.

Most prisoners in the United States are allowed to use the phone, although the degree of access varies from unlimited to highly controlled (both in length and frequency). In at least one prison visited by Human Rights Watch, the Florida State Prison, inmates did not have any access to telephones. All telephone conversations in U.S. prisons, except those with lawyers, are monitored by prison staff.

There are no limits on the number of letters prisoners may write or receive, though letters in both directions may be opened unless they are properly marked as legal matter.

LIVING CONDITIONS ON DEATH ROW

More than 2,500 Americans currently live under a sentence of death. As of this writing, thirty-six states provide for the death penalty in their laws. Before all appeals have been exhausted, many inmates can actually live on death row for ten years or longer.

Inmates on death row in different states whom Human Rights Watch was able to interview reported a number of problems related specifically to their situation. They complained about lack of medical treatment, about bad cell conditions, and about total mind-numbing idleness. One inmate summarized these complaints by saying: "The mentality is that since we are going to die anyway, why bother to do anything [for us]?" We received many reports of staff insensitivity toward the condemned. One inmate in Tennessee said that when he returned to prison from a court hearing, a prison clergyman asked him: "So, when are they going to fry you?" An inmate in Florida said that after his friend had been executed, he overheard a guard saying: "It's about time to get rid of some Niggers here." A woman whose death sentence had been commuted by the time we interviewed her said that while under the death sentence, she had been held in total isolation because she was the only woman on death row.

ACCESS TO COURTS

The American legal system allows prisoners and pre-trial detainees to bring lawsuits when they believe that their rights are violated in detention. It does not permit prisoners to obtain redress for all the human rights violations that they experience in prisons and jails. Constitutional protections are limited in scope, and the judicial system is often slow and ill-equipped to address the miserable conditions found in so many of the country's prisons and jails. Also, the courts' ability to secure compliance with their orders is limited, particularly when corrective action is required. Nonetheless, much has been accomplished through litigation in eliminating some of the worst human rights violations in U.S. prisons.

INS DETENTION

For about a decade now, the United States has had a policy of incarcerating foreigners who have been arrested for lack of proper documentation. This policy is ostensibly intended to assure that aliens appear at all hearings on their legal status, yet the Immigration and Naturalization Service officials acknowledge that its main purpose is to discourage aliens from illegally entering the U.S. to seek political asylum or other means of establishing themselves in the country. As of early 1993, the INS estimates it held 7,200 such illegal aliens in its custody.

Illegal immigrants are often held for a year or more in typically overcrowded institutions. They sleep in dormitories, alongside as many as 100 detainees. They wear government-issue orange jumpers, and when taken outside for an asylum hearing or medical treatment, they are handcuffed. Most have nothing to do and spend day after day, month after month, watching TV or sitting in the courtyard. Families are separated by sex and allowed only brief weekly visits together. Individuals from distant countries face severe isolation due to the lack of a common language with their jailers and fellow detainees. In addition to holding illegal aliens in its own institutions, the INS has also confined detainees in local jails, where they are routinely housed alongside dangerous offenders.

ZAIRE

In theory, Zaire has been in a state of transition from one- party rule since April 24, 1990. Its long time dictator, Mobutu Sese Seko, has refused to yield any real power, however. The result has been a prolonged economic and political crisis punctuated by acts of violence perpetrated by Mobutu's forces. Human Rights Watch conducted an investigation of conditions in prison and police detention in Zaire from March 22 to April 5, 1993. A representative visited the central prison of Makala in Kinshasa, Luzumu detention camp in Bas Zaire, Kasapa prison in Lubumbashi and Buluo detention camp, near Likasi. Our representative also visited a number of police lockups in the urban Kinshasa area. The investigation was undertaken with the informal cooperation of a number of judicial and prison officials and with the active collaboration of Zaire's human rights groups.

Zaire's prisons are an apt reflection of the disintegrating Zairian state. Years of neglect and corruption have now given way to complete abandonment. Left to their own devices, prisons have become private enterprises and prisoners are slave laborers. In the past year, only the intervention of humanitarian and religious associations has prevented mass starvation. Even so, the rate of death and disease is extremely high, dwarfing any of the other problems faced by the prison population.

THE SYSTEM

There are 208 prisons officially reporting to the Ministry of Justice in Zaire. In 1991, the last year for which relatively reliable statistics are available, there were close to 30,000 prisoners in those prisons, including both civilians and soldiers. The number has diminished since then, although it is hard to know how substantially. The central prison administration in the capital of Kinshasa has largely stopped functioning and communication with the interior is rare and unreliable. President Mobutu announced an amnesty in December 1992 which should have affected the large majority of convicted prisoners, but has not, at least in part because the order has never been received by prison directors outside Kinshasa. On the other hand, the prison population in Kinshasa has substantially diminished both because of the amnesty and because of the dire conditions at the central prison of Makala. In 1992, the Justice Ministry instituted a policy to release those prisoners who were sick.

Of the total prison population, only about 15 percent are convicts, the remainder being prisoners facing trial. There are no absolute limits on pre-trial detention and many prisoners will remain in jail for as long as two years before a final judgment.

The official figures for the prison population, which in 1991 stood at about 80 per 100,000, do not reflect the entire prison population. In addition to police lockups, which are theoretically subject to judicial oversight, there are an undisclosed number of "secret" and informal prisons under the control of various security and intelligence forces. These prisons escape any oversight by the ministry of justice. Some of them, including the prisons belonging to the military and civilian intelligence services, are quite substantial in size. In the capital of Kinshasa alone, there are at least a half dozen with a capacity for more than 100 prisoners each.

The informal prisons are essentially outside the law. Many were not built as prisons and have no facilities for preparing food or meeting the hygienic needs of prisoners. In addition, visitors are frequently banned and the law requiring a magistrate's intervention after forty-eight hours is openly flouted. While a very small number of detainees are purely political prisoners, the vast majority are held for common crimes or personal vendettas. In the past two years, long-term political detention has substantially diminished, except in the military.

As for prison lockups—of which there are sixty-one in the capital of Kinshasa alone—there was an effort to improve enforcement of the forty-eight hour rule after 1990. But the effort is currently collapsing in the face of financial troubles, which prevent magistrates from making regular visits.

FOOD AND MEDICAL CARE

By 1991, the number of officially recognized deaths in prison reached 2,229 or 8 percent of the entire prison population. Since then, there are anecdotal reports from around the country that suggest a continuing rise. The underlying causes are severe malnutrition and the absence of any significant medical care. Large numbers of prisoners are reported to be dying from causes that are easily treated, such as "severe diarrhea" or dysentery. The number of deaths at Makala prison in Kinshasa reached two or three people per day until the International Committee of the Red Cross (ICRC) intervened in the summer of 1991. At Kasapa prison in Lubumbashi, an average of nine prisoners a month have died since the beginning of 1993 (out of a total prison population of 350).

It is easy to understand the cause of the current desperation. Since independence there has been no noticeable investment in prison maintenance and upkeep by the state. The basic infrastructures were allowed to decay and workshops, which were often a source of income for the prisons, were diverted to the profit of prison staff and run into the ground. Whatever the official budget, the actual amount of money that reached the prisons was never sufficient to assure adequate food and health resources, particularly in the interior. Most of the national budget (75 percent in 1989) was spent in a vain effort to make the central Makala prison into a model. In any event, corruption at all levels of the prison administration meant that money, medicine and food were siphoned off before reaching the prisoners.

The inconsistent flow of funds slowed to a trickle in 1992 and effectively ended in 1993. As one prison official unabashedly stated, "As long as we aren't paid, the prisoners aren't fed."[1] In 1993, no salaries have been paid to prison staff and only minimal subsidies have reached the prisons for food and upkeep. For example, from 1992 until the present, the prison camp of Buluo, with between fifty-four and 120 prisoners, received in total state subsidies money sufficient to pay for twelve (50 kilogram) sacks of corn flour.

The same dire conditions exist with respect to medical care. None of the prisons we visited had adequate facilities for drinking water or waste disposal. Malnutrition and unhygienic living conditions contribute to an extremely high rate of disease. The director of Kasapa prison in Lubumbashi reported that 173 of 350 prisoners were sick. Because of a lack of salaries and transportation, doctors are an increasing rarity at the prisons. But the absence of medicine is even more severe, making it practically impossible to treat any significant disease. Finally, it is often impossible to transfer severe cases to hospitals because of transportation costs and hospital expenses. The hospitals themselves

---

[1] Interview with prisons administrator, Makala prison, March 24, 1993.

require patients to provide the necessary drugs and payment in advance, further complicating the possibility of obtaining care.

The only significant food and medical care that has reached the prisons over the past two years has come from foreign missionaries, local benevolent associations and international humanitarian groups. In July 1991, the ICRC took the extraordinary measure of instituting a temporary nutrition program inside Makala prison. The program, which ICRC was able to prolong until the end of March 1993, treated up to 200 severely malnourished inmates each day on the basis of height/weight statistics. The ICRC also repaired broken water pipes and provided medical assistance and basic necessities such as soap. The Belgian branch of Médecins sans Frontiers has provided some medicine and assisted in rebuilding a long abandoned septic tank at Buluo prison in Shaba.

The bulk of the responsibility for prisons has been taken over by the diminished foreign missionary community. Most of the missionaries in the country were evacuated in the fall of 1991 following violent rampages by soldiers. Many, though far from all, have returned since then. In many prisons throughout the country, the missionaries provide the only certain meals served each week. In order to maintain access to the prisons, missionaries are required to operate discreetly. Ten years ago, missionary nuns were banned from Makala prison for several months when news was leaked of a cholera epidemic inside the prison. The missionary community is still sensitive to such a threat; nevertheless, it is a sign of the new desperation that prison officials have openly courted their assistance during the current times.

PHYSICAL CONDITIONS

The country's prisons are in an advanced state of decay. Most of the prisons date from the period prior to independence in 1960. At most, only limited quantities of drinking water are available in the prisons. Sanitary facilities are, at best, semi-functional. In many of the prisons, including Makala, prisoners clean out the contents of non-functional toilets by hand. Where kitchen facilities exist, they consist of no more than a common pot on a makeshift wooden stove.

The living quarters of prisoners range from individual cells to group pavilions. There is generally no artificial light, except in the cells allocated to wealthy prisoners or those with political connections. The same is true of beds and mats. Perhaps the majority of prisoners are forced to sleep either on concrete or a burlap sac. Many of the buildings are dilapidated and out of use. Others are still used despite their dilapidated condition and flooding that occurs whenever it rains.

Crowding, which has been a problem in the past, had eased at least temporarily this past spring. Makala prison was built for 500 prisoners and housed 540 at the end of March 1993. This is unusual, however, and reflects the sudden drop in the prison population. As recently as two years ago, the number reached as high as 2,000 people; the average number of prisoners in the spring of 1992 was still over 1,000. The crowding which has been reported lately results from the effect of recent political and economic turmoil on the prisons. Reduced staff and damaged facilities have forced prison directors to consolidate prisoners in a number of prisons. In Kasapa prison, for example, 110 prisoners are living in three rooms eight by five meters each.

Many prisons were equipped with workshops for carpentry, blacksmithing, sewing, printing and other crafts. The workshops are largely non-functional. Where equipment remains, it is usually in unusable condition. One exception is the saw-mill at the Kasapa prison, which prison officials have succeeded in keeping operational. Despite its precarious nature, it now serves as the main source of income for the prison.

The typical police lockup is little more than an enclosed concrete cell attached to a neighborhood police station. Those visited by Human Rights Watch were without light or sanitary facilities. Inside, the smell of urine was so intense, in some cases, that it burned the eyes within moments of entering. There were no beds or mattresses.

DISCIPLINE

The prison director sets the basic regime for the prison. Prisoners are usually locked in their cells or pavilions from about 7:30 P.M. until 5:30 or 6:00 A.M. The cells, which house one or at most two prisoners, are theoretically for hardened criminals. In some prisons, however, new prisoners are put into the cells for initial observation. Final living assignment is made by the prison administration although, in some cases, it appears that other prisoners have a say. Prisoners are segregated by their social position and then, primarily by the nature of their crime. Most prisons have a place for privileged prisoners—wealthy prisoners and those with political connections. They tend to live well, with few restrictions, and employ other prisoners as their servants. The cells for privileged inmates at Makala resemble small college dormrooms and are often equipped with videos and televisions.

During the day, inmates may be subject to work duty, if they are convicted prisoners. Otherwise they are usually left to their own devices within a limited area, for example, the courtyard. In some of the smaller sub-regional prisons, like the Mbanza Ngungu facility, prisoners are forced to sit all day under the command of one of the guards. In larger prisons including Kesapa prison in Lubumbashi and Buluo detention camp, where staff has been reduced, large areas have been put off limits to the prisoners.

One of the most striking factors in Zairian prison life, however, is the power and control exercised by the prisoners themselves. Inside the prison, prison authorities are rarely visible. The rules that govern most behavior are dictated and enforced by a strict hierarchy of prisoners, usually chosen by the prisoners themselves with the agreement of the director. Every prison has a "Kapita General," a "chief of staff." Under him are regional governors, pavilion leaders, and guards, all of whom are prisoners.

Nowhere is this system more in evidence than at Makala prison. There, prisoners prepare and distribute the food, tend the sick, adjudicate disputes, organize the day and mete out most penalties. The advantages of the system for the prison administration are clear. With the crisis of salaries and transportation, some prisons have been virtually abandoned by their staffs. It is not unlikely to find a prison of 150 inmates operating with an effective non-prisoner staff of five. However, the abuses are also apparent. Inmates are subject to the whim of the prison hierarchy, most of which, not surprisingly is in the hands of the long-term prisoners. At Makala, prisoners effectively decide who will eat and how much. New prisoners and younger prisoners are forced to service the more senior prisoners—working their garden plot for example, or providing sexual favors.

Formal discipline may only be ordered by the prison director. In theory there is a whole range of punitive measures beginning with a ban on visitors. Whippings have been reported in cases relating to attempted escapes. However, most prisons appear to favor short term lockup in isolation cells, some of which—like police lockups—have no windows or ventilation. Up to forty-five days of detention is possible. Leg chains and metal spans are used in many of the prisons in the interior. The type used in Zaire are welded together, often causing severe burns to the skin. To remove them requires a hacksaw. Three prisoners interviewed by Human Rights Watch while still in chains, were delivered to Luzumu prison from Mbanza Ngungu. They remained chained there for four months because, the director claimed, he did not have access to the necessary blade.

CORRUPTION

The crisis in Zaire's prisons is exacerbated by corruption at all levels of the prison hierarchy, from the minister of Justice to the jail guard. At its simplest, corruption requires paying and feeding the jail guards in order to visit the prison or bring food to prisoners. This practice, which is common to all of Zaire's prisons was banished for a few months from Makala prison in the latter part of 1992. A reform minded Justice Minister under the transition government of Prime Minister Etienne Tshisikedi placed a sign at the entrance saying, "Visits are free" and effectively threatened guards into enforcing it. The sign was gone as soon as the transition government was displaced by President Mobutu several months later and the practice has quickly returned.

Corruption is responsible for the fact that prisons are without functioning vehicles or machinery for workshops. Much of this has been sold or converted to private use over the years. In one recent case a prison director has succeeded in identifying key machinery sold to private businesses by his predecessor. Corruption also explains why major contributions of food and medicine disappear quickly from the prisons. Missionaries and humanitarian groups have had to fight to maintain control over their own contributions in order to insure that they benefit the prisoners.

Finally, corruption in some prisons has created situations where prisoners are forced to work for the director, either in prison fields or in private fields. Directors justify this activity by referring to the needs of the prison. But there are no controls to ensure that the proceeds actually go to its benefit. In one case, it seemed likely to Human Rights Watch that the prison director had deliberately failed to implement President

Mobutu's December amnesty order because he feared losing an essential workforce.

The problem of corruption extends to other aspects of the judicial system. In the view of many—including many prosecutors—the majority of Zairians who land in prison are those who were not in a position to pay off the policeman or the prosecutor who ordered their detention. When a policy was instituted at Makala prison to release sick detainees, it was quickly distorted to allow other prisoners out on dubious grounds. Even the prison doctor was not given access to the official list of detainees released.

CONTACTS WITH THE OUTSIDE

Official prison rules usually permit visitors on two days during the week. These days prison directors tend to permit visits at any time, because they are a major source of food for the prisoners. However, because of the increasingly dire economic situation, the number of visits has dropped off precipitously since 1991. This has been exacerbated by the demands made on visitors by prison guards. Travel back and forth, even to the urban prisons, is extremely expensive and, in the case of Makala prison, dangerous. Rural prisons, like Luzumu or Buluo, rarely receive visitors. Although access to the prisons appears relatively unrestricted, some prisoners complained, nevertheless, that certain of their visitors were not allowed in for political reasons.

APPENDICES

APPENDIX A

PRISON PROJECT ADVISORY COMMITTEE

Nan Aron
Vivian Berger
Haywood Burns
Alejandro Garro
William Hellerstein
Edward Koren
Sheldon Krantz
Benjamin Malcolm
Diane Orentlicher
Norman Rosenberg
David Rothman
Herman Schwartz
Clarence Sundram

APPENDIX B

INTERNATIONAL COVENANT ON CIVIL AND POLITICAL RIGHTS

Article 7

No one shall be subjected to torture or to cruel, inhuman or degrading treatment or punishment. In particular, no one shall be subjected without his free consent to medical or scientific experimentation.

Article 10

1. All persons deprived of their liberty shall be treated with humanity and with respect for the inherent dignity of the human person.

2. (a) Accused persons shall, save in exceptional circumstances, be segregated from convicted persons and shall be subject to separate treatment appropriate to their status as unconvicted persons;

(b) Accused juvenile persons shall be separated ffrom adults and brought as speedily as possible for sjudication.

3. The penitentiary system shall comprise treatment of prisoners the essential aim of which shall be their reformation and social rehabilitation. Juvenile offenders shall be segregated from adults and be accorded treatment appropriate to their age and legal status.

APPENDIX C

STANDARD MINIMUM RULES
FOR THE TREATMENT OF PRISONERS

Adopted by the First United Nations Congress on the Prevention of Crime and the Treatment of Offenders, held at Geneva in 1955, and approved by the Economic and Social Council by its resolutions 663 C (XXIV) of 31 July 1957 and 2076 (LXII) of 13 May 1977

PRELIMINARY OBSERVATIONS

1. The following rules are not intended to describe in detail a model system of penal institutions. They seek only, on the basis of the general consensus of contemporary thought and the essential elements of the most adequate systems of today, to set out what is generally accepted as being good principle and practice in the treatment of prisoners and the management of institutions.

2. In view of the great variety of legal, social, economic and geographical conditions of the world, it is evident that not all of the rules are capable of application in all places and at all times. They should, however, serve to stimulate a constant endeavour to overcome practical difficulties in the way of their application, in the knowledge that they represent, as a whole, the minimum conditions which are accepted as suitable by the United Nations.

3. On the other hand, the rules cover a field in which thought is constantly developing. They are not intended to preclude experiment and practices, provided these are in harmony with the principles and seek to further the purposes which derive from the. text of the rules as a whole. It will always be justifiable for the central prison administration to authorize departures from the rules in this spirit.

4. (1) Part I of the rules covers the general management of institutions, and is applicable to all categories of prisoners, criminal or

civil, untried or convicted, including prisoners subject to "security measures or corrective measures ordered by the judge.

(2) Part 11 contains rules applicable only to the special categories dealt with in each section. Nevertheless, the rules under section A, applicable to prisoners under sentence, shall be equally applicable to categories of prisoners dealt with in sections B, C and D, provided they do not conflict with the rules governing those categories and are for their benefit.

5.   (1) The rules do not seek to regulate the management of institutions set aside for young persons such as Borstal institutions or correctional schools, but in general part I would be equally applicable in such institutions.

(2) The category of young prisoners should include at least all young persons who come within the jurisdiction of juvenile courts. As a rule, such young persons should not be sentenced to imprisonment.

PART I

RULES OF GENERAL APPLICATION

Basic principle

6.   (1) The following rules shall be applied impartially. There shall be no discrimination on grounds of race, colour, sex, language, religion, political or other opinion, national or social origin, property, birth or other status.

(2) On the other hand, it is necessary to respect the religious beliefs and moral precepts of the group to which a prisoner belongs.

Register

7.   (1) In every place where persons are imprisoned there shall be kept a bound registration book with numbered pages in which shall be entered in respect of each prisoner received:

(a) Information concerning his identity;

(b) The reasons for his commitment and the authority therefor;

(c) The day and hour of his admission and release.

(2) No person shall be received in an institution without a valid commitment order of which the details shall have been previously entered in the register.

Separation of categories

8. The different categories of prisoners shall be kept in separate institutions or parts of institutions taking account of their sex, age, criminal record, the legal reason for their detention and the necessities of their treatment. Thus,

(a) Men and women shall so far as possible be detained in separate institutions; in an institution which receives both men and women the whole of the premises allocated to women shall be entirely separate;

(b) Untried prisoners shall be kept separate from convicted prisoners;

(c) Persons imprisoned for debt and other civil prisoners shall be kept separate from persons imprisoned by reason of a criminal offence;

(d) Young prisoners shall be kept separate from adults.

Accommodation

9.   (1) Where sleeping accommodation is in individual cells or rooms, each prisoner shall occupy by night a cell or room by himself. If for special reasons, such as temporary overcrowding, it becomes

necessary for the central prison administration to make an exception to this rule, it is not desirable to have two prisoners in a cell or room.

(2) Where dormitories are used, they shall be occupied by prisoners carefully selected as being suitable to associate with one another in those conditions. There shall be regular supervision by night, in keeping with the nature of the institution.

10. All accommodation provided for the use of prisoners and in particular all sleeping accommodation shall meet all requirements of health, due regard being paid to climatic conditions and particularly to cubic content of air, minimum floor space, lighting, heating and ventilation.

11. In all places where prisoners are required to live or work,
(a) The windows shall be large enough to enable the prisoners to read or work by natural light, and shall be so constructed that they can allow the entrance of fresh air whether or not there is artificial ventilation;
(b) Artificial light shall be provided sufficient for the prisoners to read or work without injury to eyesight.

12. The sanitary installations shall be adequate to enable every prisoner to comply with the needs of nature when necessary and in a clean and decent manner.

13. Adequate bathing and shower installations shall be provided so that every prisoner may be enabled and required to have a bath or shower, at a temperature suitable to the climate, as frequently as necessary for general hygiene according to season and geographical region, but at least once a week in a temperate climate.

14. All parts of an institution regularly used by prisoners shall be properly maintained and kept scrupulously clean at all times.

Personal hygiene

15. Prisoners shall be required to keep their persons clean, and to this end they shall be provided with water and with such toilet articles as are necessary for health and cleanliness.

16. In order that prisoners may maintain a good appearance compatible with their self-respect, facilities shall be provided for the proper care of the hair and beard, and men shall be enabled to shave regularly.

Clothing and bedding

17.   (1) Every prisoner who is not allowed to wear his own clothing shall be provided with an outfit of clothing suitable for the climate and adequate to keep him in good health. Such clothing shall in no manner be degrading or humiliating.

(2) All clothing shall be clean and kept in proper condition. Underclothing shall be changed and washed as often as necessary for the maintenance of hygiene.

(3) In exceptional circumstances, whenever a prisoner is removed outside the institution for an authorized purpose, he shall be allowed to wear his own clothing or other inconspicuous clothing.

18. If prisoners are allowed to wear their own clothing, arrangements shall be made on their admission to the institution to ensure that it shall be clean and fit for use.

19. Every prisoner shall, in accordance with local or national standards, be provided with a separate bed, and with separate and sufficient bedding which shall be clean when issued, kept in good order and changed often enough to ensure its cleanliness.

Food

20.   (1) Every prisoner shall be provided by the administration at the usual hours with food of nutritional value adequate for health and strength, of wholesome quality and well prepared and served.

(2) Drinking water shall be available to every prisoner whenever he needs it.

Exercise and sport

21.   (1) Every prisoner who is not employed in outdoor work shall have at least one hour of suitable exercise in the open air daily if the weather permits.

(2) Young prisoners, and others of suitable age and physique, shall receive physical and recreational training during the period of exercise. To this end space, installations and equipment should be provided.

Medical services

22.   (1) At every institution there shall be available the services of at least one qualified medical officer who should have some knowledge of psychiatry. The medical services should be organized in close relationship to the general health administration of the community or nation. They shall include a psychiatric service for the diagnosis and, in proper cases, the treatment of states of mental abnormality.

(2) Sick prisoners who require specialist treatment shall be transferred to specialized institutions or to civil hospitals. Where hospital facilities are provided in an institution, their equipment, furnishings and pharmaceutical supplies shall be proper for the medical care and treatment of sick prisoners, and there shall be a staff of suitable trained officers.

(3) The services of a qualified dental officer shall be available to every prisoner.

23.   (1) In women's institutions there shall be special accommodation for all necessary pre-natal and post-natal care and treatment. Arrangements shall be made wherever practicable for children to be born in a hospital outside the institution. If a child is born in prison, this fact shall not be mentioned in the birth certificate.

(2) Where nursing infants are allowed to remain in the institution with their mothers, provision shall be made for a nursery staffed by qualified persons, where the infants shall be placed when they are not in the care of their mothers.

24. The medical officer shall see and examine every prisoner as soon as possible after his admission and thereafter as necessary, with a view particularly to the discovery of physical or mental illness and the taking of all necessary measures; the segregation of prisoners suspected of infectious or contagious conditions; the noting of physical or mental defects which might hamper rehabilitation, and the determination of the physical capacity of every prisoner for work.

25.   (1) The medical officer shall have the care of the physical and mental health of the prisoners and should daily see all sick prisoners, all who complain of illness, and any prisoner to whom his attention is specially directed.

(2) The medical officer shall report to the director whenever he considers that a prisoner's physical or mental health has been or will be injuriously affected by continued imprisonment or by any condition of imprisonment.

26.   (1) The medical officer shall regularly inspect and advise the director upon:
(a) The quantity, quality, preparation and service of food;
(b) The hygiene and cleanliness of the institution and the prisoners;

(c) The sanitation, heating, lighting and ventilation of the institution;

(d) The suitability and cleanliness of the prisoners' clothing and bedding;

(e) The observance of the rules concerning physical education and sports, in cases where there is no technical personnel in charge of these activities.

(2) The director shall take into consideration the reports and advice that the medical officer submits according to rules 25 (2) and 26 and, in case he concurs with the recommendations made, shall take immediate steps to give effect to those recommendations; if they are not within his competence or if he does not concur with them, he shall immediately submit his own report and the advice of the medical officer to higher authority.

Discipline and punishment

27. Discipline and order shall be maintained with firmness, but with no more restriction than is necessary for safe custody and well-ordered community life.

28.   (1) No prisoner shall be employed, in the service of the institution, in any disciplinary capacity.

(2) This rule shall not, however, impede the proper functioning of systems based on self-government, under which specified social, educational or sports activities or responsibilities are entrusted, under supervision, to prisoners who are formed into groups for the purposes of treatment.

29. The following shall always be determined by the law or by the regulation of the competent administrative authority:

(a) Conduct constituting a disciplinary offence;

(b) The types and duration of punishment which may be inflicted;

(c) The authority competent to impose such punishment.

30.   (1) No prisoner shall be punished except in accordance with the terms of such law or regulation, and never twice for the same offence.

(2) No prisoner shall be punished unless he has been informed of the offence alleged against him and given a proper opportunity of presenting his defence. The competent authority shall conduct a thorough examination of the case.

(3) Where necessary and practicable the prisoner shall be allowed to make his defence through an interpreter.

31. Corporal punishment, punishment by placing in a dark cell, and all cruel, inhuman or degrading punishments shall be completely prohibited as punishments for disciplinary offences.

32.   (1) Punishment by close confinement or reduction of diet shall never be inflicted unless the medical officer has examined the prisoner and certified in writing that he is fit to sustain it.

(2) The same shall apply to any other punishment that may be prejudicial to the physical or mental health of a prisoner. In no case may such punishment be contrary to or depart from the principle stated in rule 31.

(3) The medical officer shall visit daily prisoners undergoing such punishments and shall advise the director if he considers the termination or alteration of the punishment necessary on grounds of physical or mental health.

Instruments of restraint

33. Instruments of restraint, such as handcuffs, chains, irons and straitjackets, shall never be applied as a punishment. Furthermore, chains or irons shall not be used as restraints. Other instruments of restraint shall not be used except in the following circumstances:

(a) As a precaution against escape during a transfer, provided that they shall be removed when the prisoner appears before a judicial or administrative authority;

(b) On medical grounds by direction of the medical officer;

(c) By order of the director, if other methods of control fail, in order to prevent a prisoner from injuring himself or others or from damaging property; in such instances the director shall at once consult the medical officer and report to the higher administrative authority.

34. The patterns and manner of use of instruments of restraint shall be decided by the central prison administration. Such instruments must not be applied for any longer time than is strictly necessary.

Information to and complaints by prisoners

35.   (1) Every prisoner on admission shall be provided with written information about the regulations governing the treatment of prisoners of his category, the disciplinary requirements of the institution, the authorized methods of seeking information and making complaints, and all such other matters as are necessary to enable him to understand both his rights and his obligations and to adapt himself to the life of the institution.

(2) If a prisoner is illiterate, the aforesaid information shall be conveyed to him orally.

36.   (1) Every prisoner shall have the opportunity each week day of making requests or complaints to the director of the institution or the officer authorized to represent him.

(2) It shall be possible to make requests or complaints to the inspector of prisons during his inspection. The prisoner shall have the opportunity to talk to the inspector or to any other inspecting officer without the director or other members of the staff being present.

(3) Every prisoner shall be allowed to make a request or complaint, without censorship as to substance but in proper form, to the central prison administration, the judicial authority or other proper authorities through approved channels.

(4) Unless it is evidently frivolous or groundless, every request or complaint shall be promptly dealt with and replied to without undue delay.

Contact with the outside world

37. Prisoners shall be allowed under necessary supervision to communicate with their family and reputable friends at regular intervals, both by correspondence and by receiving visits.

38.   (1) Prisoners who are foreign nationals shall be allowed reasonable facilities to communicate with the diplomatic and consular representatives of the State to which they belong.

(2) Prisoners who are nationals of States without diplomatic or consular representation in the country and refugees or stateless persons shall be allowed similar facilities to communicate with the diplomatic representative of the State which takes charge of their interests or any national or international authority whose task it is to protect such persons.

39. Prisoners shall be kept informed regularly of the more important items of news by the reading of newspapers, periodicals or special institutional publications, by hearing wireless transmissions, by lectures or by any similar means as authorized or controlled by the administration.

Books

40. Every institution shall have a library for the use of all categories of prisoners, adequately stocked with both recreational and instructional books, and prisoners shall he encouraged to make full use of it.

Religion

41.   (1) If the institution contains a sufficient number of prisoners of the same religion, a qualified representative of that religion shall be appointed or approved. If the number of prisoners justifies it and conditions permit, the arrangement should be on a full-time basis.

(2) A qualified representative appointed or approved under paragraph (1) shall be allowed to hold regular services and to pay pastoral visits in private to prisoners of his religion at proper times.

(3) Access to a qualified representative of any religion shall not be refused to any prisoner. On the other hand, if any prisoner should object to a visit of any religious representative, his attitude shall be fully respected.

42. So far as practicable, every prisoner shall be allowed to satisfy the needs of his religious life by attending the services provided in the institution and having in his possession the books of religious observance and instruction of his denomination.

Retention of prisoners' property

43.   (1) All money, valuables, clothing and other effects belonging to a prisoner which under the regulations of the institution he is not allowed to retain shall on his admission to the institution be placed in safe custody. An inventory thereof shall be signed by the prisoner. Steps shall be taken to keep them in good condition.

(2) On the release of the prisoner all such articles and money shall be returned to him except in so far as he has been authorized to spend money or send any such property out of the institution, or it has been found necessary on hygienic grounds to destroy any article of clothing. The prisoner shall sign a receipt for the articles and money returned to him.

(3) Any money or effects received for a prisoner from outside shall be treated in the same way.

(4) If a prisoner brings in any drugs or medicine, the medical officer shall decide what use shall be made of them.

Notification of death, illness, transfer, etc.

44.   (1) Upon the death or serious illness of, or serious injury to a prisoner, or his removal to an institution for the treatment of mental affections, the director shall at once inform the spouse, if the prisoner is married, or the nearest relative and shall in any event inform any other person previously designated by the prisoner.

(2) A prisoner shall be informed at once of the death or serious illness of any near relative. In case of the critical illness of a near relative, the prisoner should be authorized, whenever circumstances allow, to go to his bedside either under escort or alone.

(3) Every prisoner shall have the right to inform at once his family of his imprisonment or his transfer to another institution.

Removal of prisoners

45.   (1) When the prisoners are being removed to or from an institution they shall be exposed to public view as little as possible, and proper safeguards shall be adopted to protect them from insult, curiosity and publicity in any form.

(2) The transport of prisoners in conveyances with inadequate ventilation or light, or in any way which would subject them to unnecessary physical hardship, shall be prohibited.

(3) The transport of prisoners shall be carried out at the expense of the administration and equal conditions shall obtain for all of them.

Institutional personnel

46.   (1) The prison administration, shall provide for the careful selection of every grade of the personnel, since it is on their integrity, humanity, professional capacity and personal suitability for the work that the proper administration of the institutions depends.

(2) The prison administration shall constantly seek to awaken and maintain in the minds both of the personnel and of the public the conviction that this work is a social service of great importance, and to this end all appropriate means of informing the public should be used.

(3) To secure the foregoing ends, personnel shall be appointed on a full-time basis as professional prison officers and have civil service status with security of tenure subject only to good conduct, efficiency and physical fitness. Salaries shall be adequate to attract and retain suitable men and women; employment benefits and conditions of service shall be favourable in view of the exacting nature of the work.

47.   (1) The personnel shall possess an adequate standard of education and intelligence.

(2) Before entering on duty, the personnel shall be given a course of training in their general and specific duties and be required to pass theoretical and practical tests.

(3) After entering on duty and during their career, the personnel shall maintain and improve their knowledge and professional capacity by attending courses of in-service training to be organized at suitable intervals.

48. All members of the personnel shall at all times so conduct themselves and perform their duties as to influence the prisoners for good by their example and to command their respect.

49.   (1) So far as possible, the personnel shall include a sufficient number of specialists such as psychiatrists, psychologists, social workers, teachers and trade instructors.

(2) The services of social workers, teachers and trade instructors shall be secured on a permanent basis, without thereby excluding part-time or voluntary workers.

50.   (1) The director of an institution should be adequately qualified for his task by character, administrative ability, suitable training and experience.

(2) He shall devote his entire time to his official duties and shall not be appointed on a part-time basis.

(3) He shall reside on the premises of the institution or in its immediate vicinity.

(4) When two or more institutions are under the authority of one director, he shall visit each of them at frequent intervals. A responsible resident official shall be in charge of each of these institutions.

51.   (1) The director, his deputy, and the majority of the other personnel of the institution shall be able to speak the language of the greatest number of prisoners, or a language understood by the greatest number of them.

(2) Whenever necessary, the services of an interpreter shall be used.

52.   (1) In institutions which are large enough to require the services of one or more full-time medical officers, at least one of them shall reside on the premises of the institution or in its immediate vicinity.

(2) In other institutions the medical officer shall visit daily and shall reside near enough to be able to attend without delay in cases of urgency.

53.   (1) In an institution for both men and women, the part of the institution set aside for women shall be under the authority of a responsible woman officer who shall have the custody of the keys of all that part of the institution.

(2) No male member of the staff shall enter the part of the institution set aside for women unless accompanied by a woman officer.

(3) Women prisoners shall be attended and supervised only by women officers. This does not, however, preclude male members of the staff, particularly doctors and teachers, from carrying out their professional duties in institutions or parts of institutions set aside for women.

54.   (1) Officers of the institutions shall not, in their relations with the prisoners, use force except in self-defence or in cases of attempted escape, or active or passive physical resistance to an order based on law or regulations. Officers who have recourse to force must use no more than is strictly necessary and must report the incident immediately to the director of the institution.

(2) Prison officers shall be given special physical training to enable them to restrain aggressive prisoners.

(3) Except in special circumstances, staff performing duties which bring them into direct contact with prisoners should not be armed. Furthermore, staff should in no circumstances be provided with arms unless they have been trained in their use.

Inspection

55. There shall be a regular inspection of penal institutions and services by qualified and experienced inspectors appointed by a competent authority. Their task shall be in particular to ensure that these institutions are administered in accordance with existing laws and regulations and with a view to bringing about the objectives of penal and correctional services.

PART II

RULES APPLICABLE TO SPECIAL CATEGORIES

A. PRISONERS UNDER SENTENCE

Guiding principles

56. The guiding principles hereafter are intended to show the spirit in which penal institutions should be administered and the purposes at which they should aim, in accordance with the declaration made under Preliminary Observation I of the present text.

57. Imprisonment and other measures which result in cutting off an offender from the outside world are afflictive by the very fact of taking from the person the right of self-determination by depriving him of his liberty. Therefore the prison system shall not, except as incidental to justifiable segregation or the maintenance of discipline, aggravate the suffering inherent in such a situation.

58. The purpose and justification of a sentence of imprisonment or a similar measure deprivative of liberty is ultimately to protect society against crime. This end can only be achieved if the period of imprisonment is used to ensure, so far as possible, that upon his return to society the offender is not only willing but able to lead a law-abiding and self-supporting life.

59. To this end, the institution should utilize all the remedial, educational, moral, spiritual and other forces and forms of assistance which are appropriate and available, and should seek to apply them according to the individual treatment needs of the prisoners.

60.   (1) The regime of the institution should seek to minimize any differences between prison life and life at liberty which tend to lessen the responsibility of the prisoners or the respect due to their dignity as human beings.

(2) Before the completion of the sentence, it is desirable that the necessary steps be taken to ensure for the prisoner a gradual return to life in society. This aim may be achieved, depending on the case, by a pre-release regime organized in the same institution or in another appropriate institution, or by release on trial under some kind of supervision which must not be entrusted to the police but should be combined with effective social aid.

61. The treatment of prisoners should emphasize not their exclusion from the community, but their continuing part in it. Community agencies should, therefore, be enlisted wherever possible to assist the staff of the institution in the task of social rehabilitation of the prisoners. There should be in connection with every institution social workers charged with the duty of maintaining and improving all desirable relations of a prisoner with his family and with valuable social agencies. Steps should be taken to safeguard, to the maximum extent compatible with the law and the sentence, the rights relating to civil interests, social security rights and other social benefits of prisoners.

62. The medical services of the institution shall seek to detect and shall treat any physical or mental illnesses or defects which may hamper a prisoner's rehabilitation. All necessary medical, surgical and psychiatric services shall be provided to that end.

63.   (1) The fulfilment of these principles requires individualization of treatment and for this purpose a flexible system of classifying prisoners in groups; it is therefore desirable that such groups should be distributed in separate institutions suitable for the treatment of each group.

(2) These institutions need not provide the same degree of security for every group. It is desirable to provide varying degrees of security according to the needs of different groups. Open institutions, by the very fact that they provide no physical security against escape but rely on the self-discipline of the inmates, provide the conditions most favourable to rehabilitation for carefully selected prisoners.

(3) It is desirable that the number of prisoners in closed institutions should not be so large that the individualization of treatment

is hindered. In some countries it is considered that the population of such institutions should not exceed five hundred. In open institutions the population should be as small as possible.

(4) On the other hand, it is undesirable to maintain prisons which are so small that proper facilities cannot be provided.

64. The duty of society does not end with a prisoner's release. There should, therefore, be governmental or private agencies capable of lending the released prisoner efficient after-care directed towards the lessening of prejudice against him and towards his social rehabilitation.

Treatment

65. The treatment of persons sentenced to imprisonment or a similar measure shall have as its purpose, so far as the length of the sentence permits, to establish in them the will to lead law-abiding and self-supporting lives after their release and to fit them to do so. The treatment shall be such as will encourage their self-respect and develop their sense of responsibility.

66.   (1) To these ends, all appropriate means shall be used, including religious care in the countries where this is possible, education, vocational guidance and training, social casework, employment counselling, physical development and strengthening of moral character, in accordance with the individual needs of each prisoner, taking account of his social and criminal history, his physical and mental capacities and aptitudes, his personal temperament, the length of his sentence and his prospects after release.

(2) For every prisoner with a sentence of suitable length, the director shall receive, as soon as possible after his admission, full reports on all the matters referred to in the foregoing paragraph. Such reports shall always include a report by a medical officer, wherever possible qualified in psychiatry, on the physical and mental condition of the prisoner.

(3) The reports and other relevant documents shall be placed in an individual file. This file shall be kept up to date and classified in such a way that it can be consulted by the responsible personnel whenever the need arises.

Classification and individualization

67. The purposes of classification shall be:
(a) To separate from others those prisoners who, by reason of their criminal records or bad characters, are likely to exercise a bad influence;
(b) To divide the prisoners into classes in order to facilitate their treatment with a view to their social rehabilitation.

68. So far as possible separate institutions or separate sections of an institution shall be used for the treatment of the different classes of prisoners.

69. As soon as possible after admission and after a study of the personality of each prisoner with a sentence of suitable length, a programme of treatment shall be prepared for him in the light of the knowledge obtained about his individual needs, his capacities and dispositions.

Privileges

70. Systems of privileges appropriate for the different classes of prisoners and the different methods of treatment shall be established at every institution, in order to encourage good conduct, develop a sense of responsibility and secure the interest and co-operation of the prisoners in their treatment.

Work

71.   (1) Prison labour must not be of an afflictive nature.

(2) All prisoners under sentence shall be required to work, subject to their physical and mental fitness as determined by the medical officer.

(3) Sufficient work of a useful nature shall be provided to keep prisoners actively employed for a normal working day.

(4) So far as possible the work provided shall be such as will maintain or increase the prisoners' ability to earn an honest living after release.

(5) Vocational training in useful trades shall be provided for prisoners able to profit thereby and especially for young prisoners.

(6) Within the limits compatible with proper vocational selection and with the requirements of institutional administration and discipline, the prisoners shall be able to choose the type of work they wish to perform.

72.   (1) The organization and methods of work in the institutions shall resemble as closely as possible those of similar work outside institutions, so as to prepare prisoners for the conditions of normal occupational life.

(2) The interests of the prisoners and of their vocational training, however, must not be subordinated to the purpose of making a financial profit from an industry in the institution.

73.   (1) Preferably institutional industries and farms should be operated directly by the administration and not by private contractors.

(2) Where prisoners are employed in work not controlled by the administration, they shall always be under the supervision of the institution's personnel. Unless the work is for other departments of the government the full normal wages for such work shall be paid to the administration by the persons to whom the labour is supplied, account being taken of the output of the prisoners.

74.   (1) The precautions laid down to protect the safety and health of free workmen shall be equally observed in institutions.

(2) Provision shall be made to indemnify prisoners against industrial injury, including occupational disease, on terms not less favourable than those extended by law to free workmen.

75.   (1) The maximum daily and weekly working hours of the prisoners shall be fixed by law or by administrative regulation, taking into account local rules or custom in regard to the employment of free workmen.

(2) The hours so fixed shall leave one rest day a week and sufficient time for education and other activities required as part of the treatment and rehabilitation of the prisoners.

76.   (1) There shall be a system of equitable remuneration of the work of prisoners.

(2) Under the system prisoners shall be allowed to spend at least a part of their earnings on approved articles for their own use and to send a part of their earnings to their family.

(3) The system should also provide that a part of the earnings should be set aside by the administration so as to constitute a savings fund to be handed over to the prisoner on his release.

Education and recreation

77.   (1) Provision shall be made for the further education of all prisoners capable of profiting thereby, including religious instruction in the countries where this is possible. The education of illiterates and young prisoners shall be compulsory and special attention shall be paid to it by the administration.

(2) So far as practicable, the education of prisoners shall be integrated with the educational system of the country so that after their release they may continue their education without difficulty.

78. Recreational and cultural activities shall be provided in all institutions for the benefit of the mental and physical health of prisoners.

Social relations and after-care

79. Special attention shall be paid to the maintenance and improvement of such relations between a prisoner and his family as are desirable in the best interests of both.

80. From the beginning of a prisoner's sentence consideration shall be given to his future after release and he shall be encouraged and assisted to maintain or establish such relations with persons or agencies outside the institution as may promote the best interests of his family and his own social rehabilitation.

81. (1) Services and agencies, governmental or otherwise, which assist released prisoners to re-establish themselves in society shall ensure, so far as is possible and necessary, that released prisoners be provided with appropriate documents and identification papers, have suitable homes and work to go to, are suitably and adequately clothed having regard to the climate and season, and have sufficient means to reach their destination and maintain themselves in the period immediately following their release.

(2) The approved representatives of such agencies shall have all necessary access to the institution and to prisoners and shall be taken into consultation as to the future of a prisoner from the beginning of his sentence.

(3) It is desirable that the activities of such agencies shall be centralized or co-ordinated as far as possible in order to secure the best use of their efforts.

B. INSANE AND MENTALLY ABNORMAL PRISONERS

82.   (1) Persons who are found to be insane shall not be detained in prisons and arrangements shall be made to remove them to mental institutions as soon as possible.

(2) Prisoners who suffer from other mental diseases or abnormalities shall be observed and treated in specialized institutions under medical management.

(3) During their stay in a prison, such prisoners shall be placed under the special supervision of a medical officer.

(4) The medical or psychiatric service of the penal institutions shall provide for the psychiatric treatment of all other prisoners who are in need of such treatment.

83. It is desirable that steps should be taken, by arrangement with the appropriate agencies, to ensure if necessary the continuation of psychiatric treatment after release and the provision of social-psychiatric after-care.

C. PRISONERS UNDER ARREST OR AWAITING TRIAL

84.   (1) Persons arrested or imprisoned by reason of a criminal charge against them, who are detained either in police custody or in prison custody (jail) but have not yet been tried and sentenced, will be referred to as "untried prisoners" hereinafter in these rules.

(2) Unconvicted prisoners are presumed to be innocent and shall be treated as such.

(3) Without prejudice to legal rules for the protection of individual liberty or prescribing the procedure to be observed in respect of untried prisoners, these prisoners shall benefit by a special regime which is described in the following rules in its essential requirements only.

85.   (1) Untried prisoners shall be kept separate from convicted prisoners.

(2) Young untried prisoners shall be kept separate from adults and shall in principle be detained in separate institutions.

86. Untried prisoners shall sleep singly in separate rooms, with the reservation of different local custom in respect of the climate.

87. Within the limits compatible with the good order of the institution, untried prisoners may, if they so desire, have their food procured at their own expense from the outside, either through the administration or through their family or friends. Otherwise, the administration shall provide their food.

88.   (1) An untried prisoner shall be allowed to wear his own clothing if it is clean and suitable.

(2) If he wears prison dress, it shall be different from that supplied to convicted prisoners.

89. An untried prisoner shall always be offered opportunity to work, but shall not be required to work. If he chooses to work, he shall be paid for it.

90. An untried prisoner shall be allowed to procure at his own expense or at the expense of a third party such books, newspapers, writing materials and other means of occupation as are compatible with the interests of the administration of justice and the security and good order of the institution.

91. An untried prisoner shall be allowed to be visited and treated by his own doctor or dentist if there is reasonable ground for his application and he is able to pay any expenses incurred.

92. An untried prisoner shall be allowed to inform immediately his family of his detention and shall be given all reasonable facilities for communicating with his family and friends, and for receiving visits from them, subject only to restrictions and supervision as are necessary in the

interests of the administration of justice and of the security and good order of the institution.

93. For the purposes of his defence, an untried prisoner shall be allowed to apply for free legal aid where such aid is available, and to receive visits from his legal adviser with a view to his defence and to prepare and hand to him confidential instructions. For these purposes, he shall if he so desires be supplied with writing material. Interviews between the prisoner and his legal adviser may be within sight but not within the hearing of a police or institution official.

D. CIVIL PRISONERS

94. In countries where the law permits imprisonment for debt, or by order of a court under any other non-criminal process, persons so imprisoned shall not be subjected to any greater restriction or severity than is necessary to ensure safe custody and good order. Their treatment shall be not less favourable than that of untried prisoners, with the reservation, however, that they may possibly be required to work.

E. PERSONS ARRESTED OR DETAINED WITHOUT CHARGE

95. Without prejudice to the provisions of article 9 of the International Covenant on Civil and Political Rights, persons arrested or imprisoned without charge shall be accorded the same protection as that accorded under part I and II, section C. Relevant provisions of part II, section A, shall likewise be applicable where their application may be conducive to the benefit of this special group of persons in custody, provided that no measures shall be taken implying that re-education or rehabilitation is in any way appropriate to persons not convicted of any criminal offence.

APPENDIX D

THE HUMAN RIGHTS WATCH QUESTIONNAIRE
FOR PRISON VISITS

I. General Information Regarding Country's Prison System

    A. Basic Data
        1. Number of institutions and capacity
        2. Number of prisoners
        3. Ratio of prisoners per 100,000

    B. Different kinds of facilities
        1. Police lock-ups (maximum time of confinement under the law)
        2. Pretrial detention centers: do they exist or are pre-trial detainees held in prisons?
        3. What is the maximum time of pre-trial confinement under the law and in practice?
        4. Different security levels prisons for sentenced prisoners
        5. Women - find out the % of women, number of institutions holding women, and rules regarding infants and young children
        6. Does the country have security prisoners? Are they held in special prisons or prisons' sections?

    C. Jurisdiction
        Under whose jurisdictions are pre-trial facilities and facilities for sentenced prisoners?

II. Additional Issues Worth Checking (either ahead of time or in the course of interviews with experts or officials)

    A. Is there mixing of juveniles with adults, pre-trial with sentenced, recidivists with first offenders, etc.

B. Length of time spent in facilities for pre-trial detainees (whether sentences are in fact served there)

C. Find out the principal differences in rules for sentenced and pre-trial prisoners (for example non-contact visits only in pre-trial detention in some places)

D. Are inmates medicated by staff as a means of control?

E. Are there reports of widespread sexual abuse (inmate-to-inmate or staff-to-inmate)

F. AIDS
    1. policy on testing
    2. percentage infected
    3. treatment of those infected
    4. treatment of those sick

III. Interview with the warden or other official in the prison

A. General information about the institution
    1. Type (security level, pre-trial or sentenced, etc.)
    2. The length of average sentence and/or length of average stay
    3. Capacity of the institution
    4. Number of inmates on the day of your visit
    5. Age of the institution
    6. Type of housing in the institution
        a. what kinds of cells?
        b. how many inmates in each type?
    7. Number of staff

B. Work
    1. are inmates required to work?
    2. how many are employed?
    3. how many are paid?
    4. how much are they paid?
    5. how many hours a day and days a week do they work?

6. are there inmates who wish to work for whom there are no jobs? How many?

C. Rules regarding visits
    1. who can visit?
    2. how often?
    3. contact/non-contact
    4. conjugal visits?
    5. are inmates/relatives searched? always? occasionally/when?
    6. what can the visitors bring?

D. Disciplinary infractions
    1. range
    2. the most frequent type

E. Disciplinary measures
    1. what are the disciplinary measures (from most lenient to most severe)?
    2. what is the most often used measure?
    3. is suspension of visits or correspondence ever used as a disciplinary measure?
    4. are physical restraints used as a disciplinary measure?

F. How do inmates know about what the rules are?
    Can they appeal the disciplinary ruling?

G. Is there inmate-to-inmate violence within the institution?
    1. number of assaults in the last 12 months
    2. number of assassinations in the last 12 months

H. In women's institutions - rules regarding pregnant inmates, infants and small children (whether allowed to stay with mothers and for how long). Rules regarding mothers' contacts with other children.

IV. Individual Interviews With Inmates

NOTE: No need to ask the name or why is the inmate imprisoned (crime committed). But do try to identify the inmate for yourself in your notes. Make sure they understand you will not be sharing the contents of your interview with the staff. Always try to interview one person at a time, if possible out of the earshot of others. Even when you cannot avoid the presence of others, it is best to interview one person at a time.

A. General information about the inmate.
   1. How long have you been in this institution?
   2. How long is your sentence?
   3. How old are you?
   4. How long were you in pre-trial detention?

B. Physical conditions
   1. How long have you been in this cell?
   2. How much time a day are you locked in the cell?
   3. What is your cell like in different seasons (temperature, etc)?
   4. Has anything changed in the cell or in the institution the last few days?
   5. What was the highest number ever of people in your cell and when?
   6. Within your prison, is your cell considered good, bad or average type of housing?
   7. Which cells or cellblocks are the worst? (get the name or number and ask to be taken there)

C. Sanitary conditions
   1. How often can you shower?
   2. Is there hot water in the showers?
   3. How often do you get a clean change of clothes? of sheets?
   4. Do you have a razor or any other shaving instrument? If not, how do inmates shave?
   5. Does the prison provide you with soap, toothpaste, toilet paper, sanitary napkins (for women)?

6. Do you have any complaints regarding sanitary conditions?

D. Food

1. Do you eat in the cell or in a dining room?
2. Is there sufficient amount?
3. Any health problems related to food?
4. Can you supplement your food with purchases from the commissary or packages from home (find out about the rules regulating both)?

E. Activities

1. Describe your average day.
2. What do you do in your free time?
3. Are you allowed to have a radio or TV in your cell?
4. Can you have books in your cell?
5. How do you get them?
6. Are there any restrictions on the kinds of books?
7. What kind of recreational and sports opportunities do you have?
8. Can you study in prison? Describe
9. Can you practice your religion?

F. Work

1. Describe your work
2. Are you being paid?
3. How much?
4. Have you witnessed any work accidents? When? What sort? How often?

G. Contacts with the outside

1. How often can you have visits?
2. Who can visit you?
3. For how long?
4. Are you and/or your visitors searched?
5. Are there any special rules about visiting your visitors have to obey?
6. Did you have visits in pre-trial detention, how often, contact or non-contact?

7. How many letters can you send and receive every month?

8. To and from whom?

9. Are they read by the staff?

10. Are there any problems with the mail?

11. Will the prison provide you with paper, envelopes and stamps if you can't afford them?

12. Can you use the phone? How often?

H. Prison rules

1. Do you know the rules in the institution?

2. How do you know them?

3. Are any of them particularly burdensome?

I. Disciplinary measures

1. What are the disciplinary measures (from most lenient to most severe)?

2. What is the most often used measure?

3. Is suspension of visits or correspondence ever used as a disciplinary measure?

4. Are physical restraints used as a disciplinary measure?

5. Have you ever been in a punishment cell? If yes, for how long? Describe conditions there. If not, who can I talk to who has been there?

6. Do guards ever beat inmates? (if the answer is yes, find out exactly how does your witness know. Dates and detailed descriptions of incidents, to be confirmed by interviews with other witnesses).

7. Are there any measures that are particularly unfair?

8. What do inmates do when they feel they are unjustly punished (you want to find out if there are self-mutilations, hunger strikes, protest actions, etc. without specifically asking about them)

J. What is the medical care like?

1. Can you see a doctor when you are sick?

2. How soon after reporting illness?

3. What happens if someone gets sick at night?

4. (for women) Have you been seen by a gynecologist while in prison?

K. What are the biggest problems between inmates?
1. Do inmates have a self-government body? Is it official? Is it effective? Does it treat everybody fairly? (try to find out without leading if there are gangs within the prison)
2. Have you heard of or witnessed any assaults? When? (get details)

L. What do you consider the biggest problem here (aside from being confined)?

M. Is there something I should have asked you and didn't?

V. Note on police lockups investigations.

If the institution you are visiting is a police lockup, pay a particular attention to issues such as beatings, torture, prolonged incommunicado detention. In many countries, this is where most of the physical abuses associated with deprivation of freedom occur.

BIBLIOGRAPHY

Human Rights Watch Reports

Africa Watch. *Kenya: Taking Liberties.* New York: Human Rights Watch, 1991.

_____. "Zaire: Two Years without Transition." *A Human Rights Watch Short Report,* vol. 4, no. 9 (July 1992).

Americas Watch. *A Certain Passivity: Failing to Curb Human Rights Abuses in Peru.* New York: Human Rights Watch, 1987.

_____. "Cuba: Behind A Sporting Facade, Stepped-up Repression." *A Human Rights Watch Short Report,* vol. 3, no. 9 (August 1991).

_____. "El Peru de Fujimori" (Spanish only). *A Human Rights Watch Short Report* (August 1992).

_____. *El Salvador's Decade of Terror: Human Rights since the Assassination of Archbishop Romero.* New Haven: Yale University Press, 1991.

_____. "Frontier Injustice: Human Rights Abuses Along the U.S. Border with Mexico Persist Amid Climate of Impunity." *A Human Rights Watch Short Report,* vol. 5, no. 4 (May 1993).

_____. *Human Rights in Cuba: The Need to Sustain the Pressure.* New York: Human Rights Watch, 1989.

_____. *Human Rights in Peru One Year after Fujimori's Coup.* New York: Human Rights Watch, 1993.

_____. *In Desperate Straits: Human Rights in Peru after a Decade of Democracy and Insurgency.* New York: Human Rights Watch, 1990.

_____. "Notorious Jail Operating Again in São Paulo." *A Human Rights Watch Short Report,* vol. 1, no. 11 (October 1989).

_____. *Peru under Fire: Human Rights since the Return to Democracy.* New Haven: Yale University Press, 1992.

_____. "[Cuba] Perfecting the System of Control Human Rights Violations in Castro's 34th Year." *A Human Rights Watch Short Report,* vol. 5, no. 1 (February 1993).

_____. *Police Abuse in Brazil: Summary Executions and Torture in São Paulo and Rio de Janeiro.* New York: Human Rights Watch, 1987.

_____. *Police Violence in Argentina: Torture and Police Killings in Buenos Aires*. New York: Human Rights Watch, 1991.

_____. *Prison Conditions in Brazil*. New York: Human Rights Watch, 1989.

_____. *Prison Conditions in Jamaica*. New York: Human Rights Watch, 1990.

_____. *Prison Conditions in Mexico*. New York: Human Rights Watch, 1991.

_____. "Prison Conditions in Puerto Rico." *A Human Rights Watch Short Report*, vol. 3, no. 6, (May 1991).

_____. "Prison Massacre in São Paulo." *A Human Rights Watch Short Report*, vol. 4, no. 10 (October 1992).

_____. "Tightening the Grip: Human Rights Abuses in Cuba." *A Human Rights Watch Short Report*, vol. 4, no. 1 (February 1992).

_____ and Jorge Valls. *Twenty Years and Forty Days: Life in a Cuban Prison*. New York: Human Rights Watch, 1986.

_____ and the Women's Rights Project. *Untold Terror: Violence against Women in Peru's Armed Conflict*. New York: Human Rights Watch, 1992.

Asia Watch. *Anthems of Defeat: Crackdown in Hunan Province 1989-1992*. New York: Human Rights Watch, 1992.

_____. "China: Political Prisoners Abused in Liaoning Prison as Official Whitewash of Labor Reform System Continues." *A Human Rights Watch Short Report*, vol. 4, no. 23 (September 1992).

_____. "Forced Labor Exports From China: Update No. 1." *A Human Rights Watch Short Report*, vol. 3, no. 19 (September 1991).

_____. "Forced Labor Exports From China: Update No. 2." *A Human Rights Watch Short Report*, vol. 3, no. 25 (November 1991).

_____. "Democracy Wall Prisoners: Xu Wenli, Wei Jingsheng and Other Jailed Pioneers of the Chinese Pro-Democracy Movement." *A Human Rights Watch Short Report*, vol. 5, no. 6 (March 1983).

_____ and Women's Rights Project. *Double Jeopardy: Police Abuse of Women in Pakistan*. New York: Human Rights Watch, 1992.

_____. *Kashmir under Siege: Human Rights in India*. New York: Human Rights Watch, 1991.

_____. *Political Prisoners in Tibet*. New York: Human Rights Watch, 1992.

_____. *Prison Conditions in India.* New York: Human Rights Watch, 1991.

_____. *Prison Conditions in Indonesia.* New York: Human Rights Watch, 1990.

_____. "Prison Labor in China." *A Human Rights Watch Short Report,* vol. 3, no. 11 (April 1991).

_____. *Punjab in Crisis: Human Rights in India.* New York: Human Rights Watch, 1991.

_____. *Two Years After Tiananmen: Political Prisoners in China.* New York: Human Rights Watch, 1991.

Helsinki Watch. *Broken Promises: Torture and Killings Continue in Turkey.* New York: Human Rights Watch, 1992.

_____. "Lockups in Romania." *A Human Rights Watch Short Report,* vol. 5, no. 2 (January 1993).

_____. *Prison Conditions in Czechoslovakia: An Update.* New York: Human Rights Watch, 1991.

_____. *Prison Conditions in Czechoslovakia.* New York: Human Rights Watch, 1989.

_____. *Prison Conditions in Poland: An Update.* New York: Human Rights Watch, 1991.

_____. *Prison Conditions in Poland.* New York: Human Rights Watch, 1988.

_____. *Prison Conditions in Romania.* New York: Human Rights Watch, 1992.

_____. *Prison Conditions in Spain.* New York: Human Rights Watch, 1992.

_____. *Prison Conditions in Turkey.* New York: Human Rights Watch, 1989.

_____. *Prison Conditions in the United Kingdom.* New York: Human Rights Watch, 1992.

_____. *Prison Conditions in the United States.* New York: Human Rights Watch, 1991.

_____. *Prison Conditions in the Soviet Union.* New York: Human Rights Watch, 1991.

Middle East Watch. *Behind Closed Doors: Torture and Detention in Egypt.*
New York: Human Rights Watch, 1992.
_____. *Throwing Away the Key: Indefinite Political Detention in
Syria.* New York: Human Rights Watch, 1992.
_____. *Human Rights in Iraq.* New Haven: Yale University
Press, 1990.
_____. *Prison Conditions in Egypt.* New York: Human Rights
Watch, 1993.
_____. *Prison Conditions in Israel & the Israeli-Occupied West
Bank & Gaza Strip.* New York: Human Rights Watch, 1991.
_____. *Syria Unmasked: The Suppression of Human Rights by the
Asad Regime.* New Haven: Yale University Press, 1991.

Other Publications

Amnesty International. "Cuba: Silencing Voices of Dissent." London:
1992.
Bergman, Catherine M., Nancy Neveloff Dubler, Hon. Marvin E.
Frankel. "Management of HIV Infection in New York State Prisons."
Columbia Human Rights Law Review (Spring 1990).
Breytenbach, Breyton. *The True Confessions of an Albino Terrorist.* New
York: Farrar, Straus & Giroux, 1985.
Henkin, Alice H., Mary Jane Camejo, Richard J. Miller, Michael Posner,
Stephen J. Ritchen and Kenneth Roth. "Human Rights in Cuba." *The
Record of the Association of the Bar of the City of New York,* vol. 43, no. 7
(November 1988).
Neier, Aryeh. "In Cuban Prisons." *New York Review of Books* (June 30,
1988).
City of New York Department of Investigation. *Report to the Mayor: The
Disturbance at the Rikers Island Otis Bantum Correctional Center, August 14,
1990; Its Causes and the Department of Corrections Response.* New York:
1991.
Rodley, Nigel. *The Treatment of Prisoners under International Law.* Oxford:
Clarendon Press, 1987.
United Nations. *Compendium of United Nations Standards and Norms in
Crime Prevention and Criminal Justice.* New York: United Nations
Publications, 1992.

United Nations. *Human Rights: A Compilation of International Instruments.* New York: United Nations Publications, 1988.

van Zyl Smit, Dirk and Frieder Duenkel, eds. *Imprisonment Today and Tomorrow: International Perspectives on Prisoners' Rights and Prison Conditions.* Boston: Kluwer, 1991.

van Zyl Smit, Dirk. *South African Prison Law and Practice.* Durban: Butterworth, 1992.

Williams, Paul R. *Treatment of Detainees: Examination of Issues Relevant to Detention by the United Nations Human Rights Committee.* Geneva: Henry Dunant Institute, 1990.